War, Journalism and the Shaping
of the Twentieth Century

War, Journalism and the Shaping of the Twentieth Century

The Life and Times of Henry W. Nevinson

ANGELA V. JOHN

BLOOMSBURY ACADEMIC
LONDON • NEW YORK • OXFORD • NEW DELHI • SYDNEY

BLOOMSBURY ACADEMIC
Bloomsbury Publishing Plc
50 Bedford Square, London, WC1B 3DP, UK
1385 Broadway, New York, NY 10018, USA
29 Earlsfort Terrace, Dublin 2, Ireland

BLOOMSBURY, BLOOMSBURY ACADEMIC and the Diana logo are
trademarks of Bloomsbury Publishing Plc

First published in Great Britain by I.B. Tauris 2006
Paperback edition published by Bloomsbury Academic 2023

A catalogue record for this book is available from the British Library.
A catalog record for this book is available from the Library of Congress.

ISBN: HB: 9781845110819
        PB: 9781350382060
        eISBN: 9780755628568
        ePDF: 9780857717832

Typeset by RefineCatch Limited, Bungay, Suffolk

To find out more about our authors and books visit
www.bloomsbury.com and sign up for our newsletters.

This book is dedicated to the memory of two remarkable women of the twentieth century:

Marjorie Mathias (née Scott)
(1909–2001)

Mabel Smith (née Lovering)
(1910–2000)

Contents

Maps

I am very grateful to Valeri Bayura and Alik Aliaoutdinov for producing these three specially commissioned maps.

Illustrations

Every effort has been made to trace copyholders. The following illustrations are reproduced by permission of: James Nisbet & Co., Cover, 10, 11; The Bodleian Library, University of Oxford, 1; Shrewsbury School, 2; Myrna Goode, 3; Nancy Nichols, 5; The British Library, 13, 14, 15; RHUL Archives, 16.

Acknowledgements

Historical biography – and biographical history – may appear to be the work of one person but in reality the research and writing form part of a cumulative, collaborative process. In documenting Henry Nevinson's life I have been generously aided by many institutions and individuals. At the outset I was awarded a Charter Fellowship for a year at Wolfson College, Oxford. For this opportunity to undertake sustained research I am indebted to the President and Fellows of Wolfson College and to the School of Humanities at the University of Greenwich. I was especially fortunate that the Henry Nevinson Papers, along with the Evelyn Sharp Nevinson Papers, were housed in the Modern Papers Reading Room at the Bodleian Library, University of Oxford where Colin Harris and his staff could not have been more helpful. I was generously assisted in completing the book with grants from both the Authors' Foundation of the Society of Authors and the Helen Heroys Foundation.

I am grateful for permission to use or quote from unpublished material: the Michael Ayrton Estate (Nevinson and Sharp Papers); the Society of Antiquaries of London (John L. Nevinson Papers); Berg Collection of English and American Literature the New York Public Library Astor, Lenox and Tilden Foundations; Cadbury Schweppes plc (Cadbury Papers, University of Birmingham); the Bodleian Library Department of Special Collections and Western Manuscripts (Henry Nevinson Papers, Evelyn Sharp Nevinson Papers, Hammond Papers); the Bodleian Library of Commonwealth and African Studies at Rhodes House (Anti-Slavery Society Papers); the British Library (Dryhurst Papers; Dunlop-Smith Papers, Gokhale Papers, Morley Papers, Minto Papers); Bristol University Library, Special Collections (Penguin Archives); the Dartington Hall Trust Archive (Elmhirst Papers), the Syndics of the Fitzwilliam Museum (Blunt MS); the Provost and Scholars of King's College, Cambridge (E. M. Forster Papers); the *Guardian* (*Manchester Guardian*, the John Rylands University Library, University of Manchester); Leeds University Library (the Brotherton Collection); the Trustees of the Liddell Hart Centre for Military Archives (Hamilton Papers, King's College London); National Library of Ireland (Casement Papers); the Robinson Library,

University of Newcastle Special Collections; Archives, Royal Holloway, University of London (Bedford College for Women Council Minutes); RUKBA (Elizabeth Robins Papers at the Fales Library and Special Collections, New York University); Marion Shaw (Winifred Holtby Collection, Hull Local Studies Library); Sheffield Libraries (Carpenter Collection), the Board of Trinity College, Dublin (Campbell MS); Vaughan Williams Library, Cecil Sharp House; West Sussex Record Office (Blunt MS). Every effort has been made to trace copyright holders.

I received assistance from archivists and librarians at Birmingham Museum and Art Gallery, Art Department; the BBC Written Archives Centre, Caversham Park; the British Library of Political and Economic Science; the British Newspaper Library, Colindale and British Library Sound Archive; Camden Local Studies and Archives; the Campden Society; Christ Church Archives and Picture Gallery; Cumbria Record Office, Carlisle; Dulwich College; Edinburgh University Library, Special Collections; Eton College Library; the University of Greenwich Library; the Guild of St George; House of Lords Record Office; the Imperial War Museum, Department of Art; the Isle of Wight Record Office; Stadtarchiv Jena; London Metropolitan Archives; Keats House Museum; McGill University Library, Rare Book Department; the National Archives, Public Record Office and Family Records Centre; the National Arts Club, New York; the National Portrait Gallery; National Library of Scotland; National Library of Wales; New York Public Library; Norwich Record Office; Reading University Library; the Royal College of Music; University of St Andrews Library; Institute of Historical Research, School of Slavonic and East European Studies, and Senate House Library, University of London; Sherborne School Archives; Shrewsbury School Archives; Sotheby's; the Tate Archive; Thomas Hardy Memorial Library, Dorchester; Tower Hamlets Local History Library and Archives; University of Wales, Aberystwyth Information Services; the Warburg Institute; Westminster School Archives; the Women's Library; Woolwich Public Library, Reference Department.

I am extremely grateful to Dryhurst descendants Nancy Nichols and Pat Paget for enabling me to read family papers. Thanks to Geoffrey Haskins for Nevinson family insights and to Michael Walsh, biographer of C. R. W. Nevinson, and Barbara Smith and Clare Hardy of 'The Nevi(n)son News'. Lady Vaughan Williams kindly shared her recollections of Henry Nevinson. Nevill New recalled wartime Chipping Campden. Shantibhai Banarsi and Harish Chandra Banazi enabled me to see the Nevinson home. Tom Buchanan allowed access to privately owned Nevinson/Woodd correspondence. Liz Staff drove me over precipitous mountain routes in northern Greece tracking Henry Nevinson's first war and helped in New York Public Library. Michael and Catherine Gaum took me to Mons. Thanks also to people in Chipping Campden, especially Allan Warmington and Bob McClement.

I owe much to former colleagues at the University of Greenwich, especially staff and students in the School of Humanities where I worked for many years. Many individuals made specific contributions. They include June Balshaw, Diana Banks-Conney, Paula Bartley, Jo Baylen, Katherine Bradley, Alun Burge, Gina Burrows, Noel Campbell, David Cannadine, Pat Caplan, Lionel Caplan, Elaine Chalus, Laurence Clark, Ross Davies, Lord Deedes, Jean L'Esperance, Martyn Everett, Edward Fenton, the Rt. Hon. Michael Foot, Dominik Geppert, Steve Goldsmith, Lesley Gordon, Galina Gornostaeva, Wendell V. Harris, Jess Hounsell, Jocelyn Hoyle, Fred Hunter, Ken John, Aled Jones, Bob Jones, Elin Jones, Lis Jones, Chandrika Kaul, Hilda Kean, Ann Keen, Seth Koven, Patrick Larkin, James Lawson, Fred Leventhal, Adrian Marsh, Christopher Martin, Mary Clare Martin, Neville Masterman, Sowon Park, Mark Pottle, June Purvis, Richard Rathbone, Ellen Ross, Lady Jenny Rudge, Jutta Schwarzkov, Wendy Scott, Peter Searby, Kathy Stansfield, Anne Summers, Marvin J. Taylor and Linda Walker. Ross Davies deserves special thanks. Hara Kastanaki generously supplied me with Greek translations. The assistance of Lynne Beesley, Helen Moss and Steve Peacock is much appreciated, as is that of Lis Evans and Elfed Evans. Diolch yn fawr iawn. Naomi Symes assiduously tracked down Nevinson books.

I am very grateful to my publisher I.B. Tauris, especially Lester Crook and Kate Sherratt, and indebted to those who read the manuscript and experts who commented on specific sections: Linda Edmondson, Peter Doyle, Gary Peatling and Vesna Goldsworthy. Jacky Beaumont and Nick Owen not only read chapters but also kindly let me see drafts of forthcoming publications. I thank Dinah Wiener for her faith in me. Judith P. Zinsser's discussions on biographical method have greatly enriched my understanding of the genre. Paul Stigant provided wise comments on the manuscript as it evolved, for which I remain immeasurably grateful.

Angela V. John
Newport, Pembrokeshire
3 February 2005

Abbreviations

APS	Aborigines' Protection Society
ASR	Anti-Slavery Reporter
ASS	Anti-Slavery Society
BEF	British Expeditionary Force
BLCAS	Bodleian Library of Commonwealth and African Studies at Rhodes House, Oxford
CIR	*Criminal Intelligence Reports*
CO	conscientious objector
DC	*Daily Chronicle*
DH	*Daily Herald*
DN	*Daily News*
DORA	Defence of the Realm Act
EB	Edward Bonney (Henry's brother)
EFDS	English Folk Dance Society
ESNev.	Evelyn Sharp Nevinson Papers, The Bodleian Library, University of Oxford
HMM	*Harper's Monthly Magazine*
HWNP	Henry W. Nevinson Papers, The Bodleian Library, University of Oxford
INC	Indian National Congress
IOR	India Office Library and Records, The British Library
LMA	London Metropolitan Archives
MG	*Manchester Guardian*
MGA	Manchester Guardian Archives, The John Rylands University Library, University of Manchester
MPU	Men's Political Union for Women's Enfranchisement
MRC	Macedonian Relief Committee
NCCL	National Council for Civil Liberties
NevJ.	Henry Nevinson's diaries
NL	*New Leader*
NUWSS	National Union of Women's Suffrage Societies
PEN	Poets, Essayists and Novelists
RAMC	Royal Army Medical Corps

RHUL   Royal Holloway, University of London
TNA: PRO The National Archives: Public Record Office, Kew
US   United Suffragists
WFL   Women's Freedom League
WSPU   Women's Social and Political Union

See Appendix 1 for abbreviations in the Notes of Henry Nevinson's book titles.

Henry Nevinson's Life and Travels at a Glance

For publications see the Appendices.

1856   Born in Leicester, England.
1872   Shrewsbury School.
1875   Christ Church, Oxford.
1879   Graduates. School teaching.
1880   Visits Germany.
1884   First book published (on Herder). Marriage to Margaret Wynne Jones. University of Jena, Germany. Birth of Philippa Nevinson.
1885   Returns to London. History lecturer, Bedford College for Women. Moves to East End. Works with Toynbee Hall.
1887   Moves to John Street, Hampstead.
1889   C. R. W. Nevinson born.
1891   Secretary to the London Playing Fields Committee.
1892   Meets Nannie Dryhurst.
1896   Moves to Savernake Road, Hampstead.
1897   Begins career as war correspondent for Graeco-Turkish War (mainland Greece and Crete). First visit to Ireland.
1898   Spain (for Spanish–American War in Cuba).
1899   Edits Literary Page for *Daily Chronicle*. Second Anglo-Boer War (in Siege of Ladysmith 1899–1900). Ireland.
1900   Ireland.
1901   Moves to 4 Downside Crescent, Hampstead. Meets Evelyn Sharp.
1902   Returns to South Africa.
1903   Macedonia for the Macedonian Relief Committee.
1904   Travels in France for Hallam Murray's book. To Angola.
1905   Returns from Portuguese Angola, San Thomé and Principe and begins campaigning against slavery. Reports on revolution in Russia.
1906   Baltic provinces, Russia (twice), the Caucasus.

1907   International Peace Conference, The Hague. To India. Founder
        member of Men's League for Women's Suffrage.
1908   Joins *Daily News*.
1909   Barcelona and Morocco (Spanish War against the Riff).
1910   Finland. Chairs Men's Political Union for Women's Political
        Enfranchisement.
1911   Albania (for Macedonian Relief Committee).
1912   Bulgaria (First Balkan War). Ireland.
1913   Albania (Second Balkan War). Ireland.
1914   Chairs United Suffragists. Berlin. First World War (France,
        Belgium: Quaker Ambulance Unit). Ireland.
1915   Germany. With British Army in France. Gallipoli. Salonika.
1916   Egypt. Campaigns for Sir Roger Casement.
1917   C. R. W. Nevinson becomes an official war artist.
1918   Western Front. Sees Armistice begin at Mons. Ireland. Cologne.
1919   Germany. Ireland. Denmark.
1920   United States (lecture tour and Republican Convention in
        Chicago). Ireland.
1921   Ireland (twice). United States (Disarmament Conference,
        Washington).
1922   Ireland (twice). Vienna (lecturing).
1923   Germany (twice) – the Ruhr and Rhineland, Jena.
1924   Pre-election tour of England and Wales with Ramsay
        MacDonald.
1926   Turkey, Lebanon, Palestine, Syria, Iraq.
1929   United States with Ramsay MacDonald. Canada. Vienna (PEN).
1931   The Hague (PEN).
1932   Margaret dies.
1933   Marries Evelyn Sharp.
1936   President of the National Council for Civil Liberties.
1937   President of PEN.
1938   Czechoslovakia (with PEN).
1940   Hampstead home bombed. Moves to Chipping Campden,
        Gloucestershire.
1941   Dies in Chipping Campden aged eighty-five.

Note To The New Edition

Since this biography first appeared in 2006, Angela V. John has published the following about Henry Nevinson and/or his family: *Evelyn Sharp. Rebel Woman, 1869–1955*, Manchester, 2009; 'A Family at War: The Nevinson Family' in M. J. K. Walsh (ed.), *A Dilemma of English Modernism. Visual and Verbal Politics in the Life and Work of C. R. W. Nevinson (1889–1946)*, Newark, Delaware, 2007; 'Henry W. Nevinson: *Neighbours of Ours* (1895)' in A. Whitehead and J. White, *London Fictions*, Nottingham, 2013; 'Gender and National Identity: Margaret Wynne Nevinson' in *Rocking the Boat: Welsh Women who Championed Equality 1840–1990*, Cardigan, 2018 and 'What the Papers Say: Evelyn Sharp, Author, Journalist, Suffragette and Diarist', *The Bodleian Library Record*, 23/1, 2010.

Introduction

Henry W. Nevinson and the Drafting of History

War was to be the making of Henry Nevinson. From tracking ancient hostilities in the mountains of Greece to reporting from the Western Front in the final days of the Great War, he brought warfare to British breakfast tables. It was a perilous pursuit. But writing about war was his trade and, as he told a friend, 'It is always rather hard for me to live in peace unless there is a war.'[1] He covered civil wars, national struggles and total war, witnessing in the process many of the seminal conflicts that helped mould the world as we know it today.

Henry Nevinson was not solely a war correspondent. He travelled round India observing 'unrest' and alarming the British authorities. Passionate about what today we call human rights, he journeyed into the interior of Angola and exposed an illegal slave trade. His account of these horrors vies with the most vivid of boys' adventure stories. He travelled at a time when it might take weeks to reach a destination and getting copy home could be a huge challenge. In 1935, when he was seventy-nine, his fellow correspondent and friend H. N. Brailsford asked whether there existed 'in this island, any man who has seen more, any man indeed, who has seen half as much of the events that shaped our time?'[2]

In a period when newspapers were particularly influential, he informed contemporaries about many of the conflicts of their day. Along with other eminent correspondents, he followed up his journalism with books on the countries and conflicts he had covered, combining compelling prose with a riveting tale. He published over thirty books and they have helped shape later historical interpretations of events.[3] They were perceived as important contributions to the political sensitivities of the time. For, as the modern correspondent Martin Bell has put it, such observers have 'a front row in the making of History'.[4] Having watched law and order collapse in Russia during the heady days of 1905 when freedom was briefly glimpsed, Henry Nevinson's account of the problems facing the Russian Empire was described as 'The finest book about Russia ever written'.[5]

He was a scrupulous and fortunate journalist. Not only did he encompass a vast spatial and temporal sweep but he also possessed the knack of being in the right place at the right time. He was already installed in Ladysmith when the long siege began. He happened to be at the Indian National Congress when it erupted. He attended historic meetings of the Irish Dáil and Russian Duma. He just made it to Mons in time to witness the beginning of the Armistice in 1918 and was the first to report sympathetically on the privations of a ravaged Germany. In the 1920s he visited both Palestine and Iraq. One of three assignments in the United States covered the first visit from a British Prime Minister to an American President. In the process he anticipated the United States' cultural and political dominance.

A lifetime of international reportage accorded Henry Nevinson a privileged position in observing the uneven shifts towards democratic rights across the globe.[6] In turn his perspectives illuminate the gradual dismantling of the old and the shaping of the modern world order. He could be remarkably prescient. As early as 1917 he wrote that it was the end of the European Age of History. Historians use this periodization today.[7]

He wrote for the leading Liberal newspapers of the day, notably the *Daily Chronicle, Manchester Guardian* and *Daily News*. Much of his finest work first appeared in the *Nation* between 1907 and the early 1920s when H. W. Massingham was its editor. Much more than a progressive weekly paper, it suggested a state of mind, providing a valuable forum for the intelligentsia. It brought together, not least through weekly lunches, some of the key thinkers who had helped shape new Liberalism, men such as J. A. Hobson and J. L. Hammond. An increasingly disillusioned Liberal, after the First World War Henry Nevinson supported Labour. But an atavistic suspicion of authority ensured that he never toed party lines for long. As a young man he had briefly flirted with the far Left. In the 1890s he lived in London's East End and worked with the new Toynbee Hall settlement.

His commitment to social justice was recognized internationally. When Harold Laski asked Gopal Krishna Gokhale how India might best be served, he replied 'Try to see us with Nevinson's humanity.'[8] Committed to the self-determination of small nations such as Georgia, some of his most terrifying times and eloquent prose emanated from the conflict in Ireland. He helped ensure that Irish nationalist perspectives were aired in the English press. Michael Collins praised him for fighting Ireland's battles with his pen.[9]

Like the wider world he commented upon, Henry Nevinson was a curious combination of old and new. He may have been passionate about exposing injustices in Ireland and a leading advocate of justice for Sir Roger Casement but he was also a very English gentleman who had been born in mid-Victorian times and enjoyed a privileged upbringing. His distinctive style was sculpted from a classical education that he revered. The Henry Nevinson of the Edwardian years was ill at ease with the Victorian Henry Nevinson. The new man tried, not always successfully, to shake off his Evangelical and imperial heritage. His espousal of modernity took many forms. He was one of the leading male supporters of women's suffrage. Both of his wives, Margaret Wynne Nevinson and Evelyn Sharp, were prominent suffrage activists. His passionate love affairs and the sense he made of them in his diary help our understanding of the shaping of modern masculinity. They suggest, too, a complex and equivocal nature, displaying elements of a remarkably modern man alongside a quintessentially Victorian Gent.

Henry Nevinson was a biographer, poet and writer of short stories long before he became a freelance war and special correspondent.[10] He gained a reputation as a writer of middles. A superb stylist, these exquisite essays or belles-lettres, laced with a generous dose of irony, were his hallmark. He ranged widely, from essays on literary heroes such as Thomas Carlyle, John Ruskin or Thomas Hardy (who praised his prose[11]) to informed comments on world events. Like Jonathan Swift, one of the writers he most admired, he believed in 'the unity of life with literature'.[12] From 1899, for three and a half years, he edited the Literary Page of the *Daily Chronicle*. It was the closest he came to a managerial post. He spotted talented reviewers, giving figures like the poet Edward Thomas all-important 'breaks'.

Riding on the crest of New Journalism, which came into its own in the 1890s, his paper had the largest circulation of any daily London newspaper.[13] With mechanical typesetting, the modern business world of Fleet Street enjoyed unprecedented distribution, symbiotically linked to an increasingly mobile, educated and voting population whose opinions it reflected, influenced and helped shape. John Masefield wrote that the *Chronicle* in Nevinson's day was 'possibly the very best of the literary papers of the world'.[14] Appreciated as a writers' writer, he was said to be the only journalist whom 'all men of letters looked up to as a writer and as a judge of writing'.[15]

But, unlike many literary men, Henry Nevinson was irresistibly attracted to a world of action. He was familiar with the theory and practice of military training. For his motto he reversed Shakespeare's epithet to read 'The better part of Discretion is Valour.' Yet although known as the king of war correspondents, he was no advocate of war, even arguing that it was murder sanctioned by a State. He protested against militarism and supported conscientious objectors. His second wife was a pacifist. His son, the eminent artist C. R. W. Nevinson, questioned, through his paintings, the glorification of war. Henry

Nevinson used the metaphor of war to create rather than to destroy: 'The battle of Freedom is never done and the Field is never quiet'.[16]

He features in at least half a dozen novels of his day and one modern novel. In a satire by his friend John Galsworthy, he is Charles Courtier, former soldier of fortune who has written a book against war.[17] 'Mounted on a lost cause, he had been riding through the world ever since he was eighteen', was said to have 'killed some men, and loved some women' and was now standing in a by-election in the cause of peace. Henry Nevinson protested that his causes were not lost. They were simply battles waiting to be won. Philip Gibbs fictionalized him as Henry Carvell, 'who had seen more of wars, big and little, than any man in England . . . a knight-errant of the pen in most countries of the world'.[18]

Recently described by a historian as a 'brilliant observer of men and manners',[19] Henry Nevinson's capacity for courting controversy ensured that he created enemies. More remarkable, though, is the adulation he received from men as well as women. Colonel T. E. Lawrence, who was fashioned into the 'superstar' Lawrence of Arabia, admitted that he was one of 'the several legions of men of my generation in your debt'.[20] The combination of pen and sword proved irresistible. 'Wherever democracy is at grips with reaction and rebels are fighting and freedom is in the balance, he is never far away' wrote one journalist in 1915.[21] He added that 'he has lived the romance that other men dream of, and shared the travails and hardships of the men and women who have fought for liberty everywhere'. He represented the last of a dying breed, 'the noblest of that band'[22] of Victorian war correspondents, witnesses of significant developments both in the technology of warfare and in how they worked and transmitted their stories. Since he lived into his mid-eighties, fulminated against fascism to the end and died (in 1941) at a moment when much of what he had stood for was threatened, the principled and courageous Henry Nevinson assumed a symbolic importance. Moreover, he was a rebel who managed not to eschew tradition.

His distinguished appearance added to the legend. Above average height, his five foot eleven inches became elevated to six foot three in the autobiography of an admiring American judge![23] Passport photographs reveal a strikingly handsome man, even in his late seventies, with what is called a noble bearing. White-haired by his mid-thirties, and bearded, with grey-blue eyes, descriptions evoked earlier eras or the romance of legend. He was compared to a Viking, a Crusader, Sir Francis Drake, a Velasquez portrait, a Confederate General and a handsome Prometheus. Time and again he was called a fearless knight. Yet he claimed not to recognize himself in such descriptions, suggesting in 1933 that friends' kindly and chivalrous imaginations had forged this figure: 'you fixed upon me merely to impersonate the kind of man you might like to find existing – one whom I myself should be very glad to meet'.[24] In some ways this 'Grand Duke', as friends called him, had come to stand for the best of the old and new. But although praised for his modesty and often self-censorious, his comment contained a customary touch of meiosis.

Henry Nevinson colluded in the creation of his own history, validating a figure said to be 'the embodiment of the heroic spirit in modern life'.[25] So assiduous was his cultivation of the role of the rebel who championed liberty – Heine's loyal soldier holding out in the war of freedom – and so attractive was it to defy expectations, that at times the pursuit of freedom seemed to matter more than its attainment.

Yet, however carefully crafted, his focus is illuminating for the modern reader. A depressing number of the conflicts he covered and causes he championed are still being contested today, whether in the Balkans, the Caucasus or the Middle East. His reflections help to inform us about the historical shaping of both local grudges and international disputes. And at a time when the importance of war correspondents in modern conflicts is being scrutinized, the fortunes of this veteran campaigner show how their role has evolved.

Henry Nevinson wrote a three-volume autobiography, books and a vast number of newspaper articles and essays. He once commented that:

> A journalist writes but for the day and when the day is passed his work is wiped out like a child's sums upon a slate. The meaning must be clear at first glance, so that the man in the train may grasp it between his suburban station and the city.[26]

His writings were informed by history and literature yet had an immediacy and impact for both men and women. And, unlike many journalists, Henry Nevinson has left behind more than the published word. Hundreds of letters and eighty-seven detailed, frank and thoughtful diaries survive, replete with witty character sketches. They cover almost half a century, providing a rich basis for evaluating the life of this remarkable and acute observer.[27]

Note

This biography of a man and an era is divided into ten chapters. Since the primary focus is on Henry Nevinson's life as a correspondent, most chapters concentrate on a particular conflict, country or cause, examining his perspectives in context. The better-known events such as the Anglo-Boer War and the scenes in Russia in 1905–6 are not explored in as much detail as events that have received less historical attention.

CHAPTER ONE

Finding Arcadia
Greece, War and Work

Henry Nevinson was a late developer. At the age of forty, when many Victorians felt they were nearing the end of their useful lives, he entered a world defined by action and danger. On 14 March 1897 during his first visit to the National Liberal Club, he met the illustrious editor of the *Daily Chronicle*, H. W. Massingham. As Henry later recalled, 'The interview lasted less than a minute, but in that less than a minute the whole course of my life was changed. That is how I began.'[1] Three days later he set off for the Graeco-Turkish War. His career as a war correspondent was finally launched. For the next forty years he witnessed more conflict and travelled further than most Englishmen of his and the following generation. From the war of 1897 he dated his spiritual re-birth.

As he always liked to stress, the early signs had not been propitious. Henry's memoirs, published in the 1920s, open with a characteristically witty denial: 'I was not born in Arcadia.'[2] His birthplace on 11 October 1856 was 5 Southfields Place, Leicester. It was mid-century, the Midlands and he was middle class. All that he would come to revere was the antithesis of this provincial background. His father, George Henry Nevinson, a solicitor (who worked in the family firm in the centre of town with Henry's Uncle Thomas), and his mother, Maria Jane (née Woodd, a name Henry inherited), were middle-aged when he was born. The four Nevinson children were born at two-yearly intervals from 1852. Henry was the third child, following Basil George and Marian Eleanore. Then came a younger brother named Edward Bonney. They now moved to a larger house at 66 Regent Street and by the 1860s boasted as many servants as children.

They were fervently Evangelical. George Nevinson promptly marched his family out of church when the choir adopted white surplices. His mother dismissed Shakespeare's writings as immoral and Henry (who later married a writer of fairy stories) was told that fairy tales were untrue so must not be read. The Bible reigned supreme and Henry and his two brothers and sister read from it morning and evening, learning passages by heart. This must have aided his memory, sound knowledge of things scriptural and love of fine literature. It also helped nurture a

1 Henry Nevinson aged 3.

healthy disregard for taking anything too literally and an enviable ease of style.

Yet we need to read his retrospective accounts with caution. Henry's background was not exactly bourgeois. Henry chose to emphasize a family connection with the seventeenth-century highwayman William Nevinson who robbed only the rich, got deported to North Africa, imprisoned in Leicester and eventually hanged in York. But they could claim descent from a Nevinson who was Thomas Cranmer's lawyer. A more recent Nevinson had been physician to George IV. Henry's father hailed from Hampstead where he met his wife, daughter of a New Bond Street brandy and wine merchant. The autobiography omits the skating parties, seaside holidays and climbs in the mountains of north Wales. Henry was aware that he told a good tale about a stifling puritanical upbringing, and the story seems to have got better as it was retold. By the 1930s Henry was writing that 'the flames of Hell could almost be felt licking our feet'.[3] The childhood that he crafted and polished as an adult was intrinsically linked to the construction of his public persona.

How people choose to recount their family stories can be revealing.[4] Henry's insistence on a past which encapsulated some of the least imaginative features of Victoria's reign provided a dramatically different picture from that of H. W. Nevinson, new man of the new (twentieth) century and international champion of progressive causes. Henry contrasted generations and his private past and public present. In the process he conveniently deflected attention from his complicated private present. Compared to the era of domesticity that characterized the time, his childhood, his married life and his journalism (with frequent night shifts or periods overseas) reveal an extreme flight from domesticity.[5]

Henry's story reinforces but also helps explain the rebel. After all, rebels need to emerge from conventional backgrounds. Yet this rebel stuck closer to his roots than might be imagined. Although deeply critical of organized religion as an adult, Henry's writings reveal traces of the imagery and language of the Bible and Book of Common Prayer, as the title of his autobiography, *Changes and Chances*, suggests. His first teacher was the Revd Robert Burnaby, who drilled him in the rudiments of spelling, Latin and Greek. A rude shock followed in 1870 when Henry and his younger brother Edward Bonney (nicknamed EB) followed their older brother Basil (Bas) to Christ's College, Finchley. It was modelled, according to Henry, on the prison or workhouse, and boys were known by numbers not names. Henry wrote a short story based on a real teacher who ran away.[6] Yet conditions were probably no worse than in many other unreformed public schools of the time. Christ's College had a good reputation for sport. Indeed, the young Henry was passionately attached to Willie Hutchinson, a future rugby international. He reluctantly conceded that the classics master knew a good deal of Greek and he learned more mathematics in his two years there than at Shrewsbury School.

Founded in the Tudor period but modernized in Dr Butler's time, Shrewsbury also provided minimal comforts.[7] Boys were 'strenuously underfed', they sat on wooden benches and discipline was strict. Located in the centre of town (today's public library where Henry's brother's initials EBN can still be seen neatly carved into the wood panelling), the school had only 177 pupils. Henry was initially located in the Shell, between the fourth and fifth forms, even though he was seventeen. The man who was to be so proud of his classical background yet claimed that he knew less French than anyone this side of the Channel was next to bottom in classics and top in French when he entered the sixth form. But, thanks to the influence of one remarkable teacher, by his final year Henry was fifth in classics.

Each morning sixth formers had to learn forty lines of Greek or Latin verse or prose. Mornings and afternoons they had to be prepared to stand up and translate with scrupulous accuracy longish passages from texts. Evenings saw them translating English prose into Latin and English poetry into Greek iambics or Latin verse. What training for the future journalist under pressure to produce copy quickly and at a precise length! Boys were questioned weekly on Greek or Roman history but translation and grammar were paramount. Deadly accuracy mattered rather than the beauty of language or literature. Henry, who, over time, shaped himself into a Romantic Hellenist, became critical of this single-minded dedication to the rules of composition. But it produced results, most notably in scholarships to St John's College, Cambridge.

Henry's accounts of his school extol the River Severn. When he died in 1941 it was in this river that his ashes were scattered. Shrewsbury offered 'the promise of Wales' and, echoing Housman, 'a long blue vision of western mountains'.[8] The symbol and actual challenge of climbing mountains always fascinated him. He and EB were good at music and sport and enjoyed Shrewsbury's unique steeplechase known as The Hunt. It used boys as foxes and hounds. When he joined the upper sixth Henry became a 'praepostor', whose privileges included wearing a top hat. But the chief advantage, he believed, was Arthur Herman Gilkes: 'the noblest character I have ever known, my motive and model, my only true master, even apart from the knowledge he gave me'.[9] Six feet four, this former Salopian literally towered above his fellows and adopted a distinctive approach to teaching. He encouraged reflection and held dialogues on Socratic lines, leading boys on until they contradicted themselves.

Gilkes later became Master of Dulwich College where he wrote a novel entitled *Boys and Masters*, based on Shrewsbury.[10] He is recognizable as the master Mr Scott. The most intellectually promising of the boys is

2 Henry Nevinson (seated on a chair on the far right) and other praepostors at Shrewsbury School, 1875.

Barton: handsome, gifted but somewhat conceited. Personal tragedies and dedicated coaching in classics make him more likeable and win him a scholarship to Oxford. Barton is not simply based on Henry. Salopians such as Graham Wallas and Tom Thomas, a classics master at Middlesbrough High School, also acknowledged Gilkes as the one inspirational teacher.[11] Yet Scott writes to Barton about the values of life from his home at 232 Brunswick Buildings. Henry was then living at 252 Brunswick Buildings in London's East End.

Henry recognized the transformative power of a classical education. It informed his understanding and use of language, sharpened his keen irony and enabled him to feel he was part of the intelligentsia. As the eminent classical scholar Professor Gilbert Murray put it, there was found Henry's centre of gravity.[12] It spoke volumes about class and gender through its assumption of a shared common ground that effectively excluded those without such an education, and it is all too easy today to underestimate the extent to which the educated elite in Victorian society were saturated in the classical tradition. It went far beyond Byronic dreams of freedom. Especially cherished was the Athenian Age (500–350 BC). The seminal moment within this was the funeral oration Pericles delivered in 431 BC over the bodies of Athenian soldiers who had died in the first year of the Peloponnese War. In 1915, in the midst of world war, London buses carried posters with excerpts from this funeral oration to denote the meaning of democracy.[13] In 1940 the *Listener* asked well-known figures to speculate about when they would most like to have been born. In his mid-eighties and deeply saddened by the state of wartime Europe, Henry opted for the Athenian Age.[14]

Henry Nevinson may have cast off the trammels of Evangelical morality but he willingly donned an alternative faith, a Hellenism tailored to his conception of a just society and full of humanistic wisdom. He cultivated it when he went up to Oxford in 1875 with a Junior Studentship to Christ Church (a scholarship worth £120 per annum supplemented by his father's allowance of £100).[15] Henry had chosen Gilkes's former college but it was not the most appropriate place for a painfully sensitive, somewhat gauche youth convinced he was not from an appropriate background. Indeed, Henry's (unfulfilled) plans for his own son included Shrewsbury followed by Balliol College.

Unlike the wealthy and aristocratic, scholars were placed in rooms in the Meadow Buildings overlooking 'a dank and unwholesome swamp'.[16] Henry read classics or *Literae Humaniores*, known as 'Greats', the most prestigious of the Honours schools. But he had little respect for the intellectual or social skills of his tutor, Mr Madan, whom he later parodied in a short story as a man certain of 'nothing but the uses of two Greek particles'.[17] Canon Scott Holland, however, impressed him and he regularly attended lectures by T. H. Green, Professor of Moral

Philosophy at Balliol. Green's complex Hegelian ideas appealed after a surfeit of Evangelicalism and Henry became attracted to new ways of thinking about social obligations. Hints of the later rebel began to emerge. He claimed that he was the first undergraduate to refuse to attend the regulation morning chapel services.[18]

His accounts of Oxford suggest that a miserable initial two years were followed by two more years of 'radiant joy and success'.[19] Yet, although he described himself as so painfully shy that he seemed aloof, he did have friends (interestingly, given his later life, they were invariably male in this insistently masculine environment). He travelled with them in vacations, and in term time rowed and skated. He played the violin in quartets and trios with brother Bas, who was at Exeter College. Elgar later dedicated Variation XII of his *Enigma Variations* to Bas, a talented cellist.[20] But the splitting of Henry's undergraduate days into contrasting halves can be explained by two developments: one was personally devastating, the other redemptive.

He had expected to shine in his 'Mods' after two years of studying. Moderations came halfway through the four-year degree, involving detailed study of Greek and Latin texts, primarily testing linguistic ability before the final seven terms in Greats which, combining ancient history and philosophy, related classical studies to more recent thought.[21] In a letter brimming with banter and bravado he told EB, 'I should think I'm the safest plough-man that ever faced examiner, as every one agrees with me.'[22] But although his translations were highly competent, Latin prose condemned him to a second: 'It was an irretrievable fall.'[23] He fled to Herefordshire where Gilkes coached him for Greats and counselled patience: 'wait to see what time and knowledge and humility will bring you.'[24]

Then Henry met Philip G. L. Webb, one of Christ Church's Westminster scholars, an intellectual, urbane Londoner with whom he began studying literature, language and music (Webb later became secretary of the Handel Society). It was thanks to Webb that Henry came to appreciate Ruskin, whose famous course of lectures at the Parks Museum he now eagerly attended. He became devoted to Ruskin, calling him 'Master Of The Hand, The Heart, The Head'.[25] In the 1920s Henry was still emphasizing Webb's impact, claiming that nobody had 'dragged me out of the slough of despond like you'.[26] There is a remarkable symmetry here with Henry's description of school. Whether life in both institutions was quite so dramatically altered by the Gilkes/Webb figures as retrospectively suggested is perhaps open to question. But the conversion narrative makes a compelling tale.

In his eightieth year Henry wrote that nothing had ever compensated for receiving a second-class degree.[27] His reminiscences of Oxford were indubitably shaped by his results. His later radicalism and ironic wit enhanced the ambivalence. He could argue that the Oxford man was often 'self-centred, superior, contemptuous of the actual men around him, and maddeningly given to lecture and put the others to right' but he was also a product of the place and glad to be one.[28] As Gilbert Murray astutely observed, Henry displayed 'a fine example of the true Oxford manner . . . he vehemently abused her and quite obviously loved her'.[29] He gave many talks there and, as he aged, so he dwelt more on Oxford's visual appeal. In December 1939 Christ Church finally offered him an Honorary Studentship. The man who had once described himself there as 'like the pelican in the wilderness'[30] was immensely proud. But in 1879 his second-class degree seemed only to confirm precisely what he despised, mediocrity. Arcadia must have seemed a very long way away.

'For the next fifteen or twenty years I hurried on from one small employment to another, like a cinema moved too fast.'[31] Henry's description of life after Oxford seems a far cry from the world of the dashing war correspondent. He taught at Shrewsbury for one term and then briefly at Westminster School. In 1880, he travelled to Germany. Through the writings of Thomas Carlyle he had become fascinated by German thinking and by Goethe in particular. He still deployed the language of the spiritual quest, seeing Germany as his new 'spiritual friend' with Goethe his lodestone.[32] Goethe united the man of letters and the heroic man of action, positions that Henry himself would seek with difficulty to reconcile.

In 'a bug-infested attic' in London's West End, Henry wrote his first book, a 450-page tome on Johann Gottfried Herder.[33] It was dedicated 'in grateful reverence to the memory of Thomas Carlyle' and published in 1884.[34] Lacking his later crisp, ironic style, it acknowledges the help of his pious sister Marian and seems to have been influenced by an Evangelical model of what constituted an appropriate life. The notes also mention assistance from Sophie Weisse. Henry wrote later about his 'desperate love' for this young woman of German origin, five years his senior. Henry's nephew John L. Nevinson (EB's son) also mentioned this 'flame of HWN's youth' in his diary,[35] adding that, at the same time as Henry was seeing Sophie, Leicester neighbours began gossiping about his frequent Greek lessons with Margaret Wynne Jones. John Nevinson records that Henry 'suddenly decided he must marry' Margaret. Henry recalled this period as 'all very sad and unhappy': hardly an auspicious start to what would prove to be a disastrous marriage.[36]

Born on 11 January 1858 and fifteen months younger than Henry, Margaret was the only daughter of elderly parents, Timothy and Mary Jones.[37] She had five brothers (a sixth had died of croup aged two). Her father, whom she adored, was a Welsh-speaking Welshman from Lampeter and the vicar of St Margaret's Church in the centre of Leicester, after which she was named. Her mother was born in Leicester but was half-Welsh, and Margaret always chose to emphasize her own Welsh identity. 'I want to learn Latin; please let me be a boy' had been the plea of Jane Walsh, who married Thomas Carlyle.[38] Margaret was fortunate that her father, a classics scholar, included his daughter from the age of seven in the rigorous training of his children in Latin and Greek. Although her mother feared that nobody would want to marry a girl who read Greek, Margaret became passionately interested in things classical. She later published articles such as 'Juvenal on Latter-Day Problems', and the first of Henry's surviving diaries (for 1893) shows the couple working on Horace's best odes.

The location of Margaret's education largely mirrored Henry's, though its form was strictly gendered. A convent school in Oxford was followed by a year's finishing school in Paris. Her father died when four brothers were still being educated. Margaret became a governess. Keen to travel she answered an advertisement in a Cologne paper for an au pair to teach English and be a companion to a man's wife, discovering just in time that the man was an unmarried, third-rate actor living in lodgings. She then boarded with a professor's family and became a pupil teacher in Cologne, gaining a diploma in German literature and language. Four years as a Latin, German and Greek mistress at South Hampstead High School (part of the Girls' Public Day School Trust) followed, alongside what today is called distance learning. This was a degree set up in 1876 by St Andrews University, enabling young women to study from home and take examinations at local centres. Examinations were identical to those for the men's MA but the course could be completed over a longer period. In 1883 Margaret was one of sixty-three women awarded an LLA (Lady Literate in Arts).[39]

3 Margaret Wynne Nevinson (second from left) in her graduation gown at a women's suffrage demonstration.

Henry and Margaret thus had much in common. They had known each other since childhood though Timothy Jones, who had joined the Oxford movement in his youth, was far too High Church for the Nevinsons. There is evidence too that the latter saw themselves as socially superior to the Jones family, who also lived in a poorer part of town. But the couple shared many interests and Margaret too was passionate about Carlyle. Both attended the 'pops' in St James's Hall, London, where another mutual hero, Browning, could be espied in the stalls.[40] Here or in Leicester, after a gap of ten years, they met again. They suddenly and, as Henry later put it, 'mistakenly' became engaged. They married on 18 April 1884, Margaret's curate brother, Lloyd, officiating. Henry was twenty-seven and Margaret twenty-six. Reversing the usual sentiments, Henry's diary refers to being 'unhappily married' at St Clement Danes, the beautiful Wren church close to Fleet Street. He describes their honeymoon as 'a disastrous journey' to Germany. Yet these comments came years after the event and we do not have direct evidence of their sentiments at the time.

Putting together dates from German and British records reveals that Margaret was pregnant when they married.[41] Quite apart from their familiarity with Germany, travel abroad would have afforded a welcome escape from family censure. Four and a half months after their wedding, on 30 August, Margaret gave birth to Philippa Maria. They were now living in Jena, the sleepy university town amongst the mountains and forests of Thuringia which Goethe had converted into 'the true home of German thought' and where Schiller had been a professor of history. Henry enrolled at the university as a philosophy student.[42] He attended lectures on morphology by the renowned rector, Ernst Haeckel, and studied Goethe intensively and metaphysics from Kant to Lotze. He and Margaret gave private tuition in English. They lived more cheaply than was possible at home, with three furnished rooms, a garden and a maid for the equivalent of a pound a month.[43] Henry apparently gained some unofficial claim to fame by introducing proper football rules into the German game and using a real football in place of a leather casing stuffed with straw.[44]

Returning to England in the late spring of 1885, the Nevinsons took rooms in Bloomsbury where Henry wrote another rather conventional biography, a slim volume on Schiller (1889). He also became the 'right-hand man' for Lloyd C. Sanders, editor of a huge biographical dictionary, *Celebrities of the Century* (1887), which appeared initially in seventeen sixpenny parts. A Eurocentric account of men and women of the nineteenth century, it had forty acknowledged contributors and others, like Margaret, who were not mentioned.

Between 1885 and 1891, Bedford College, London, a pioneer in women's higher education, employed Henry as the head of its history department.[45] He admitted to knowing only Greek history but was now called Professor of History. He really wanted to be a writer but lacked confidence and was easily depressed. He wrote disparagingly of 'This half-hearted life, without grandeur, without concentrated aim'. It was 'worse than death'. He was 'sinking, sinking down to hell' with 'no one to help me'.[46]

The Nevinsons were also committed to another kind of teaching. Since the summer of 1885 they had been living in the East End of London at Brunswick Buildings in Goulston Street, close to Petticoat Lane and to the newly formed experimental universities' settlement, Toynbee Hall. They were not literally residents (the residents were all men) but, persuaded by the settlement's founder, the Revd Samuel Barnett, they lived round the corner, occupying two new workmen's flats with six rooms, for fifteen shillings and sixpence a week. Margaret hated the constant battle against vermin and after a year they moved to another block. But the bugs came too. Henry had already helped the Salopian Luke Paget (later Bishop of London) at the Christ Church Mission and briefly dabbled with the fledgling socialist Social Democratic Federation. Toynbee Hall, he felt, helped reconcile spiritual needs with a more fulfilling life than that offered by the day job. He could draw on Carlyle's belief in the dignity of labour and the Hegelian idealism advocated by T. H. Green (Toynbee was named in memory of Green's disciple). Henry was elected a Toynbee Associate.

It is easy to criticize settlement workers, steeped in high culture but attempting to disseminate rather than really re-fashion their ideas amongst the socially deprived. Yet such commitment would have appeared both novel and daring at a time when many went slumming just for the afternoon and probably gained infinitely more from it than did their intended recipients. Henry criticized those who babbled about 'green tea and Schopenhauer' and found the poor 'so interesting' but could not establish personal close contact with them.[47] There was a little smugness here since he was living amongst the poor. But he was also conscious of the gulf between himself and the deprived and especially scathing about the High Anglican Oxford House students, suggesting that they were 'in danger of self-sacrificial priggery'. Toynbee Hall suited him better but it was appropriate that he lived outside the fellowship, not least because he understood the difference between sympathy and empathy and recognized his own ambivalence about helping the very poor. Believing that the degradation of their minds was a major problem, he taught classes at Toynbee. Learning about Goethe and Homer was, however, most popular with clerks and teachers. Margaret held French and dancing classes and EB, now an architect, taught drawing. Henry also sat on the committee of the Whittington Boys' Club and assisted the Toynbee resident Ernest Aves in research into the building trades for Charles Booth's massive investigation of London's life and labour.

Margaret was a rent-collector or lady visitor in two large blocks of artisans' dwellings. Some of her insights helped Henry's book *Neighbours of Ours* (1895).[48] In ten inter-linked stories united by one narrator he joined those who put the East End under the microscope. Henry's fiction avoided the common representation of its people as prone to violence or totally bowed down by circumstances. Character matters more than class in his stories and there is a slight tendency to downplay some of the real hardships and sheer grind in the focus on developing the individual's strength of character against the odds. Recent assessment of Henry's stories has earned him the label of 'the first distinctive writer of the Cockney School', with particular interest paid to two stories with unconventional romances: cross-class in 'The "St. George" of Rochester' and inter-racial in 'Sissaro's Return'. Both were reprinted in the 1970s.[49] Yet the latter still reinforces a number of predictable stereotypes. Henry's views would, though, become more sophisticated over time, not least because on his own travels he would sometimes find himself the outsider.

The final tale about cadets covered a subject few were so well qualified to write about. For over a decade a working-class cadet corps, St George's in the East Company, was under the command of Captain Henry Nevinson. This was a time when a gender-specific 'youth' was discovered and carefully cultivated to deflect the newly defined hooliganism. Henry's company was the first for the working class of London and in 1891 he united it to a battalion. The First Cadets, The Queens, Royal West Surrey Regiment was based in Southwark. Henry's diaries for the early 1890s are peppered with references to their drill, parades, manoeuvres and camp life. He did his own drill with the Grenadier and Coldstream Guards, worked his way up from private to major and 'passed school' with 98 per cent.

His commitment to a cadet corps does not at first sight sit easily with Nevinson the passionate champion of freedom and rebellion. Neither does his belief in a national army and universal conscription but, inspired by Germany and Comtean notions of solidarity, he gave his plans a democratic twist by arguing that a national army could actually be the basis for eliminating class distinctions and a university for the poor.[50] Yet, as he began to see war at first hand and as others took up ideas of national service, so he began to espouse very different beliefs.

A second volume of short stories appeared in 1896.[51] *In The Valley of Tophet* focused on the Black Country and was slightly more successful than *Neighbours*. The Fabian novelist Edith Nesbit was sufficiently impressed to write to Henry praising these stories. Replying, Henry admitted how hard he found it to write:

For nearly twenty years I have been trying to learn how to write but I perceive that I shall never succeed in learning that great art in this life. For what others do so easily day by day, still costs me endless distress, and gives me no satisfaction when it is done. So I have to follow my business – which takes most of my time, and I can only practise at learning to write in my odd moments.[52]

Following his business was all the more important after the birth in August 1889 of a second child, Christopher Richard Wynne Nevinson (called Richard by the family). Henry briefly considered a post at the Museum of the Guild of St George, the small Ruskin Museum in Sheffield, and then was rescued from history teaching in February 1891 when he became the part-time Secretary to the London Playing Fields Committee at £100 a year.[53] This sought to support cricket and football in a capital city with five million inhabitants and dwindling space for playing fields. It worked with local clubs to secure land for sports grounds and opposed building on open spaces. But much of Henry's time was spent in administration. On his thirty-fifth birthday he penned a poem with the words:

> Now in the centre of life's arch I stand
> And view its curve descending from this day.[54]

His diary makes sad reading. In March 1893 all seemed wretched, 'my spirits nearer suicide than ever'. On reaching forty he lamented 'That I who can write sh. [*sic*] spend my life directing envelopes.' Yet his fortunes soon changed dramatically and irrevocably.

Henry had visited Greece once before his 1897 mission. At Easter three years earlier he had accompanied the Toynbee Travellers' Club on one of their annual European tours.[55] He recalled his initial sensations on numerous occasions: 'Every stone and clod of its brilliant surface was consecrated by the noblest memories in all the history of men', and:

> The whole country is endowed with exquisite beauty – deep inlets of purple sea, so brilliant that you might think you could take up the water like amethyst in your hand; high mountains, some gleaming with snow; and deep valleys, some dark with the ilex, some brilliant with peach-blossom in spring, or ripening maize and stunted vineyards in summer; and over all the clear Greek air, a nurse of genius.[56]

Ironically, his first glimpse of Arcadia was not a romantic one: it was a cold, grey day and the travellers saw only a wet, marshy plain almost encircled by high mountains. But he was entranced by the country he dubbed his spiritual home. And soon Greece, and more particularly the fate of the Cretans, was in the news. Abdul Hamid II, 'The Red Sultan', had instigated massacres of Armenians in Constantinople and Turkish Asia, rekindling the British indignation that had surfaced in Gladstonian times. Towards the end of 1896 Crete made a bid for independence from

Turkish control. Colonel Vassos sent a Greek battalion to support the insurgents. In February 1897 Henry approached the Byron Society in London, unsuccessfully suggesting the formation of a British volunteer force. On 5 March, however, a new group, the Liberal Forwards, held a meeting at London's Queen's Hall. Standing on his seat, Henry urged action in place of words. At first he was howled down and grabbed by stewards (the first of many such occasions) but his proposal for forming a British Legion was endorsed and passed to the Greek Minister. A few days later enlistment began for a Philhellenic Legion bound for Epirus. Henry enrolled under the command of an ex-regular officer, so was about to go to Greece when he met Massingham at the National Liberal Club.

Henry's memoirs suggest that Massingham, also a Graecophile, immediately engaged him for the *Daily Chronicle*.[57] Other accounts are less dramatic, with Massingham casually remarking, 'Well, you might send me a letter or two.'[58] Once Henry was in Athens, Henry Norman (the assistant editor) explained that Massingham was appointing him as temporary correspondent. He was to go to Thessaly until the veteran resident correspondent Charles Williams arrived. Henry was certainly with the right newspaper. Known as the soldier's paper and a respected organ of Liberalism, the *Chronicle* was at its height under Massingham's editorship. It had a good reputation in Greece: Henry claimed that he got past sentries in Crete by shouting the Greek for *Daily Chronicle*.[59] He had earlier approached the paper to enquire about openings abroad. The Sudan and India had been mentioned but nothing had materialized. Now 'One of the smallest and poorest nations in the world had dared to defy an empire more than twenty times its size.'[60] To witness and write about a struggle for freedom from a foe represented as a monstrous slaughterer, to return to his beloved Greece and to be paid for all this as a 'war special' must have made Henry feel as though at last those Greek gods were smiling on him.

From mid-March 1897 the notebook in which he wrote his diary is blank, the pages suddenly and pointedly empty. It resumed in October with a new volume. But a public record exists through Henry's newspaper articles and the book he wrote on his return home. The Graeco-Turkish War, prompted by the Greek attempt to annex Crete, lasted but a month. It is not remarked upon much today, even on the soil where it was fought, not least because it formed one of the less glorious moments in Greece's long and impressive military history. Not until 1913, after the Balkan Wars, did Crete become part of Greece. But it was a seminal event for Henry: six weeks of 'higher happiness than any man has ever known'.

Leaving on 17 March he travelled via Turin to Brindisi and then by steamer to Athens. Borrowing from Thucydides, he wrote that 'Ignorant of war, Athens stood a-tiptoe with excitement.'[61] He was now forced to take note of the Greek present as well as its past. He saw refugees and heard about the massacre at Canea (Chania) in January. Volunteers and reservists were everywhere. Athens seemed like 'a modern play enacted on a background of Aeschylus'.[62] Classical comparisons were never far away and the tale of Henry's journey suggests something of ancient Greek myths. Norman gave him £25 and told him to travel from Thessaly over the mountains to Arta. It was a perilous plan given both the terrain and the need to cross the frontier before war was actually declared.

Henry and Scaramangar, his interpreter, sailed to Volos and then took a train to Larissa in the centre of Thessaly. They travelled light: Henry had a small canvas knapsack, a rug and a mackintosh. They went down the Vale of Tempe, close to the Turkish border. From the village of Kalambaka they saw the Meteora, gigantic sandstone needles, 1,820 feet high, said to be meteors hurled by angry gods. Henry was wound up by windlass in a basket for a night in one of the monasteries perched on the columns like storks' nests. The following morning was bright and the snow-capped mountains looked peaceful 'yet that day for the first time I was to see the shedding of blood and to hear the cries of the wounded'.[63] Henry climbed the steep pass to Metsovo, marvelling that this was probably the route by which Caesar had brought his army from the Adriatic to triumph over the Pompeians at Pharsalia.

Before the formal declaration of war there were various skirmishes aimed at occupying border stations. Defying orders, a few thousand Andarti, volatile and intensely patriotic irregulars, crossed the frontier, burned blockhouses and besieged the main Turkish station. With them were cold and hungry young Italian volunteers, 'Garibaldians' in distinctive red shirts, armed only with rifles. In the village of Baltino in Turkish Macedonia was a large blockhouse and 129 Turks besieged by animated Andarti. A snowstorm helped the Turks to escape that night. Henry telegraphed the story to the *Chronicle* and got an unexpected 'scoop' since it was the first account of the fighting printed in Britain. When he found some Andarti driven back from the Turkish village of Krania, Henry reflected on the making and telling of history. It was a little skirmish, never to be heard of again. The fighting had just ended. Henry was on the spot, in the middle of eyewitnesses and 'Any historian would envy such materials, but the truth of the event was undiscoverable by me.' He admitted that 'I could hardly put down a single definite sentence and be sure it was really true.'[64] Descriptions of historic battles had always filled him with admiration but this event caused him to begin thinking critically about the apparent insight and accuracy with which historians managed to describe 'almost every minute in the enormous conflicts of the world, even many years later'.

Henry and Scaramangar slept where they could find shelter. In words evocative of a child's farmyard story, Henry described a cacophonous scene with one family of peasants: 'The suckling wailed, the chickens clucked, the cats howled, the women snored, the horses sighed, the pig grunted inquisitively, and we all enjoyed a good medieval sort of night together.'[65] The Turks were now firing at random and Henry had to modify his plans. They returned to Kalambaka and then went a little south to Trikala. A telegram arrived from Charles Williams, who was now in Larissa watching the Thessalian frontier. He suggested that Henry try to cross the Pindos Mountains to cover the Epirus frontier. Locals were sceptical, not least because of the deep snow. Scaramangar had already walked enough so Henry set off without him, helped by the loan of a horse from the correspondent W. T. Maud. The horse got him to the foot of the mountains.

The war correspondents on mainland Greece were mainly in Thessaly. Bertram Christian, who later published several of Henry's books, dined with some of them in Larissa. He recalled how, dressed in 'blue collar', Henry stood out from the others. He 'simply radiated quiet distinction'.[66] By the time of the Greek Palm Sunday, Henry was in a remote village acquiring ponies and the services of two local men, one of whom, Spero, readily confessed to being afraid of the Turks and the snow. Despite the pacific setting, enhanced by decorated churches, war had now started officially.

It was a hazardous journey. Traversing the snowy mountain was like climbing a perpendicular ladder. In places Henry had to hold the ponies' hooves in the crevices of stones and so narrow were the tracks along the edges of the precipices that their heads and tails had to be held to prevent them from falling. The snow nearly reached the ponies' bellies. They crossed one stream by making a raft from felled pine trees and spent a night in a barn at a place known as 'the Sewer of Sorrow'. Somehow they reached Arta in just over three days. Here was ancient Ambracia. Henry had long wished to see Pyrrhus' capital with its Byzantine churches and legendary tenth-century bridge, celebrated in a ballad.

To his surprise he discovered that the Turks had fled and were retreating northwards towards Janina (Ioannina), then the capital of Turkish Epirus and in southern Albania. Greek soldiers under General Manos were in hot pursuit. Henry followed, keen to see more action. He met Scudamore of the *Daily News* and Knight of the *Morning Post*. They shared a paschal lamb, Henry noting their trappings of luxury: a large tent, effective horses, servants, messengers, cases of food, cutlery, plates and bedding. Four days followed on his own in a fortified house in the village of Karavarsavas while Spero returned to Arta for provisions. Henry ate black bread, dried figs and a maggot-ridden chicken he had shot.

The Turks had taken Larissa on Good Friday and the Greek army had fled. Henry now found himself under serious targeted rifle-fire for the first time as he walked up a steep mountain pass south of Janina with the

Evzoni. These crack mountaineer troops wore blue jackets, white kilts, red caps and shoes. The Turks were firing from only 400 yards away. Years later Henry wrote how the mountains, plants and sun 'appeared more than usually beautiful' that day as he faced serious danger. It was a sensation that would be repeated many times in his life. Unarmed, he experienced both exhilaration and fear. Yet 'the fear of exposing my fear before foreigners' also kept him in line.[67]

Firing ceased at sunset but resumed the next morning. Henry risked climbing the high ridge on the right of the pass, joining the Greek forces posted along the edge of the summit. He helped them build a defensive low parapet from loose rocks. Peering over the edge he saw the Turks advancing. Bullets bounced over their heads and an Evzoni close to Henry was hit in the neck and died. Climbing up to this position again the following afternoon, Henry watched the Greek soldiers on the summit hesitate. The Turks had renewed their assault 'with terrible vigour'. The Greeks now rushed down the mountainside. It was a complete rout: 'In straggling blue lines they came rushing down the mountain side. Hardly had they gone when the crest swarmed with black figures, shouting, waving red flags, and firing down upon us in the valley.' At the sound of the Turkish trumpet the local population took flight and fled along the track towards Arta. The village was burned that night: 'The Andarti fluttered away like blown leaves. The regulars buckled on their blankets, and hastened to join the herd of refugees. There was no attempt at defence. Officers and men just walked out of the trenches and disappeared.'[68]

Fugitives were weighed down by personal possessions: babies in cradles, rolls of bedding, iron pots. One woman had a baby tied to her back and a little calf round her neck. This was the image Henry later used in his story 'In Twenty-Four Hours'.[69] A young Greek soldier, Kephelas, shifts from hopeless hope to real fear in battle. When the line breaks and the whole army retreats he sees a young woman hand her quilt to her husband while she carries the cooking pot, calf and cradle. They are separated in the fleeing crowd but she is reunited with her husband only to find that he has abandoned the quilt, unaware that the baby was asleep in it. Kephelas goes in search of it and returns the baby unharmed to his mother. But after instinctively displaying true courage, Kephelas is fatally wounded by a Turkish bullet.

Joining this flight south at about 3 a.m., the scent of orange blossom alerted Henry that they were approaching Arta. There were so many soldiers, peasants and animals on the bridge that the goats panicked, leaping over the parapet to be drowned in the River Arachtos. A few days later Henry began a three-day ride south to Patras to establish contact with his paper. Here it seemed as though the war had ended but he wished to return one final time to Arta.

It was just as well, for there took place on 13 May a fated yet truly gallant Greek effort known as the Battle of Gribovo (Grimpobo). In torrential rain, not far from Arta, the Greeks sought to advance up slopes with the Turks ranged along the summits of successive lines of hills. Henry estimated that about 300 Greeks perished and as many as 1,000 were wounded (there were 8,000–10,000 in the division). When General Manos arrived and spoke at the Greeks' shallow graves, Henry thought of Pericles' funeral oration. He was to see many men killed in battle over the years but 'those young farmers whom I saw buried in that month of May have remained most deeply in my mind'.[70] They were, after all, the first he had seen buried on the battlefield and they were Greeks.

After sleeping in the rain for two nights Henry took shelter in an old house in Arta. He slept on planks, surrounded by pictures of saints. When he was struck down by excruciating pain, an old woman pounded his stomach with clenched fists and then placed a bread poultice with four lighted matches on it. A glass tumbler was pressed down on top and, within an hour, the pain subsided. Known as 'venduses', it was to draw out evil humours.

On 18 May, thirty days after the start of war, a telegram from Constantinople announced that, due to intervention from Britain and Russia, an armistice had been signed. Henry invited four Greek artillery officers to dine with him in an orange grove. They ate lukewarm lamb and drank to the future of Greece: 'I think it was the saddest toast ever drunk among the sons of men.'[71] He would not attribute the Greek defeat to cowardice despite having witnessed panic and retreat. Rather it was the Greeks' love of life and 'imaginative fear' that explained their behaviour, as the story of Kephelas suggests. In his book on the war Henry issued a stern warning to those predisposed to criticize:

> It is very easy for comfortable Englishmen whose greatest risks have been run in a football match, to sneer at a poverty-stricken and long oppressed people for want of courage in face of enormous odds; but when I hear them, there rises before my mind a picture of the thin blue line going into action against impregnable entrenchments at Grimbovo for a cause they knew to be hopeless.[72]

Barnett noted that Henry seemed disillusioned by the Greeks' want of seriousness. But his criticisms were largely levelled at the lack of proper preparation and training of men and officers. He was scornful of the amateur and opportunistic Andarti whom he dubbed 'the curse of the modern army', a phrase formerly used by Lord Wolseley to describe war correspondents![73] Henry praised the gunners but the army lacked sufficient horses. Fresh from working with cadets, Henry extolled valour combined with discipline. Precisely because the Greeks were 'a democratic, eloquent and imaginative people' the first signs of defeat provoked distrust and uncertainty because there was no underlying confidence in officers. Infantry officers needed to be younger and, if Greece were to persist with an army, it must be small and well trained. The American correspondent Richard Harding Davis made a similar point: 'The country was like a huge debating society. When these men were called out to act as soldiers, almost every private had his own idea as to how the war should be conducted.'[74] The Greek tradition of democracy and comradeship militated against the hierarchical structures of the army and the tight discipline so imperative in wartime.

Henry now spent ten days in Athens. Here he met for the first time another journalist inspired by ancient Greece, H. N. Brailsford. He had joined the Philhellenic Legion. Despite similar outlooks, Brailsford was painfully aware of the physical contrast between them:

> My ill-fitting uniform was ragged and dirty and I was limping on a wounded foot. The man I met made on me, at first glance, an impression of physical perfection. He was tall and well-proportioned . . . he seemed older and also younger than the rest of us.[75]

They spent an evening together, Brailsford discovering that Henry not only looked like a soldier and athlete but was also a scholar and poet. It was the start of a long friendship.

Henry was now ordered to Crete to investigate the insurgents' demands. The sight of Britain helping to protect Turkish Crete was galling for him. Camped along the Venetian ramparts in Candia (Heraklion/Iráklion) which looked out towards the birthplace of Zeus, he saw some 350 Welsh Fusiliers, 400 Seaforth Highlanders and a mule battery. They were placed there to protect the Turks from 'the unorganized Christian inhabitants who are struggling for freedom and existence against their ancient murderers'.[76] Ships and troops from the Great Powers (excepting Germany) surrounded the island, upholding the sovereignty of the Turks in 'European Concert'. But although attempting to rebuff Greek occupation and stop Greek massacres of Muslims, they sought also to prevent Constantinople (Istanbul) from making significant gains from victory. And the Great Powers were carefully watching each other's actions. Henry deplored such a 'shameful alliance' just as he had earlier condemned the combined fleets' bombardment.[77] Yet he also believed that there was a vast gap between official gestures and dutiful soldiers' true sentiments. He ended one article on Crete by asking: 'Was the British army ever before engaged on a service in which the sympathy of nearly every officer and man was on the side of the so-called enemy?'[78]

Seeking to be entertaining, he came dangerously close to farce in his accounts of meeting Crete's patriotic rebels. He told how he stumbled upon the insurgents' eastern headquarters in a cottage filled with rifles, revolvers, Cretan knives and 'fine Cretan males, all wearing the black handkerchief round their heads, and trousers like an undivided bag'.[79] They placed him on a table while three officers sat on a bed. They drank goats' milk and told Henry and his interpreter Sigalas about their demands for the immediate withdrawal of Turkish troops from the island and ultimate union with Greece. Years later Henry wrote that one of the three insurgents was probably Venizelos, Prime Minister of Greece from 1910.

Granted a pass to cross the lines, Henry also visited insurgents in the devastated west of the island. Warning shots greeted him as he approached an orange grove at Alikianu. He tied a handkerchief to a stick, finding 'the usual crowd of picturesque men with rifles and knives'. It was 'like an early English wapentake'.[80] He returned the next day, travelling by gunboat, accompanied by a Cretan lexicographer. He then struck out into the mountains on his own. He had a secret letter for the insurgents stitched into his waistcoat lining but did not divulge who exactly gave him this in Athens or what this mysterious message said. He handed it to Michalis (Hadji Mikhali), hero of the Cretan insurrection of 1866–9, talked to him under the olive trees and slept on a bench in his kitchen. A few days later he sailed away to the Messenian coast and then rode on to Sparta. Musing on its former distinction he was suddenly struck down with his first attack of malarial fever. A nightmarish journey back to Athens followed. He was treated by an English doctor and cared for by Sigalas before sailing home from one of the century's last wars and his first conflict.

Henry also credited it as the first war in which censorship was firmly established.[81] His telegrams and letters took some time to reach the paper, not least because the Greek censors in Patras were not over-keen to send the depressing news. Henry complained that it was a far cry from the freedom enjoyed by the pioneer war correspondents. He had wandered on foot or on a 'crawling war-horse' for twelve hours daily, lived off black bread and an occasional lamb or dried fig, slept on the ground and been exposed to fire four times in one week yet his telegrams did not get through.[82] In fact most of his material eventually reached home though was not always printed in the intended order. This was also the last war to use the black or smoky powder that enabled every rifle to be traced by a telltale puff of smoke. It had helped Henry estimate the number and position of troops. A short war, at the *fin de siècle*, it appropriately combined the old with a little of the new.

So how had Henry fared? One modern writer suggests that he was too wrapped up in the ancient, evincing more interest in proximity to Actium than in modern dangers.[83] Yet contemporaries would have had an empathy with this approach that it is difficult to appreciate today. For Henry, Ancient Greece set the standard for modern civilized behaviour. Not all educated people would have agreed but many late Victorian readers would have felt comfortable with his comparisons since they were more familiar with the legends and histories of classical times than with the modern developments of a faraway country they would probably never visit. Others also made similar allusions. Hugh Hankey's article on the aftermath of the war was called 'Thermopylae in the Armistice'.[84]

The majority of Henry's articles – and by no means all were attributed – focused overwhelmingly on present and imminent dangers. And since the facts were being reported elsewhere in the paper, passages such as the one alluding to ancient Actium can anyway be appreciated for their lyrical qualities:

> Across the little strait is Actium, and it was there the Queen of men turned back, and was irresistible in charm. A little to the right is the great mass of Leukas [Corfu]; and much further off, Cephallonia rises, round and grey; and one of the line of hills between them is actually the little island that was good for goats but bad for horses – the island from which Ulysses longed to see the smoke leaping up again.[85]

Henry sent his paper half a dozen unsigned long letters on the Greek–Turkish frontier. Here his descriptions of the region's natural beauty make his words on war all the more chilling. He tells of the anemones, white primroses and violets on the journey from Kalambaka to the top of the Pindos Mountains and how a cuckoo sang throughout the firing at Baltino.

Massingham was pleased with his discovery, telling Margaret that 'I have nothing but praise for his work which under circumstances of great difficulty has been unequalled for dispatch, finish and critical faculty.'[86] This war effectively launched the middle-aged Henry on a new, long and illustrious career as a war correspondent and respected journalist. It may not have ended financial and other uncertainties but it freed him from his old job. In October he left the London Playing Fields post (Margaret had valiantly covered during his absence) and joined the *Daily Chronicle* staff. At the end of November he replaced Norman editing the Literary Page and took over from Williams for overseas campaigns. That Greek spring had become emblematic of Henry belatedly finding his vocation and voice. The man who had once found writing difficult now became an accomplished essayist who always got his copy in on time and a helpful editor. But it was reporting on the Greek war that inspired him. In the final verse of his poem 'Pilgrim's Song' he wrote:

> Dear land, my more than mother,
> Receive me to my home!
> Count me among thy children,
> Though late in time I come;
> Though late in time I come,

> Give me thy children's peace
> When like a saint I'm buried
> In the shirt that went to Greece.[87]

In 1898 his *Scenes in the Thirty Days' War between Greece and Turkey, 1897* was 'published, praised & neglected'.[88] Its title played on the famous Thirty Years' War of 1618–48. It included Henry's drawings and photographs and somewhat disingenuous claims that it was about personal experience rather than a history of war and free from politics and controversy. It was, though, a highly partisan account. Nowhere in the analysis of why the Greeks were so easily crushed is there any suggestion of the superior skills of the Turks. It is presented as a modern Greek tragedy, not as a Turkish triumph. Indeed, it ends with an impassioned romantic flourish encapsulating what Greece meant for Henry and the heirs of Byron and invoking the stock representation of the wicked Turk:

> In the near [*sic*] East, Greece is still what she was of old, the one point of enlightenment and freedom, the one barrier against Oriental darkness and oppression. When greater Powers were hesitating through fear or selfishness, she alone had the courage to strike another blow against the barbarian despotism which still holds so many of her race in bondage.[89]

In the same year as the war, Henry wrote the Introduction and text for a book of pictures of Greece by his neighbour, the artist and architect John Fulleylove, RI. Henry claimed in print that his Introduction was written in 'The Insurgents' Headquarters, Halikanu Crete 1897'.[90] It was actually composed in Hampstead that summer. His visits to Greece in 1894 and 1897 also helped produce *The Plea of Pan* (1901), furthering the fashion for this grotesque creature who sought refuge in Arcadia. The *Manchester Guardian* declared it to be the best of the genre since *Sartor Resartus*. Henry would have enjoyed this comparison with what he believed to be Carlyle's most profound and imaginative work.[91] For Brailsford, the beauty of the writing and its insight made it the 'most perfect thing Nevinson accomplished'.[92] But precisely because it was so much a product of its time, its appeal today is limited. The first of its stories is set in Arcadia. Arcadia also featured in three of Fulleylove's plates. And in the first spring of the new century Henry found himself in yet another Arcadia, this time a place in South Africa.

CHAPTER TWO

Into Africa

The South African War

When the twentieth century began, Henry's celebrations were muted and modest. He was in the midst of the 118-day Siege of Ladysmith in the South African or Second Anglo-Boer War. He had left Britain on 9 September 1899. He had been recalled from observing another, less famous siege: the Siege of Guérin and the 'Anti-Juifs' in Paris. Sent to cover developments in the Dreyfus Affair that had, for the last five years, gripped and split the French press and politics, he had waited for the surrender with other journalists at the end of Rue de Chabrol.[1] Now he was relieved to be sent at last by the *Daily Chronicle* to the place the world was watching.

At sea Henry encountered officers such as Colonel Frank Rhodes, Cecil Rhodes's brother, and correspondents like Harry Pearse (*Daily News*) and the rather boisterous Bennett Burleigh of the *Daily Telegraph*. Arriving in Cape Town, he quickly established useful contacts, one of whom was Olive Schreiner's brother, the Cape Prime Minister. Aware that time was not on his side he quickly made for the Dutch Republics. At Pretoria he found a bright young lawyer. This 'slender and pallid youth' was Jan Smuts. War was imminent. Henry crossed the frontier into Natal. On the train he interviewed General Piet Joubert, hero of the earlier Boer victory at Majuba Hill and now commanding the Boer army. Courteous and seemingly opposed to war, he told Henry that 'the heart of my soul is bloody with sorrow'.[2] Reaching Ladysmith in northern Natal on 5 October, Henry engaged an 'elderly Cape boy', a young Zulu servant and horses. He rode round the area, gauging the terrain and sending wires to the paper. Six days later, on his forty-third birthday, the war began. The following day he witnessed the invasion of Natal.

Henry's diary had charted the deteriorating situation in the Transvaal. The discovery of gold there had transformed the prospects of South Africa. He saw the Jameson Raid as the beginning of the trouble, broadly agreeing with his colleague J. A. Hobson, whose economic analysis would be articulated in *Imperialism: A Study* (1902). Henry was unequivocal: 'our real objects were to paint the country red on the map and to exploit the gold-mines'.[3] During 1899, negotiations, conferences and proposals between the British High Commissioner to the Cape, Sir Alfred Milner, and President Kruger of the Transvaal had failed to resolve the 'Uitlander' (overseas immigrant) franchise question in the Transvaal. When Britain did not respond to an ultimatum to withdraw border reinforcements, the Boers launched offensives into British-held Natal and Cape Colony. Two of the world's smallest agrarian states, the Transvaal and Orange Free State, were now at war with Great Britain. It was the most expensive and protracted conflict for British forces since 1815. Not since Henry V's time had such a large army left British shores.[4]

Yet, despite the distance, British public opinion was kept informed at a speed that showed just how much had changed over the century. It was the most widely reported British war to date, with about 200 correspondents representing papers from Britain and the Empire.[5] Their roles and methods had altered considerably from early in the century when newspaper editors 'lifted' news from foreign papers and obtained accounts of conflicts from junior officers.

There have been various claims for the 'Father' of the profession of war correspondent. Many nominate the Irishman William Howard Russell, *The Times*' correspondent during the Crimean War. In Henry's view, his words 'upset a Government and inspired Florence Nightingale', helping stimulate wider political change and army reform.[6] Knightley highlights Thomas Chenery, the paper's Constantinople correspondent.[7] Henry's preference was for Henry Crabb Robinson, a Greek scholar and associate of English poets who was a 'special' in the Peninsular War and covered Napoleon's campaign along the Elbe in 1807. Yet his dispatch reporting Napoleon's victory over the Russians at the battle of Friedland took several weeks to reach London and he was not at the scene of battle.[8] Henry personally liked to be close to action but believed that these early correspondents had some advantages. The range of muskets and guns was so limited that they could, if they wished, witness fighting at close quarters without great danger.

The telegraph prompted changes. In 1870 Archibald Forbes, a Scot and former private in the Royal Dragoons, covered the Franco-Prussian War for the *Daily News*. He was instructed to send neither letters nor telegraphic summaries but to telegraph in full. This effectively ended the system of leisurely composition free from competition or censorship. Now the aim was to outdo rivals, to get first to the wire with a 'scoop'. Relations with the military became less amicable. Commanding officers and governments were increasingly wary of what correspondents might divulge. And telegraphic dispatches prompted field censorship. Reports of an army's movements might be printed within a few hours and so become accessible to an enemy.

At a time of mass literacy and unprecedented opportunities for extending readership, the South African War was also the first media war.[9] Much was made of photographs and illustrations from special war artists such as the monocled Melton Prior of the *Illustrated London News*. Cameras from the Biograph and Mutoscope Company of London filmed General Sir Redvers Buller as he sailed to South Africa, and hand-held cameras recorded action at the front. From 1900 the Brownie camera made photography cheaper and easier. Reuters, the largest telegraphic agency in the world, already had correspondents in South Africa and supplied close on a hundred stringers and staff including the Welshman H. A. Gwynne, in Henry's opinion 'one of the best war correspondents living'.[10] At first the War Office permitted a maximum of two accredited correspondents per paper (M. H. Donohoe was the *Chronicle*'s other journalist) but newspapers built up teams with local reporters.[11]

Lamenting the lost golden age of the war correspondent, Henry argued that this war gave them a hard time.[12] They had to find their own food and shelter, servants and horses. Such 'housekeeping' could occupy over half a day, time that should have been spent watching the campaign and writing telegrams. Censors were 'unpunctual, unbusinesslike, never present where they ought to be found, irascible and discourteous'. They regarded correspondents as 'something between traitors, scoundrels and bores' and seemed keen to thwart them whenever possible.[13] Censors, who were often junior officers, had other tasks they found more interesting. Henry suggested, from the safety of 1930, that censors were those 'unfit to be appointed to anything at all' but conceded that some at Ladysmith were talented.[14]

Many who wrote about the South African War became household names: men such as Conan Doyle, Rudyard Kipling and Edgar Wallace. Winston Churchill reported for the Unionist *Morning Post*. His aunt, Lady Sarah Wilson, was a pioneering woman correspondent for the *Daily Mail*. Henry differed in age and attitudes from many of his colleagues. He was in his forties but, understandably, this profession was largely the prerogative of young men. Unlike men such as Lionel James or Burleigh, he was not from a military or colonial background. He was somewhat more intellectual and cultured than many though one of his closest friends in Ladysmith, G. W. Steevens, was also an Oxford classical scholar. Yet Henry had experience with the cadets and was athletic. Pakenham acknowledges that he was slightly set apart from the experienced Victorian correspondents who were experts in 'the vicarious war'.[15] And unlike some colleagues, he was prepared to work long hours and face danger head-on. He stated that there were three rules for war correspondents. They should always be on the spot just before trouble started, keep as near as possible to the front lines and never get killed![16]

Not many shared his radical politics. Stearn's depiction of late-nineteenth-century correspondents in colonial wars sharing officers' attitudes and believing in 'the beneficence of British rule and of "the white man's burden"' covers Burleigh but does not describe Henry.[17] In

October 1900 Samuel Barnett noted that Henry had returned from the war 'a strong Pro Boer' and was influencing his paper.[18] Before the war Henry and his colleague Harold Spender had been unhappy about official British policy towards the Boers and their editor's lack of forth-right criticism. By mid-July 1899 neither of them was permitted to write about the developing crisis. But by early September the views of his editor Massingham had shifted: as the war developed so did his criticisms. Within Africa the *Chronicle* obtained news from Albert Cartwright of the *South African News*, a paper close to the Bond Party at the Cape and sympathetic to the views of Boer leaders.[19] In November a leader criticizing Chamberlain's war policy offended the paper's propri-etor, and Massingham was required to maintain silence on government policy in South Africa for the duration of the war. Not prepared to accept this, he resigned, as did Spender and Vaughan Nash. This was a severe blow for radical Liberals. The *Manchester Guardian* opposed official policy but the only London daily consistently pro-Boer was the *Morning Leader* for which Brailsford wrote. Henry was shocked by the belated news of the resignations: 'an overwhelming blow for me – all my hopes & position & power gone at once'.

During the first weeks of war there were small engagements such as the battle of Elandslaagte. Here the British had gained 'a stony and muddy little hill strewn with the bodies of dead and wounded peasants, clerks, lawyers, and other kinds of men'. At the end of October Henry witnessed 'Black Monday' when, in addition to many deaths and casualties, over a thousand prisoners were taken after an engagement extending about fifteen miles from Nicholson's Nek, just north of Lady-smith, to Lombard's Kop. Two days later, on 2 November, the Siege of Ladysmith began.

The Boers had invaded British territory in four places, coming across the Orange River into the Cape Colony, moving south west towards Kimberley, towards Mafeking in the north west and east into Natal. Their invasion routes were aimed at strategic railway lines. Ladysmith, at the junction of two railway lines and on the line to Durban, had become the headquarters of the Natal British forces and was commanded by Sir George White. It held about 21,300 people including over 12,000 troops. Surrounded by a 'horseshoe of heights'[20] occupied by the Boers, the main British force in South Africa was effectively boxed in. From 2 November 1899 until 28 February 1900 this small town on the Klip river, less than three miles in length and breadth, battled with privation and provocation and was catapulted into the minds and memories of the British public.

About twenty correspondents stayed in Ladysmith. On the day the siege began Henry's diary records guns opening on the town from all four points of the compass. Burleigh got out, but for Henry 'To stay was not a question of courage, but simply of common behaviour.' They were 'in the very front line, and for a war correspondent that is the choice of all the positions in the world'.[21]

At first the greatest hardship was the lack of mail from home and problems in sending out copy. Wire and rail links had been cut. Native runners could be used but cost lives and cash, as they had to break through Boer lines. The courier conveying Henry's longest message, about the fighting at Wagon Hill on 6 January, was killed. Months later the Boer who shot him returned this message to Henry. The army would not permit the use of their runners and sometimes seemed to exacerbate the correspondents' work. When the sun shone, a military heliograph service could send Morse code to outlying stations but permitted only thirty words at a time and, to keep morale high at home, Henry and other correspondents had their precious words censored.[22] From 2 November until early December no news got beyond the neutral camp just outside Ladysmith. Despite Henry's earlier words, correspondents were no longer in a choice position. Of the besieged towns of Kimberley, Mafeking and Ladysmith, it was Ladysmith that was perceived as the most important militarily so had the 'crack' correspondents. Yet these journalists, whose very livelihoods were defined by their ability to communicate, were now denied it.

Anxious to keep a record of events so that the public could, if only belatedly, gain some sense of daily life, many of the besieged became diarists. They included Gunner Netley of the 13th Battery and Isabella Craw, a volunteer nurse.[23] Sibbald refers to 'the mood of resigned boredom' pervading the diary of A. J. Crosby of the Natal Carbineers.[24] The truncated, staccato style of this sort of diary was enhanced by diurnal repetition. Yet life in Ladysmith did not remain static but changed as hopes of relief were raised and dashed and food supplies dwindled. Henry's personal diary suggests something of the tension. When Buller suffered serious defeat at the battle of Colenso, the intelligence officer Altham read the 'lamentable news' to the correspondents. Henry wrote 'all indefinite again. I dare not think.' During that week in mid-December the British lost three separate battles.

Although he had not originally planned to write a book, Henry did contribute to the printed diary genre. Methuen published his *Ladysmith: The Diary of a Siege* in the summer of 1900.[25] Although a daily record, it is something of a misnomer, being a series of carefully composed letters Henry had written for the *Daily Chronicle*. They had not appeared as events unfolded or at regular sequential intervals. Only three letters got through during the siege but at the end of March 1900 'an avalanche of fifteen letters' covering mid-November onwards poured into the office at once. They were printed over the next month or so (even several in one edition) although events had overtaken them.

The book has twenty-one chapters and is very similar but not identical to the original printed letters. The latter omitted some sensitive

4 Henry Nevinson at Ladysmith.

military information and, because of the belated timing of their appearance, editorial intervention and the fact that the paper's 'military critic' summarized events in his own printed 'diary', not all of Henry's words appeared in the *Chronicle*. The book therefore enabled the expansion of some information.[26] Although not the first or last to publish a volume on Ladysmith, Henry's account helps illuminate the varieties of danger facing the besieged and the insidious growth of hunger.[27]

The army controlled food supplies. Before the siege, trucks full of food were rushed up from Durban. Colonel Ward of the Army Service Corps then requisitioned everything possible, earning the nickname of Moses of the Commissariat. Strict rationing was maintained and non-rationed items were very expensive: an egg could cost four shillings and sixpence.

Henry sensibly suggested that jam or some sort of fruit should be available as an essential item rather than an extra.[28] One culinary invention was soup made from adding hydrochlorine and pepsine to the essence of horse. Known as chevril and flavoured with almond hair-oil, it 'smelt like a vulgar woman's hair and neighed in the throat'. For this twenty-eight horses were sacrificed daily from January. The very sick received this efficacious delicacy.[29]

Despite such tales, Henry was concerned about the plight of the horses. Many were casualties not so much of battle or chevril as of sickness and starvation. Thousands never even reached South Africa, having perished on the long sea voyage from South America. When he gave slide-shows at home Henry used the starving horse as the symbol of war. He spent much of his time riding round soldiers' camps and defences. He ended his Christmas Day letter lamenting the sorry state of the horses.

As for humans, enteric fever (a form of typhoid) and dysentery killed 571 at Ladysmith, about twice the number lost through shell- or rifle-fire. Nevertheless, civilians and soldiers alike were constantly under threat from the thirty-three Boer guns fixed on the town. The most distant were only 7,000 or 8,000 yards from its centre, and the four six-inch Creusot guns, known as Long Toms, threw ninety-six-pound shells. Henry wrote a parody called 'Omar on the River Bank' for the correspondents' satirical newspaper, the *Ladysmith Lyre*: 'One thing is certain in this town of lies, If Long Tom gets you on the head, you dies.'[30] It was claimed that 250 shells were flung into town or against the forts daily though the religious Boers held back on Sundays. A few shells fell on Christmas Day but did not spoil the children's party. Henry found this party evocative: 'Strange smell of feminine garments & hair, as fr. [*sic*] a different world.' The men ate a pig and pretended that they had whisky. Three days later the Boers fired a shell charged with plum-pudding.

Henry stressed that war was unglamorous. Nine days after the siege began he wrote:

> It would be a good thing if the army could be marched through Regent Street as the men look this morning. It would teach people more about war than a hundred pictures of plumed horsemen and the dashing charge. The smudgy khaki uniforms soaked through and through, stained black and green and dingy red with wet and earth and grass; the draggled great-coats, heavy with rain and thick with mud . . . the blackened, battered faces . . . unwashed and unshaved . . . the peculiar smell – there is not much brass band and glory about *us* [my emphasis] now.[31]

He effectively punctured any suggestion of romanticization.

It was difficult knowing how to treat 'an indeterminate situation'. As

Henry admitted in mid-December, 'The siege is already too long for modern literature.'[32] He was aware that readers would not be enthralled by accounts of daily chores, incessant rain or scorching sun (it was now sometimes over 100 degrees fahrenheit in the shade). Yet his articulation of the sheer helplessness and problem of communication reveals once more his poetic side: 'We are thrown back into the infinite, and can fix no limit on which hope can build even a rainbow.'[33] Sibbald argues that the press manufactured the 'siege epic', *The Times*, along with other papers, focusing on the gallantry and suffering of the besieged since little was happening elsewhere and papers wanted exciting stories, not tales of tedium.[34] Yet Henry continued to record the 'flat days'. He, an old Scottish carpenter and two colonials from Maritzburg lived in a little tin cottage on the main street. He 'largely wasted' the final day of the nineteenth century in a futile attempt to obtain leave to visit Intombi. This refugee and hospital camp on neutral ground about four miles south of Ladysmith now cared for about two thousand.[35]

On 6 January the Boers challenged the legend that they would not fight in the open. Before dawn they made, in Henry's words, 'a gallant and terrible' attempt to storm the long ridge of Caesar's Camp and Wagon Hill in the south west, held by the 7th Brigade under the command of Colonel Ian Hamilton. Henry later argued that Joubert should either have ordered the attack immediately after the battle of Colenso or waited until famine had done its worst. But he conceded that it was 'a bold and well-devised assault'.[36] For once, though, Henry was in the wrong place. Presuming that the main attack would come in the north east, he had been at Observation Hill since 4 a.m. In over sixteen hours of fighting, both sides suffered. The British lost 114 men. The Boers were not ultimately victorious but their bravery and determination had been evident. The next day a brief truce enabled the dead to be buried. Henry helped, his diary referring to 'the pools of blood, all black, the helmets and hats drenched with blood'. His reporting humanized rather than demonized, as did his stories. In 'The Fire of Prometheus' the narrator finds a man stooped over a body: ' "Why, he's one of the enemy!" I said, seeing the badge on his cap. "No", the other answered; "he is dead." '[37]

Just over a week later Henry had to face the death of a friend. His closest companions at Ladysmith were the 'true-hearted, sunny tempered' illustrator W. T. Maud and the thirty-year-old *Daily Mail* 'correspondent of genius', George Steevens.[38] Maud would die in Somaliland a few years later from the effects of the Ladysmith siege. Steevens succumbed much sooner with enteric fever. Maud nursed him for five weeks but on 15 January 1900 he died and was buried under 'a clouded moon'. Ironically, his death helped validate the position of the Ladysmith war correspondents. They occupied a curious, indeterminate position, lacking the status of soldiers yet not seen as civilian victims. Steevens's death demonstrated their sacrifice.

In early December Henry had a violent attack of fever with terrible headaches lasting a fortnight. On 17 December he wrote simply 'We are sick of the siege.' In one of his stories the hero, 'worn thin by starvation and fever', finds that 'the ghosts would not lie still in the crowded cemetery of his mind'.[39] Boer hopes of victory through attrition seemed to be succeeding. By the final month many soldiers could not even stand upright. Hunger drove them to eat grass. They smoked the unravelled fringes of their tents. Covered with lice, they were fatally weakened by enteric and dysentery. Their consensus, Henry recorded, was that 'there is no glory in this war'.

He had suffered from rheumatism for some time. Early in February fever struck. Hearing about a significant defeat at Spion Kop and a failed confrontation at Vaal Krantz and Doornkop, he struggled up to Caesar's Camp but the next day, unable to stand, he was carried by Hindu stretcher bearers to a makeshift hospital in a Congregational chapel. He remained there for two weeks. At home Margaret dreamed that he was ill in hospital. Henry had sunstroke compounded by hunger and 'some impalpable kind of malaria'.[40] The usual remedies for sunstroke, such as ice, were unobtainable. Seeking to relieve the 'atrocious, unbearable' pain, 'they plunged needles into my head "to trace the nerve", they lighted cups of spirit on my neck, they flayed my temples alive, they shaved my head & boiled it'.[41] Morphine provided some relief. A trim figure, he now lost over three stone. Not until mid-March did he stop 'crawling instead of walking & gasping like a fish when I talked'.

Yet he still penned reports. On 17 February he commented that people had become indifferent to attacks. Few now bothered to take refuge in the caves by the river. The siege had become 'inexpressibly tedious' though news of the Relief of Kimberley lifted spirits. Three days later, recovering in hospital, he sent a heliograph: 'Two hundred Boer wagons, with large escort, were seen to-day trekking from Colenso, behind Bulwana.'[42] British troops had also been espied on a hill commanding the Tugela heights.

With impeccable timing, Henry was back in his corrugated iron cottage a few days before the final drama. On 27 February, Majuba Day, rations were cut still further. But Buller was at last defeating the Boers. The next day Henry observed lines of Boer wagons moving away from the Tugela heights. A triumphant heliogram arrived from Buller and soon Henry saw 'strange figures riding on fat, shining, luscious horses'.[43] The four months of siege were over. Henry's personal diary declares 'Day of Deliverance'. Yet he was still unwell. When his book was published, he wrote in his own copy after the final paragraph describing the evening of 27 February:

The last part was written in extreme illness and pain. I had to hold my head on with one hand while I wrote with the other, and often both hands were needed. This accounts for a certain dulness [*sic*] towards the end.[44]

Fiercely critical of Buller, Henry later sought to counteract the myth that developed around his triumphant entry into Ladysmith. He stressed that, when Buller first entered the camp, it was in secret. His famed formal entry was staged a few days later. Henry pointedly described his strong, healthy troops that had taken so long to come to their rescue.[45] Those lining the route in his honour, too weak to stand, sat like resurrected skeletons.

Henry now travelled to the coast where correspondents, including the 'young Winston', had gathered at Durban. He was still slightly feverish but could obtain medicine and found great pleasure in taking a bath, sleeping in white sheets and eating bread and butter. But now Maud was battling against enteric. Borrowing Joubert's words, Henry wrote in his diary, 'my heart is bloody with sorrow at everything'. His new editor, W. J. Fisher, complained that Henry's wire on the Relief was too short. He kept 'screaming for immediate news' but Henry's long account had been stolen from his saddlebag on the train.

He expected to be sent, along with other correspondents, to cover the advance from Bloemfontein towards Pretoria. But he was ordered back to Ladysmith. In this 'city of the dead' he felt 'rather like a ghost who has escaped for a week, and now returns to his former tomb . . . on almost every rock there sits a ghost, who nods his head and speaks quietly to me as I pass'.[46] Yet proximity to death meant appreciation of survival: 'it is a grand thing to be alive'. He scouted and camped in the hills and rode out several times to Arcadia. He briefly came under fire during a Boer attack near Elandslaagte. He now suspected that Buller was insane. He sat 'sullen and violent' in the convent in Ladysmith, detested by all.[47] Lord Roberts had replaced him as Commander-in-Chief in South Africa. Finally, in early May, Henry received instructions to join Roberts at Bloemfontein. But he was delayed en route for a fortnight with jaundice and in order to catch up with the army had to travel 300 miles across the veldt in ten days. After purchasing 'the last cart, the last horse, and the last can of milk' he set off with two men. Two of their horses died. There were problems with the cart and not enough food. It was often difficult to find water. When they trekked by night they found their way from the stench of the carcasses of army horses strewn along the route. Henry still managed to write to his paper and to read *Villette* and, interestingly, *Don Quixote*!

Finally, at dawn on 5 June Henry glimpsed Roberts and Kitchener flanked by the army, on the road to Pretoria. The Boers had set alight the dry veldt and there were long lines of smoke. Mid-morning, two Boer officials drove up in a carriage sporting a white flag and formally surrendered the keys of the city. The Guards rode ahead to prevent disturbances. Henry went too, reaching Pretoria's main square just before them: 'The unhappy citizens gathered round me in the market place, offering gifts as though I were a pagan god.'[48] The Grenadier Guards appeared, clearing the square of both Henry and 'my misguided worshippers'. Roberts finally appeared. The flag was raised, the National Anthem sung and the army marched past. But the real triumph for Henry was the sound, coming from a Boer home, of the last movement of Beethoven's Waldstein Sonata. He presents a fascinating imperial picture, with Roberts as a hero. Alert to the value of public spectacle, Roberts was popular with Henry and the press, not least because he handled them skilfully and seemed to care for his battalions. But the story has another message. Although Henry has elevated himself to the role of mistaken hero, enabling humour to counteract the pomp and ceremony, he nevertheless stressed that the correspondent got there first.

After covering the battle of Diamond Hill, where an attempt was made to cut off the main Boer force holding a line of hills east of Pretoria, Fisher wanted Henry to return home, believing the end to be in sight. Although Henry argued that this was a naïve approach – any suggestion by Fisher was met with scorn – by mid-March he was privately voicing similar sentiments, writing in a letter that 'I have an idea the war is almost over.'[49]

Once back in Cape Town, Henry and Donohoe analysed the 'Lessons of the War' for the *Chronicle*.[50] They stressed the need for big and long-range guns and praised the superior Boer marksmanship. They denounced those who called the Boers cowards for taking cover: 'The old idea that duty and heroism require an officer to strut about under fire waving his sword is dead.' It was the Boers who had taught the British army the importance of cover and defence. They called for new and permanent mounted infantry to replace some of the cavalry. Echoing Henry's earlier writings, they drew on Moltke's maxim that the soldier used to be drilled and must now be educated. A wider approach to soldiering was needed, linked to a 'true education of life' and a real knowledge of the terrain.[51] Those in charge at home should not focus solely on the fighting. They emphasized the importance of supply and communication and dissatisfaction with censorship. They ended with a plea for a clarification of the war correspondent's role so that he could receive just treatment and respect from the censor.

Returning home, Henry did not adjust easily. Soon 'that horrible mood of failure & self-distrust' was 'creeping over me again'. People could never fully empathize with what he had been through, and all the 'noble faces' had gone from work, their ideals vanishing too. Diary entries complained frequently that his leaders were emasculated. The paper now supported Kitchener. Henry found Fisher 'unendurable in ignorance and brutality'. E. T. Cook had become chief leader writer and, although Henry respected his fairness in representing government policies, he could not sympathize with his views (Cook had left the *Daily News* when it became pro-Boer).

The atmosphere at work enhanced Henry's pro-Boer sympathies especially now that farms and villages were being deliberately burned on the veldt (the 'scorched earth' policy). Jingoism stimulated Henry's alliance with the underdog as did being back amongst radical comrades with very different views from some of his Ladysmith companions. He had also heard Olive Schreiner address a meeting of about 1,500 in Cape Town where she raged against the destruction of land: 'though she stood perfectly still, she was transfigured into flame'.[52] Deeply impressed, Henry had a long talk with her the next day, discussing the need for conciliation and Boer freedom.

Much of the British press depicted the Boer as an enemy with inherent national defects. Henry, in contrast, stressed the democratic nature of their army. They were farmers simply fighting for their country. He was prepared to praise courage and leadership on both sides and described the Boer General De Wet as 'the soldier of instinctive genius'.[53] He discussed the situation with leading pro-Boer intellectuals such as Leonard Courtney, Emily Hobhouse and her brother Leonard.

One summer's evening in 1901 Henry attended a large pro-Boer gathering at the Queen's Hall and was impressed by a 'fine, slim, young' man, a 'born orator' called David Lloyd George. His speech was 'one of the finest I have heard' and he seemed 'courageous, enthusiastic, indifferent to consequences'. Henry needed to leave quickly to get to work but a huge crowd of opponents had gathered outside. The police suggested that Henry make his getaway by pretending to be a protester whom they were forcibly ejecting. They would manhandle him a little to convince the crowd. But the police acting was a bit too realistic for Henry's liking. To add (literal) insult to injury, the crowd was unconvinced, immediately denouncing Henry as pro-Boer, 'as if I did not know that already'. He escaped by jumping on to an omnibus and arrived at the office bleeding and with torn clothes, having been spat at and battered by umbrellas. 'You went as a sympathiser, I suppose!' was his editor's response. 'Certainly', Henry replied and 'I have learnt how right Ibsen's Enemy of the People was when he advised never to go battling for truth and justice in one's best trousers.'[54] Relations deteriorated still further.

Margaret also disagreed with Henry. Before the war she had met Olive Schreiner and even attended a peace meeting at Trafalgar Square. But she became concerned about the suffering of soldiers as well as her husband during the Ladysmith siege and was increasingly supportive of the government's position.[55] When she heard Canon Scott Holland preach a pro-Boer sermon she was so angry that 'I had an impulse to throw my shoe at him.'[56] Too much the lady to display her feelings, particularly in St Paul's Cathedral, she nevertheless made them clear to her family. Henry noted in his diary that Emily Hobhouse's report on the South African concentration camps was 'received with jeers & laughter by my family – encouraged by their mother'. Richard's autobiography refers to his father attending pro-Boer meetings at Parliament Hill 'at which all manner of cranks' were present. He claimed that he paid for his father's views by being thrown into a pond by patriots.[57]

The Hobhouse report of June 1901 revealed the sufferings of women and children in camps in the Cape and Orange River colonies. The Americans had pioneered concentration camps during the recent Spanish–American War over Cuba but it was now that they became infamous. From November 1900 Kitchener rapidly expanded them. Ten months later there were thirty-three camps for whites with 110,000 inmates. Food was meagre and those with relatives still fighting were more strictly rationed. Over 27,000, mostly women and children, perished in what Henry called the 'devastation camps', more than double the number of men killed fighting on both sides. Vast numbers of black and 'Coloured' Africans died but their plight did not receive attention.

Years later Emily Hobhouse told Henry that she had talked to Milner on her voyage home in the spring of 1901. He had urged her to say nothing of what she had seen. She delayed publicity, hoping that something would be done. Silence provoked her into exposing the situation. The government urged proprietors to refuse her venues for talks.[58] Henry continued to protest though, perhaps surprisingly, his leader of February 1902 applauded Mrs Fawcett's 'stronghearted bluebook on camps'.[59] Although this Ladies' Commission on the Refugee Camps (the first all-female government commission) criticized individual camps, it broadly supported the British administration, blaming Boer inmates for their plight and accepting the high death rate as a fact of war. Mrs Fawcett, an imperialist feminist and patriot as well as a humanitarian, had been concerned about the denial of the voting rights of 'Uitlanders'. Henry presented her recommendations as just and sensible because he believed that the worst features of the camps had been eradicated. With impending peace his paper sent him back to Pretoria. Travelling round the countryside in the spring of 1902, he visited camps for the first time, writing that the 'appalling mismanagement that had raised so just an outcry in the middle of the war' had ended.[60]

On 2 June 1902, the *Daily Chronicle* printed War Office dispatches announcing the end of the war. Immediately below was Henry's news that peace had just been signed. His first war had been of thirty days' duration. This one had rumbled on for thirty months. Henry provided his readers with a stirring, somewhat Shakespearean finale:

Pile the arms in stacks, fold up the tents, cut away the barbed entanglements. Let this trampled earth rest and nature begin once more her ancient task of healing. Call in the sentries that the sons of stout-hearted peoples may meet us better friends than ever yet before . . . leave the earth open to the wind and sun . . . The long and bitter war is done.[61]

Before leaving South Africa Henry travelled in the northern Transvaal, seeing an area almost entirely inhabited by natives 'supposed to be savage and formidable, though as usual they met me with entire politeness and hospitality as I wandered far out among their kraals'.[62] Indigenous black Africans had suffered in a war not of their own making or shaping. They became internees and victims of a visceral racism permeating official and unofficial actions. Land, crops and livestock were destroyed. Some now estimate that as many as 120,000 African, 'Coloured' and Indian men performed armed or non-combatant military service.[63] Unlike many contemporaries, Henry did not ignore their presence in his factual writing and fiction. Beaumont comments that he wrote about everybody he met, 'be they British, Colonial, Boer, Zulu, or Indian' and 'as he found them'. This helped mark him out as 'arguably, one of the best of the correspondents who reported this war'.[64]

His story 'The Relief of Eden' exposes and mocks the ignorance of those who brag of racial superiority. Mrs Ferguson comments that 'what I do hate to see is yellowish whitey-brown sort of people dressing themselves up and giving themselves airs side by side with British Colonials that were born white, like me'.[65] Here Henry is echoing Milner who had told him: 'What we must most carefully avoid is a mongrel population of grey, drab, and whitey-brown.'[66] Yet the modern reader is also struck by the racial stereotypes of 'imagined Others' in Henry's description of the 'Kaffir boy' in this story. Travel across Zululand provided material for a story called 'Izwa' (the term, meaning 'smell him out', was used by witch doctors to detect who had placed an evil spirit on a sick person).[67] Henry's African stories are based on but a fleeting acquaintance with local customs. But his focus was markedly different from the usual diet of stories that fed the imperial imagination.

So, what did South Africa do for Henry Nevinson? Bouts of malaria recurred periodically for the rest of his life. Yet although he would tell friends 'I am too ill with Africa to move', malarial fever had first struck him in his beloved Greece.[68] Then there was the psychological legacy of Ladysmith, the memory of personal horrors and loss that could not be eradicated, though Henry's diary is silent on the subject of nightmares and the trauma associated today with the stress of war reporting.

Although he recoiled from the views of men like Kitchener and missed intellectual stimulation, especially during the long voyages, the courage and spirit of military men of all ranks impressed him. Certain aspects of military manhood appealed. There was inevitably some bond between those who had been in South Africa and 'understood'. As late as 1936 he was appealing in *The Times* on behalf of the South Africa War Veterans' Association.[69] He attended numerous annual Ladysmith dinners. On 28 February 1913 he had lunch with militant male supporters of women's suffrage. Dinner was at a Ladysmith reunion. The only correspondent there, he wrote in his diary, 'it is always a joy to be with such people: they are what I ought to be'. But perhaps the most revealing comment came after the first Ladysmith dinner on 28 February 1902: 'I changed from a mouse into a man.'

Henry reviewed *The Times'* official *History of the War in South Africa*, contrasting its unemotional, matter-of-fact descriptions with his own perspectives. An account of how a flying column was detailed to try to intercept the routed enemy is set alongside his interpretation of the same event. With carefully chosen adjectives and deceptively simple phrasing he describes this 'flying' column:

> Every few hundred yards one fell down or dragged himself on all fours into the rocks . . . From every side arose the stupefying smell of horses that had cheated the soup cauldron by starvation . . . Doubled together with dysentery, twisted with rheumatism, green with hunger, so the flying column crawled out to intercept the routed enemy.[70]

Africa, and Ladysmith in particular, contributed to the making of Henry Nevinson as a hero. At the same time as the South African War was being fought, history became a compulsory subject in secondary schools in England.[71] This, the availability of toy soldiers from the 1890s and the popularity of boys' adventure fiction in books and magazines, as well as the celebrations associated with the liberation of the besieged towns, helped create an aura of glamour surrounding war and those associated with it. Although much smacked of imperial glory and a bellicosity which Henry found distasteful, he was able to turn it around to fit an alternative voice of opposition, an opposition given unusual force since he had experienced so much at first hand. This would be sharpened through his next encounter with Africa. Henry's travels and writings exposing slavery in Angola would establish him as a fighter and campaigner, not in a military sense but as a radical committed to a cause.

CHAPTER THREE

Exposing Slavery

Angola and 'The Islands of Hell'[1]

In 1904–5 Henry undertook an especially dangerous assignment in Angola and the islands of Principe and San Thomé (São Tomé/San Tomé) in the Gulf of Guinea. Most British people knew little about Portuguese Angola, roughly four times the size of the British Isles but comparable to Wales in terms of population. It was presumed that the African slave trade had ceased but Henry was instrumental in publicizing the fact that Angola and the two tiny equatorial islands were 'putrid with slavery'.[2] His excoriating accounts highlighted investigations by other humanitarians. Concerted pressure produced results. It also created enemies, notably among slavers, Portuguese officials and cocoa magnates.

The challenges Henry faced helped create the heroic Nevinsonian figure. In 1913 John Harris of the British and Foreign Anti-Slavery Society (ASS) declared that 'The evidence of slavery anywhere would inevitably call to the succour of the slaves that prince of journalists, that twentieth century knight-errant, Henry W. Nevinson.'[3] Yet in 1904 when he departed for Central Africa, Henry was middle-aged, neither adulated nor denounced and not that obvious a choice for exposing slavery. So how did this come about?

The Harper Company of New York, prompted by Tom Wells of *Harper's Monthly Magazine*, was keen for Henry to work in America. When he decided against this, they suggested he undertake, for £1,000, 'an adventurous journey'. He considered Arabia, the South Seas and the Andes; then, according to his memoirs, 'Suddenly the thought of the slave-trade occurred to me.'[4] His diary, however, tells a more prosaic tale. On 17 September 1904 he received a letter from Harper's specifically asking him to investigate the slave trade in Africa. Less than seven weeks later he was on his way, having consulted with Travers Buxton, the ASS Secretary, H. R. Fox Bourne, Secretary of the Aborigines' Protection Society (APS), and the Quaker philanthropist and industrialist William Cadbury.[5]

Boarding the SS *Fantee* at Liverpool, 'My heart rose with the sea.' Henry read E. D. Morel and Mary Kingsley on African travels, immersed himself in Catullus and Horace with a fellow passenger and played quoits. Three weeks later he went ashore on Nigerian soil. The ship passed down the coast, unloading and taking on new cargo and passengers, natives, white officials and traders. At the Niger Delta the beach disappeared, the forest extending down to the sea. Henry's description of the west coast reads like the Book of Genesis but tells of the creation of hell on earth:

> Nature has here said, 'Look, I will display all my powers of evil. I will do the worst I can. I will give querulous mankind something to whine about. I will silence the silliness that prattles of a beautiful world'. Then she took stinking slime and for hundreds of miles she laid down the mangrove swamps that never dry, and covered them with deadly growths that rot under their own darkness. The sea that washes the grey roots with its tides she filled with sharks, and in unmeasured miles of ooze, she crowded mud-fish that run like lizards, and colourless crabs, and long worms with innumerable feet, and pale slugs, and crocodiles with eyes like stones . . . [In a forest impenetrable to sun and air she placed] deadly serpents and envenomed spiders, obscene reptiles, scorpions as large as a woman's foot. Then, over swamp and forest alike, she blew dense clouds of flies and every kind of poisonous insect.[6]

Accompanied by two local men with machetes, Henry tried penetrating southern Nigeria's swampy forest. For a couple of hours they 'floundered & climbed & tore our way through . . . just like a Stanley expedition'. They emerged bleeding and covered in black slime.[7] The *Fantee* then sailed past the French Ivory Coast and German Cameroons. By the time they reached the Congo, Henry had rheumatism and a fever but could still question passengers. One woman told him Negroes were 'just children'. Close by, a native was 'reading a treatise on the human soul without a pause'. At Cabinda Henry visited a mission, run by Scots. Native girls sang 'The Wreck of the Hesperus'. On 16 December they reached the Angolan capital, St Paul de Loanda (Luanda). It was not at its best: 'There is one drain, fit to poison the multitudinous sea. So the city lies, bankrupt and beautiful.'[8] Many were dying from Angola's latest killer, sleeping sickness.

Henry had been raised on Livingstone's *Missionary Travels in South Africa*. It was fifty years since Livingstone had reached Loanda. There is a neat symmetry in Henry Nevinson, son of devout Evangelicals, following in Livingstone's footsteps. Henry saw Livingstone's 3,000-mile journey from South Africa as 'I suppose the greatest journey of exploration ever accomplished in the history of man'.[9] Henry's travels and mission may have lacked his parents' religious zeal but proselytizing against slavery owed something to the Evangelical impulse.

Much of Angola's labour supply was being diverted to the San Thomé cocoa trade but there was disquiet about how contracted labourers on mainland plantations were perceived. In Henry's view they may have legally been free but in practice were 'hardly to be distinguished from the slaves of the cruel old times'.[10] The Portuguese had been in Angola since the late fifteenth century and had originally exported its peoples as slave labour to Brazil. Now the economic and legal situation was very different. Yet in effect forced labour persisted despite legislation in the 1870s stipulating that natives and employers must agree to free and voluntary contracts approved by magistrates. In practice, either slaves were born on the estates or agents procured men, women and children from the interior in exchange for goods such as rum and rifles. In the 1900s the commission earned for an adult was equivalent to about £15 to £20 and a labourer had to work nine hours daily for five years in return for living in and monthly wages. A child was worth about £5. If estates were sold, the labourers went with them. Indeed, in the south of Angola the number of contracted labourers a man had denoted his wealth. They worked in gangs watched over by drivers with pointed staves or hippo whips (long wooden slats).

The first plantation Henry visited had the pleasant name of Monte Bello. Formerly owned by a British firm, it cultivated coffee, cocoa, bananas, oranges, mangoes, maize, sugar cane and rubber plants. Angola faced serious economic problems. Brazil now dominated the coffee business. San Thomé had cornered the cocoa trade and the Congo had control of rubber. Sugar cane was only used to produce the rum drunk by natives, an unprofitable trade, enhancing the desire for even cheaper labour. About 150 people worked at Monte Bello. Henry saw men and women with babies on their backs clearing the coffee plantation and returning to their mud huts at six o'clock. Their wake-up bell had been at 4 a.m. They collected provisions from a ganger in return for a zinc disc. These had to be traded in the company shop, like the infamous truck system of the British mining industry.

Henry spent Christmas Day walking through dense forest. His bread had turned green and he felt feverish. A lonely New Year followed in Loanda. He found it difficult to get people to speak freely. Those connected with missions could not afford to offend the Portuguese government. Henry reckoned that at least half of Angola's population was subject to some form of slavery, whether plantation slavery on the mainland or islands, domestic slavery to white people or family slavery to natives. He condemned the white slave-owners' exculpation from responsibility through their excuse that the system was endemic among natives. White slave-owners made the questionable claim that they were part of 'a higher race'. That argument, wrote Henry, implied that they should know to behave better.[11]

Henry boarded a mail-steamer travelling south to Benguella. On board was a Portuguese man with five native boys dressed in striped jerseys. Within a week of landing he had sold them all to white owners.

The purchasing of natives assumed many forms. An elderly Portuguese prospector bought a girl as his concubine to accompany him on a journey inland. Henry encountered them several times because he too made a journey into the interior and the unknown.

'He who goes to Africa leaves time behind' wrote Henry in *A Modern Slavery*.[12] Having experienced a sense of enforced time in Ladysmith, what he now encountered was not so much an abandonment of time as a new relationship to it. This was demonstrated by what might be called oxen time. Leaving Benguella in a wagon pulled by twenty-four oxen, Henry first crossed a barren mountainous region. It was six days before he saw even a trace of water. He then trekked across the high forest plateau and travelled, in drenching rain, along the watershed of the Congo and Zambesi Rivers and their tributaries. Like modern Londoners, he found that distances were estimated not by miles but by the time spent on the journey. His driver was an Englishman who had come to collect insects for the British Museum but never returned. Together they coaxed the oxen forwards. Henry had to acquire patience.

The record for travelling between Benguella and Bihé was six weeks 'but you must not complain if a wagon takes six months'.[13] The distance was less than 500 miles but it might take several days to ford a brook. They had five rivers to ford, arduous work with all their provisions. Henry learned to drive the oxen by voice. Each ox had a name and, at its sound, was trained to push the yoke forward. Henry compared steering oxen to coxing a rudderless eight. There were numerous obstacles such as sore humps (caused by rain) which needed soothing with wagon-grease. Crooked axles had to be hammered out. In the watery regions it was 'like a zoo let loose' and enormous crocodiles lay in the rivers. Native villages were stockaded against lions and leopards. Size did not matter. Tiny black and red ants could make life miserable. Oxen had to be abandoned once they reached the 'fly country' since tame animals could not withstand the tsetse fly.

Mission stations offered cleanliness and relative luxury. Henry rested for three weeks at the mission at Chisamba where he was provided with no less than sixteen native carriers to complete the journey inland. They carried his tent and all their food and provisions on their heads, fastened between two long sticks. Henry's feet became ulcerated and his rheumatism returned. At one point he feared that he was dying though the diary never ceased. They entered what was known as the Hungry Country. This was no allegorical tale of a pilgrim's progress though it was a test of endurance. The stretch of uninhabited, inhospitable land covered about 250 miles. It was late March and Henry was composing his fourth letter for Harper's. The fever returned and diary entries changed. His writing became large and much less controlled than usual. His carriers had to live up to their name, bearing him as well as everything else, and they made it clear that they were not happy.

Henry was not the first to write about the horrors of the Hungry Country. Livingstone had done so and in 1900 Colonel Colin Harding of Rhodesia provided a graphic description of the remains of slaves found along the way. Walking along a track so narrow that one foot had to be brought round in front of the other, Henry found wooden shackles hanging on trees (slaves were shackled together at night) and saw decomposed men and women, sometimes with the cleft of the axe visible in their skulls. The whole path was strewn with white bones. When Angolan slaves died from hunger and sickness, native traders hanged their bodies in trees for the jackals. Although feverish (mosquitoes abounded), Henry recognized chilling evidence of a system of slavery. It linked the interior of Angola with two tiny volcanic islands to the north, 200 miles off the coast of West Africa, all because of cocoa.

World cocoa consumption was rocketing. In Britain alone between 1870 and 1910 it rose per head by a factor of nearly six.[14] Swiss technical developments led to the creation of milk chocolate – Roderich Lindt's 'melting chocolate' was enriched with cocoa butter – and sales of eating chocolate soared. By 1906 the largest Swiss chocolate firm, Suchard, was worth nine million francs. Chocolate became a common ingredient in baking and confectionery products and was now a treat for the European working classes. Within Britain the Quaker temperance firms of Cadbury, Fry and Rowntree purchased two-thirds of all imported cocoa

5 Skeleton of a slave in the Hungry Country, Angola.

beans. They and their German and American equivalents promoted the drinking of alternatives to alcohol. They were hot chocolate and what we call cocoa (also a chocolate beverage by this stage, the raw material of cocoa beans having been roasted, rounded and mixed with sugar and other ingredients). In Britain with its chilly winters, cocoa was immensely popular as a drink, selling even better than eating chocolate up to 1914. Few cocoa drinkers, though, were fully aware of the human cost of its production. But, as H. N. Brailsford put it, Henry 'made us understand at what price we drank cocoa'.[15]

Although the Principe and San Thomé slave system had been legally abolished in the mid-1870s, it had been resumed in practice the following decade after landowners' complaints about the cost of importing free labour. A native rising by the Ovumbundu (or Bailundo) people in Angola in 1902 briefly interrupted traffic but it was increasing again by 1905 though Henry believed that traders were attempting to conceal it. He saw men armed with hide whips who hid the boys accompanying them.

With his knack for being in a place at a key moment in its history, Henry investigated these Portuguese island colonies in the very year when they were briefly the largest cocoa producers in the world. Together San Thomé and smaller Principe covered less than 400 square miles. Yet they had overtaken cocoa production in places such as Brazil and Trinidad and now played an important part in the dwindling fortunes of the Portuguese Empire. Once famous for coffee, the islands, known locally as 'okalungo' or 'abyss of hell',[16] supplied one-fifth of the world's cocoa. Essential to this business were Angolan slaves – at least 4,000 a year.

Slaves were obtained by various means including organized raids and tribal wars. They might be purchased from uncles (who had possession of their sisters' offspring unless the parents redeemed them by payment) or from rebel Congo soldiers. Native or Portuguese owners might sell their own slaves or slaves' children for a profit to 'emigration' agents. The numbers exported from interior Angola to the cocoa islands far exceeded those in domestic Angolan slavery or the plantations.

Determined to follow the entire cocoa trail, Henry came back through the Hungry Country and then took the old-established slave route down to the coast at Benguella, chief slave port for the previous 300 years. It was little more than a winding and often very steep track. It took about five weeks from crossing the Cuanza River to get to the sea. On the way Henry met traders and agents. Near Katumbella (Catumbella) he saw a slave who had escaped, been caught and would be flogged to death in front of others as an example. In a poem called 'Home, Sweet Home' Henry wrote of the meeting between slaver and merchant. The poem moves rapidly from a tone of bargaining to one of relaxation, languor and longing for the comforts of home. Then it changes gear again, nostalgia abruptly giving way to aggression as the slaver rouses himself and cries 'here! Shackle up the slaves!' Its ending is unequivocal:

> Turn out the dogs, watch all the hills,
> Have whips and rifles ready! Come,
> Ten dollars to the man who kills
> A slave that runs for home![17]

Henry stayed for some days at Katumbella, hunting crocodiles and observing processions of slaves. On the Benguella road he saw forty-three men and women marching with armed escorts to the steamer. One woman, he learned from his carrier, had been sold for twenty cartridges. 'Thus it is', he wrote, that 'England and America can get their chocolate and cocoa cheap'.

Before each fortnightly steamer left for the islands, slaves were herded in gangs. Paying lip service to a decree of 1903, they were asked whether they were going willingly as labourers (legally 'redeeming' them though they were then immediately made contract labour). Usually no answer was given and refusals were pointless. Contracts, written in Portuguese, which most did not understand, were supposed to last five years but there was no repatriation after this time or extant repatriation fund. Survivors were informed that their contracts had been renewed. Slaves wore round their necks tin discs with a number and the agent's initials. Agents made handsome profits, planters on the islands paying up to £30 for a slave delivered in good condition. The voyage took about eight days. Some died en route.

Henry missed the embarkation ritual because he was poisoned. Word had spread about a prying Englishman. A Protestant mission station had even been told that he was a Jesuit in disguise! Two nights before the steamer sailed he attended a dinner held by the engineers working on the new railway. In cloak-and-dagger style, a piece of paper was slipped into his overcoat pocket. The message stressed that he was in great peril. The next night he woke with terrible internal pains. He recorded in his diary 'Undoubtedly some kind of violent poisoning', probably aconite.

However, as in a good adventure yarn, he struggled aboard the steamer just in time. Crammed into the lower deck were 272 people (not counting babies). Just over a week later they reached San Thomé. Two had died on the way. Henry had acquired a few words of Umbundo and questioned two sisters about why they were there. They answered 'We were sold to the white man.' When asked whether this had been of their own free will, they replied 'Of course not', adding, 'Of course we are slaves!' Once landed they were all divided into gangs and sent to the plantations. San Thomé alone had about 230 plantations, some employing up to 1,000 slaves.

6 Angolan slaves wearing tin discs en route to San Thomé.

Henry stayed at the West African Telegraph Station on the island, thanks to an introduction from William Cadbury. It was extremely humid: 'I felt that now I had been plunged into one of Nature's hells.'[18] The hothouse atmosphere was perfect for the cultivation of the cocoa plant. He visited several plantations on both islands, finding that conditions varied considerably. Violent torture seemed rare but he was aware that 'The essence of slavery has nothing to do with treatment.'[19] Lack of personal freedom was what mattered and this was evident everywhere. Slaves worked the cocoa plantations until they died. Henry wrote 'If this is not the very definition of slavery, what more fiendish title can we invent?'[20]

He heard harrowing stories of attempted escapes. Many died from anaemia brought on, it was alleged, by homesickness. Tropical fevers were rife. Over 20 per cent of slaves on Principe perished annually and the mortality rate for children on both islands was much higher. The fact that children were born into 'perpetually indentured' labour suggests the unfree nature of the system despite a small wage and the legal language of contract labour.[21] With high mortality rates, low birth rates and rapid expansion in the demand for cocoa, the labour supply needed constant replenishing. The short life of the trees and increasingly labour-intensive methods of cultivation added to the pressure. Between 1880 and 1908 about 70,000 Angolans were purchased for the industry. Most followed the route Henry had taken.[22]

Now that he had followed it to the end, he could start the long journey home. He left on 2 July, arriving in Liverpool nineteen days later, racked with rheumatism and malaria. There were open sores on his legs and he had lost a lot of weight. Experts on tropical medicine prescribed ointments but there were times when he was in agony with 'the most terrible pain I have ever suffered. Tears ran dripping from my eyes.'

Henry's voyage into a 'Heart of Darkness' had more than a physical impact. What he had seen had troubled him deeply. It was not the first time he had been close to death but he had in the past, whether he liked it or not, been linked to Britain's official position in whatever war he was reporting. His Angolan experience sharpened his critique of European imperialism and of what it meant in Central Africa to be a white man and to be free. In the interior there was an elemental exposure both to his own physical vulnerability and to his attachment to what he knew as civilization. Henry's journey into the unknown and the unconscious would shift how he perceived and tested his and others' capacities for good and evil in future. In later years he would single out his journey into the Portuguese territories of Africa as his most risky and beneficial expedition. In 1925 he described his attempt to combat slavery as 'the main enterprise of my life'.[23]

The first of his seven letters on 'The New Slave-Trade' appeared in *Harper's* in August soon after he returned home. A ten-page article, lavishly illustrated, it began with Henry's own pencil sketch of the fort at Loanda. A photograph showed him looking suitably serious, and an editorial note informed American readers that Mr Nevinson was 'one of the most distinguished English war correspondents, the author of several important books'. It was also claimed, somewhat ambiguously, that he was 'a man of standing, who has already given much time to philanthropic work'.[24] To enhance the sense of an intrepid and dangerous mission, the second article was preceded by part of a 'private' letter sent from Henry to the editor after his emergence from the Hungry Country. It suggested that even worse lay ahead and made provision for his account lest he should not return. Henry was disgusted at this melodramatic ploy. The letter had been inserted without his permission. He threatened to withdraw the other articles should they 'play that game again'.[25]

Henry's skill lay in his ability to write vividly but without sensationalism. Yet, although the *Anti-Slavery Reporter* soon devoted a dozen pages to the articles, he discovered that effecting change took time.[26] Many years later E. M. Forster commented on his naivety: 'The Cadburys were so pious, and their factories at Bourneville were so model, that he expected they would receive his exposure with enthusiasm and immediately boycott all slave-grown stuff.'[27] William Cadbury wrote to Henry after reading the first two articles. When the Portuguese labour decree of 1903 had proved ineffective, Cadbury, Fry, Rowntree and Stollwerck of Cologne had commissioned an investigation by the Quaker Joseph

Burtt. Cadbury continued to trade with the islands, justifying this on the grounds that they were merely customers. At the 1906 ASS AGM (which Henry could not attend, as his son was ill) William Cadbury focused on humane treatment[28] rather than loss of liberty and urged members to understand the Portuguese position.

Neither individuals nor human rights groups jumped to attention as Henry wished. Years later, he addressed prisoners in Brixton gaol on Angolan slavery. When they suggested boycotting their regulation evening cocoa in protest, Henry replied that he wished more such gestures had been made in the mid-1900s.[29] A few principled individuals and friends gave up drinking cocoa but there was no groundswell of support and Henry's greatest ally, Fox Bourne of the APS, died in 1909. Henry tried to engage the support of Roger Casement, who had exposed the brutalities of the Belgian rubber traders in the Congo. But he had only spent a week in Angola and the Congo Reform Association was concerned lest Angola divert attention from its needs.

Henry's letters appeared in *Harper's* between August 1905 and February 1906 but, for a wider British readership, a book was needed. Working at home in the summer of 1905 Henry expanded his material.[30] There were disagreements with the publisher. Uneasy about the final chapter which widened the question, presenting it as 'part of the great contest with capitalism', the Harper Company also sought, unsuccessfully, to remove references to Irish Home Rule and to South Africa.[31]

Dedicated to his sister Marian and published in London and New York, *A Modern Slavery* did not spare the reader. Henry had read Conrad's 'very terrible' *Heart of Darkness* before going to Africa. On his return he read the novel again. Now it seemed 'not nearly terrible enough'.[32] At a time when photographs were accepted fairly uncritically as a valuable means of documenting and verifying evidence, the inclusion of pictures Henry had taken himself, accompanied by terse captions, helped to counteract his links with publishing imaginative fiction.[33] The distance and difficulties of transportation meant that he had spent seven and a half months in a place few readers had visited. This helped bolster his credibility. He seemed to be inviting readers to use their imaginations – as if they were accompanying him on a voyage into the unknown – yet simultaneously any suggestion of the imaginary was rejected. Descriptive details of, for example, Bihéan musical instruments sought to authenticate, as did the confounding of expectations, something dearly loved by investigative journalists:

The few English people who have ever heard of Bihé at all probably imagine it to themselves as a largish town in Angola famous for its slave-market. Nothing could be less like the reality. There is no town, and there is no slave-market.[34]

Humanitarian narratives tend to use the body to expose evil and elicit sympathy, thus helping establish a common bond between victim and reader.[35] Henry told a harrowing account of a woman slave with a tiny baby who, due to the rough sea, had great difficulty getting on to the steamer. He suggests the humiliation and pain of her predicament: 'bruised and bleeding, soaked with water, her blanket lost, most of her gaudy clothing torn off or hanging in strips'.[36] Here he seeks to distance himself from the gaze of the other spectators. He tells readers: 'I have heard many terrible sounds, but never anything so hellish as the outbursts of laughter with which the ladies and gentlemen of the first class watched that slave woman's struggle up to the deck.' In 1925 he added that this was 'one of those things that make me doubt whether mankind has been worth the travail of our evolution'.[37]

Questioning the notion of what it meant to be civilized and lacking the religious and moral tone that informed the observations of many humanitarians, Henry's critique had another edge. He recognized that slavery was associated with the past. In a way this made his task difficult. The great battles for emancipation had been won and who cared about places so far away, lands that were not even part of the *British* Empire? So, from its title onwards, *A Modern Slavery* challenged complacency and advanced capitalism. It plunged quickly to the point:

> What is to be the real relation of the white races to the black races? ... We need not think it has been settled by a century's noble enthusiasm about the Rights of Man and Equality in the sight of God... the whole problem is still before us, as urgent & as uncertain as it has ever been ... Laws and regulations have been altered. New and respectable names have been invented. But the real issue has hardly changed at all. It has become a part of the world-wide issue of capital, but the question of African slavery still abides.[38]

The power of Henry's prose was lauded. One critic wrote how the reader was 'lured insensibly' from the opening pages. Inflating his time in Angola to 'a year's heroic travelling', the APS journal called his book 'the fullest and most authoritative published account of the horrors of this detestable traffic'.[39]

For legal reasons, he could not name offenders, whilst his calls for British firms to boycott cocoa were initially received with 'polite or venomous incredulity'.[40] Henry was accused in Britain, Portugal, Portuguese Africa, France and Switzerland of never having visited Angola or the islands. He was even portrayed as a property speculator spreading rumours so that he could buy cheaply and denounced as a hater of Catholics and bearer of grudges against the Portuguese though he stressed that they were 'not naturally more heartless than ourselves'.[41] One Foreign Office official dismissed his findings as 'that purple report'.

When he asked Henry 'Do you expect us to act the policeman for the world?' he was told 'Yes; I thought that, in the matter of slavery, that was what England was intended for.'[42] Harris recalled how Henry's name became linked with 'the dregs of society' and 'even coupled with murderers'.[43]

The *Times* correspondent in Lisbon wrote that Henry's 'tales' (a term suggestive of fiction) had brought foreign testimony into discredit. Henry penned an indignant response.[44] A few months later Lieutenant-Colonel Wyllie put the case for the San Thomé planters: 'In his zeal for the cause of the black man, I fear Mr. Nevinson too often fails to do justice to the white.' Wyllie, who was connected with the Boa Entrada plantations on San Thomé, compared the native Angolan to a monkey rescued and taken to a zoo and depicted the islands as a 'veritable paradise'.[45] 'A vomit of poison' was how Henry's diary described the newspaper attacks from 'that slave-fed worm'. The Boa Entrada owner denounced Henry's claims as 'audacious and malevolent', as did Negreiros, a member of the International Colonial Institute. He suggested in *La Gazette de Lausanne* that Henry's claims were 'fantasmagories' and spread 'every kind of scandal and abuse' against him.[46]

In April 1907, fresh from eight months in Africa, Burtt visited Henry. They largely agreed on facts though Henry found him 'Rather secretive' and inclined to query some of his views on Portuguese control. Procrastination prevailed. The Foreign Office, wary of injuring diplomatic relations with Portugal, wanted everything kept quiet for as long as possible. The publication of Burtt's report was delayed until the autumn of the following year. But the Foreign Office did accept a consular report that focused on treatment rather than the tricky question of liberty.

The British chocolate manufacturers told Henry (at a lunch hosted by the Cadburys) that a boycott was not the way to stop trafficking. Henry thought them too subservient to the Foreign Office. He suspected that Cadbury were using delaying tactics so that their plantations on the Gold Coast would be ready before they abandoned San Thomé. They were also developing trade with Bahia in Brazil. The murder of the King of Portugal in February 1908 furthered prevarication as the new regime was given a chance to redeem itself.

The *Manchester Guardian* reported two months later that Henry had suggested (at an APS meeting) that the great cocoa merchants and manufacturers prevented reform because they did not want their vast profits threatened.[47] The firms threatened a writ for libel. The paper apologized, making clear Cadbury's assertion that there had been 'a misapprehension of facts'. The next day a letter from Henry suggested that the reporter had misrepresented him. He was sure that he had not made such a claim in public. Others backed him but his diary reveals growing concern that he *might* have said as much *informally* to the reporter. The report of the AGM in the APS journal does not mention Henry criticizing the manufacturers though does stress his appeal to government for further action and a plea for boycotting cocoa and chocolate.[48] Henry's letter stressed that he was attacking neither merchants nor manufacturers but the slave-dealers and plantation owners 'who make immense profits off the traffic'. Acknowledging the 'careful enquiry' made by the great English cocoa firms, he suggested that their findings tallied with his.

This comment needs to be seen in the context of Henry's career. For, by a curious twist in the story, he was in the process of acquiring a new employer: the Cadbury brothers! His need for regular employment had led to negotiations with the Liberal *Daily News*. Its chief proprietor was George Cadbury. The formal offer came in June 1908. Henry was contracted to write four leading articles weekly for an annual salary of £500 but there was a condition. The editor had to submit to the proprietors anything that Henry wished to write in the paper about Angolan slavery. Since Henry believed a boycott to be imminent, he agreed to the terms. He and Brailsford (now also on the paper) were later to resign from it on account of their views on women's suffrage. But in 1908 Brailsford threatened to resign if he were not allowed to write on Angolan slavery. He got his way. A. G. Gardiner, soon to be cast by Henry as another problematic editor, played at this stage a mediating role between the proprietors and the crusading journalists, speaking to the former and securing freedom of publication. When Henry and Brailsford met George Cadbury they found him amiable but anxious to ward off written attacks on Portugal since his brother William and Burtt were visiting Africa.[49]

Henry also spoke at numerous meetings. On 4 December opponents of Angolan slavery held a large gathering at Caxton Hall. It had been advertised in a letter in *The Times*. Henry had used his literary and political connections to secure support from figures such as MacDonald, Galsworthy, Wells and Barnett. St Loe Strachey, owner and editor of the *Spectator*, which had recently publicized the subject, chaired the meeting. Speakers included E. D. Morel and Brailsford. Henry briefed them first at Anderton's Hotel: 'I had to ply them with plenty of wine, but got my way at last.' His speech dwelt on the recent increase of slaves from Angola. He asked pointedly, 'What is to be done?' (Lenin's pamphlet with that title had been published six years earlier.) Recommending boycott, he criticized the firms' dilatory tactics, urging, as a last resort, sending a man-of-war to arrest a legalized slave ship. Such talk of gunboat diplomacy further outraged critics.[50]

Privately, Henry thought he was 'very bad – cold & dull with my facts. No charm or personality at all . . . Hideous failure.' Nevertheless, it was valuable publicity and a few days later came a useful meeting with the Foreign Secretary, Sir Edward Grey, 'who was very clear & straight' and proposed a consular enquiry into Benguella's indenture system. But Grey did not welcome publicity and was keen to avoid foreign complications. He summed up the government's position in 1910 when he told Henry and ASS representatives that 'The last thing we want to do is derogate in any way from the sovereign rights of the Portuguese or hurt their political susceptibilities of sovereignty in any way whatever.'[51]

Cadbury, Fry and Rowntree announced a boycott in the spring of 1909, followed by Stollwerck and Suchard. A delighted Henry suggested that Britain had 'not lost that spirit of righteousness and freedom' which had characterized earlier anti-slavery protests.[52] He told William Cadbury that 'It has been a great piece of work accomplished, and it does you great honour in every way.'[53] But rumours followed that Cadbury had made a huge shipment immediately before the announcement and unofficially trade was said to be continuing. Cadbury claimed that American buyers were purchasing cocoa at reduced prices.

Over the previous few years Henry had maintained pressure in the press. The founding of the progressive journal the *Nation* in 1907 provided an important additional platform. The Cadbury solicitor failed to dissuade Henry from publishing a ten-page article in the *Fortnightly Review* but the firm took action over an article in the *Standard*, edited by fellow war correspondent H. A. Gwynne.[54] On 26 September 1908 its leader – described by Henry as 'a fine specimen of satiric invective' – told of the joys of Cadbury model factories. It suggested a huge contrast between the firm's solicitude for its workers at home and its indifference to the fate of the Africans who ensured its success. It reminded readers that 'The white hands of the Bourneville chocolate makers are helped by other unseen hands some thousands of miles away, black and brown hands, toiling in plantations, or hauling loads through swamp and forest.' William Cadbury's undue precaution and delay in personal intervention were commented upon, as were the honesty and powers of observation of 'a writer of high character and reputation', Henry Nevinson.

Cadbury took Standard Newspapers Ltd to court. The nine-day libel case, seen by many as a case about the liberty of the press, was heard at the end of 1909.[55] Henry attended the Birmingham court as chief witness for the defence but Sir Edward Carson did not call on him since Mr Rufus Isaacs (for the prosecution) admitted at an early stage that *A Modern Slavery* was accurate. Long extracts were read from it. Not only had Burtt's report corroborated Henry's findings but it also emerged that, during his first visit to Africa for the firms, Burtt had telegraphed home a code word signifying that the report was not exaggerated and was even understated. This had been relayed to Sir Edward Grey in December 1906 though Henry had not been told about it. The lawyers' notes also imply that Henry did not appear to harbour 'any unfriendly feeling towards the Cocoa Firms'. Yet it was suggested in court that Henry had, on occasions, been so racked with fever as to be an unreliable witness. George Cadbury also made it plain that he did not see the boycott as 'a step to freedom'. The verdict was for the plaintiffs but with derisory damages of one farthing. Harris argued that this publicity did more for the liberation of the slaves than all the consuls' and the Foreign Office's work put together over the last decade.[56] In 1927 the *Millgate Monthly* stated that the libel action established Henry's veracity, giving to 'the great knight errant of the cause his first tangible result in a singularly selfless career'.[57]

In the 1960s the American historian James Duffy claimed that Henry appropriated the issue, behaving in 'what was often an arrogant and guileful way, insisting always on his share of the credit, and more, for whatever success the English campaign enjoyed'.[58] Henry's complaints that the ASS (which in 1909 amalgamated with the APS) was initially slow in taking up the campaign were not entirely fair. In the 1890s events in South and East Africa and the revelations from the Congo had focused attention on other parts of Africa, but by the early 1900s the ASS journal was reporting regularly on Angola. Nevertheless, the ASS did not exploit the wider press as keenly as it might have done. In the main it was preaching to the converted.[59] Much of the concern about conditions came from within evangelical circles though the society did appoint a special Angolan sub-committee late in 1908, urge the import-ance of the boycott and put pressure on the Foreign Office. Harris, long familiar with the Congo, visited Portuguese Africa and produced one more report.

The British campaign operated on several levels. There were questions asked in the House of Commons. In 1913, the year of Livingstone's centenary, the Earl of Mayo led a House of Lords debate on Angola. Missionaries wrote accounts. But it was Henry who crucially stimulated the early-twentieth-century interest in Angola. Indeed, Duffy acknow-ledges that Henry was 'The one man responsible for precipitating an unpleasant problem into an international controversy'.[60] He was a vital bridge between the committed anti-slavery lobby and the press. As so often, he straddled worlds. Being part of more than one sphere of influ-ence (he joined the ASS committee in 1911), he was well placed to publicize.

Duffy's criticism of Henry's 'egocentricity' and 'questionable conduct', along with his claim that the British humanitarians undertook a 'vehe-ment and often irrational campaign' against Portuguese slavery, was largely based on Foreign Office material and journals (in English and Portuguese).[61] Duffy did not use Henry's diaries written as the campaign unfolded. His critique is based on Henry's memoirs. This needs to be put into context. They were written many years after the events when Henry was an elderly man, already cast in the public eye as a champion of causes. Duffy does, though, appreciate the power of Henry's writing in *Harper's Magazine* (though barely refers to *A Modern Slavery*, which was considerably longer and the key account in Britain). He calls Henry's writing 'a classic of its kind. It was personal, it was wrathful, it was right, and it did the job.' He notes too that Henry wrote well, 'an art most humanitarians had lost by the early twentieth century'.[62]

And there were results. After Henry's articles appeared in the USA the American Frame Food Company wrote to tell him that they had ceased to use San Thomé cocoa. In July 1909 a Portuguese Royal Decree suspended recruitment from Angola for three months and this was extended over the next few years. A repatriation fund was started and the new republican government sought to impose repatriation from 1910. Henry, though, placed little faith in the new regulations. He was part of an ASS delegation to Lisbon. They and a new Portuguese anti-slavery society met the new Minister for Foreign Affairs. Henry was unimpressed by the vague assurances and refusal to turn promises into official written declarations.

About 500 Angolans were sent home annually by 1913 and the numbers were accelerating. But many were simply dumped back on the coast, money was misappropriated and in the same year at least 30,000 were thought to be working on the islands. The Portuguese government exercised little real control over the officials, slave traders and planters.

Belatedly, in 1914 a government White Book (one of five on Portuguese contract labour between 1909 and 1917) officially confirmed the situation Henry had witnessed almost a decade earlier. He had played a significant part in exposing Angolan slavery. Most of those concerned about it in Britain were Christian humanitarians or businessmen or both. They either witnessed the situation at first hand or expatiated against the system in print. Henry had the advantage of being both an eyewitness and a professional writer.

His campaigning was less patronizing than that of many of his contemporaries. In 1905 Henry was warning that 'We still think of "black people" in lumps and blocks. We do not realise that each African has a personality as important to himself as each of us in his own eyes.'[63] And his cameos of how different races treat each other are powerful. He describes a Frenchman in filthy clothes who accuses a native Angolan of being a thief. Here he reveals, in a few beautifully chosen words, just how heavily the odds are stacked in favour of the former: 'he was a white man, and he came up the ship's side with the confident air of Europe'.[64]

Yet his final words on Angola in his memoirs are much more problematic. They were written in 1925, many years after the educative experience of being with Africans on a daily basis. Intended to be amusing, they produce unwitting testimony – not least in the use of adjectives – to the confidence of those who had lived through the heyday of imperialism. Discussing how repatriation had increased, Henry added:

and when I come to die, my deep regret at leaving this beautiful
world may perhaps be tempered by a vision of 10,000 little black
men and women dancing around my bed to the sound of elfin
ochisangis [a musical instrument with iron keys on a board] or
echoing *ochingufus* [a wooden drum], and crying in grateful ecstasy:
'he sent us home He sent us home'.[65]

Henry had undergone two journeys of discovery: one literal and one
metaphorical. The first, through swamp and forest, danger and disease,
was in the footsteps of the great masculine heroes of imperial adventure.[66] The second was when he sought to convert adventure to a higher
purpose. He spoke on behalf of the truly powerless: black slaves (in
practice if not in law) belonging to another empire. Yet campaigning at
home proved to be as challenging mentally as his debilitating travels in
Africa. Henry had to learn the tough lesson that rational debate did not
easily produce the desired results. He met government intransigence and
the power of vested interests, complicated in some instances by their
humanitarian claims. Both Angola and subsequent battles for freedom –
of slaves, of speech and for change – affected him deeply for the rest of
his life.

In 1927, a year when Henry gave several talks on Angola, a missionary
told him that he was still remembered there 'with deep hatred by the
slave traders & planters'.[67] Slavery did not simply wither away. It
increased again during the First World War. When Henry died in 1941
the ASS wrote that his report had 'led to the suppression of the evil'.[68]
Yet during this time the right-wing dictatorship in Portugal, which
lasted from 1926 to 1974, condoned contract colonial labour, in effect
chattel slavery. Even in 1967 the name of Henry Nevinson was,
according to Duffy, 'still regarded with special loathing by Portuguese
colonists'.[69] Henry's book was reprinted in the United States in this
decade. Basil Davidson's Introduction suggests that his writing, showing journalism 'at its highest point', was, unfortunately, 'signally up to
date'. Davidson reminded readers that the book was also 'a capital
document in the history of modern Africa'.[70]

Modern Angola is embroiled in tragedies sparked by civil war.
Meanwhile, West Africa faces renewed concern about slavery. Reports
abound of modern slave labour with traffickers selling youths to work on
the cocoa plantations of the Ivory Coast, now the world's top cocoa
producer. In April 2001 news of a missing ship from Benin reported to
be carrying child slaves destined for Gabon fuelled concern about forced
labour. Almost a century after Henry's writings on 'The New Slave-
Trade' there were renewed efforts to exculpate and pass the proverbial
buck.[71] Although the MV *Etireno*, the purported slave ship, was not
linked with cocoa production, the adverse publicity helped air concern
about the consumption of chocolate and the importance of eating

fair-trade products. There are familiar names in the modern debate: Anti-Slavery International, chocolate firms, the Foreign Office and newer players such as UNICEF. Were Henry alive today, he might have a sense of déjà vu.

CHAPTER FOUR

The Battle for Freedom
Russia, Revolution and Empire

In 1905 Henry was sweltering in equatorial San Thomé. Within months, in deep snow, he was witnessing events in Russia that helped shape twentieth-century world history. He captured in print scenes of revolution and repression in St Petersburg and Moscow. And since 'The best journalism is the first draft of history', Henry's writings contributed to that history.[1] As Map 1 shows, he covered vast distances. He travelled almost 8,000 miles, often in inhospitable terrain, across the vast Russian Empire from the Baltic to the Caucasus, stoking his passionate commitment to freedom.

It was in Angola that he belatedly learned about the events of January 1905. In the wake of a disastrous war with Japan and galvanized by the Orthodox priest Father Gapon who had formed a Russian Workmen's Union, many thousands of workers had marched to the Winter Palace to present Tsar Nicholas II with 'A Most Humble and Loyal Address'.[2] The result was a massacre: Bloody Sunday. It prompted a vast strike movement involving, that month alone, some 414,000 across the Empire. By March Henry was describing this as a 'Russian Revolution' and wishing he were there. There followed a mutiny on the battleship *Potemkin* and a general strike in Odessa. Soon St Petersburg would have a Soviet of Workers' Deputies and for a short period the Tsar would be confronted by the power of the people.

During the summer, events in Russia directly affected Henry's friends at home. Brailsford was charged with conspiracy.[3] He sat on the executive of the Society of the Friends of Russian Freedom. It worked with Russian revolutionaries. He had secured three British passports for exiles to return undetected to Russia. When one was discovered on the body of a dead revolutionary in St Petersburg, Brailsford contacted the police. Although passports were not then treated with much seriousness in Europe – Henry claimed that 'one no more thought of getting a passport for travel on the Continent than of taking a hamper of English cooking to France' – they were required in Russia. The Russian government lodged an official complaint. Brailsford was fined £100. Henry briefly covered his friend's leaders on the *Echo* and offered financial support.

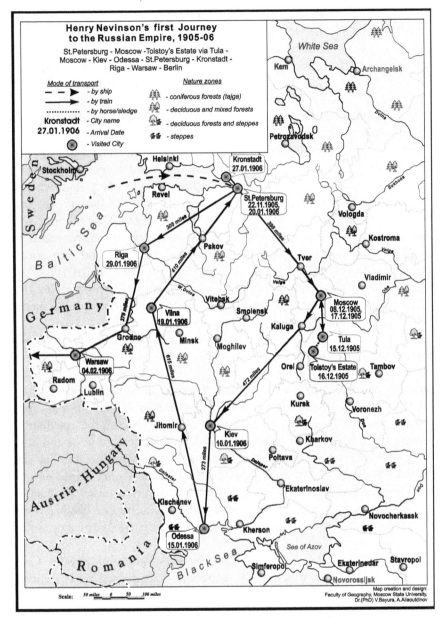

**Henry Nevinson's first Journey
to the Russian Empire, 1905-06**

St.Petersburg - Moscow -Tolstoy's Estate via Tula -
Moscow - Kiev - Odessa - St.Petersburg - Kronstadt -
Riga - Warsaw - Berlin

Mode of transport
- **- - ▶** - by ship
- **──▶** - by train
- **·········** - by horse/sledge
- **Kronstadt** - City name
- **27.01.1906** - Arrival Date
- 🔘 - Visited City

Nature zones
- 🌲 - coniferous forests (tajga)
- 🌳 - deciduous and mixed forests
- 🌿 - deciduous forests and steppes
- 🌾 - steppes

Map 1 Henry Nevinson's first journey to the Russian Empire, 1905–6.

Fired by news of a Russian general strike, Henry lay awake at night 'with crazy wishes & excitement'. The industrial proletariat represented only a tiny proportion of the total and highly fragmented population of the Russian Empire but Bloody Sunday had ensured that the intelligentsia was no longer alone in its assault upon autocracy. Four days after the strike began, the October Manifesto promised personal freedom and a constitution.

The *Daily Chronicle* agreed to send Henry to Russia for a couple of months. For £300 he was to produce about twenty letters. He had a few Russian lessons and then, still in considerable pain from 'African microbes', with suppurating sores on both arms and legs, he set sail on 17 October. The sole passenger on the *Irkutsk*, he immersed himself in Stepniak's study of the Russian peasantry: 'it gets hold of the living thing', much more illuminating than writers 'shuffling about abstractions of socialism'.[4]

Henry came ashore in Estonia, arriving in St Petersburg on 21 November, two days after the strike ended.[5] He was on the first train to run again into the city. There was 'deep & sordid poverty everywhere'. He witnessed a remarkable period known as the Days of Liberty. Lasting from 18 October (in the Russian calendar) until early December, it was a time when 'Righteousness and peace kissed each other in the streets of St. Petersburg, when professor embraced peasant, and battalions marched to the Marseillaise, and generals saluted the red flag of freedom.'[6] The government relaxed newspaper censorship. Trade and political unions mushroomed. Packed meetings produced eloquent, spontaneous speeches.

In Moscow alone over 400 public meetings were held in just over three weeks. In factories, concert-halls, cafés, lecture theatres, street corners and countless private homes, 'Without practice or tradition in public speaking, Russia was suddenly found to be a nation of orators.'[7] Henry attended numerous meetings. At an 'assembly of the educated classes' protesting against capital punishment, he noticed the 'inexhaustible patience' of Russians, the large number of women students and how the greatest applause was reserved not for the best speaker but for the person who had suffered most. The Union of Equal Rights helped ensure that women's rights were voiced. But it was precarious.[8] As Henry put it, 'Freedom at that moment was just hanging in the balance. One almost heard the grating of the scales as very slowly the balance began to swing back again.'[9]

From 4 December for ten weeks, letters from 'Our Special Correspondent' featured sporadically, generally interspersed with Reuters reports of the latest news. Henry's pictures of a revolution helped influence and inform liberal radical opinion. A century on, his diary and writings show how a correspondent tried to make sense of and negotiate his way around the disintegration of society. Henry's letters did not always arrive or get printed in the correct order. Some were adulterated. His first letter from Moscow was printed on 23 December alongside the contents of a telegram he had dispatched urgently on the day martial law was declared. He was furious. It was 'padded & stuffed full of lies & commonplace', an 'amazing abortion'. Following his remarks about people storing water in baths and pails because the water supply had been cut off were the offending words: 'and when the last drop has been drunk? Blood will flow in its place.'[10] Although not above the occasional melodramatic statement himself, he bitterly resented others intervening, writing in his diary, 'I died of shame & revived on rage.' Yet there was too much to see for indignation to detain him for long.

In London Henry had known a number of Russian émigrés. Before leaving, like any good journalist, he made the most of his contacts. One was the writer, translator and radical lawyer Dr David Soskice, who had been imprisoned in Russia in the 1890s and with whom Father Gapon had briefly stayed in Hammersmith. He found Henry an interpreter. Henry's diary records bringing with him 'S's revolver' and cartridges which he delivered to Dr Maria Vorontsova in St Petersburg. It would seem from diary entries and correspondence that this favour was for the Soskices.[11]

In St Petersburg Henry attended the first meeting of Gaponovites since Bloody Sunday as they sought to revive Gapon's Assembly of the Russian Factory and Mill Workers of the City of St Petersburg. Gapon's recent contacts with the government had left him thoroughly discredited in the eyes of the Left. He had just returned from Western Europe and did not attend the main meeting but Henry joined those who secretly met later to hear him speak in a room away from spies, Social Democrats and the police. Henry was critical of Gapon's opportunism yet recognized that here was 'the man who struck the first blow at the heart of tyranny and made the old monster sprawl'.[12] He noted too that there was 'something of a hidden child in him'. Later that day Gapon fled to Finland.[13]

In the decrepit hall of the Free Economic Society, Henry found the Central Strike Committee or Council of Labour Delegates. He learned later that Trotsky was present there and claimed that he had observed the origin of the Soviet.[14] Women wore scarlet and men brown belted blousons. Henry met the seasoned revolutionary Vera Zasulich: 'both of us spoke abominable French at each other'. He listened to debates long into the night, hearing passionate speeches on the postal strike and eight-hour day. Still in pain, he needed morphine to sleep.

Henry's autobiography states that he made many friends during that 'happy and hopeful time' though his diary reveals private exasperation with the attitudes of some fellow Englishmen. He networked extensively, lunched at the British Embassy with the first secretary, Cecil Spring-Rice (an old Oxford acquaintance), and found the consul-general, Oliver Wardrop, and his erudite sister especially helpful about Georgia. He visited several newspapers, taking advantage of an unaccustomed free press and was impressed by the remarkable flowering of artistic ability expressed through satirical cartoons.[15] He met Social Democrats, both Bolsheviks and Mensheviks, and talked to Socialist Revolutionaries such as Annesky, president of the Economic Society which appealed specifically to the peasants.

After just over a fortnight in the capital, Henry took the train to Moscow. Here he saw bedraggled soldiers finally returning from the Russo-Japanese War: 'Down the dirty streets they drifted and disappeared, the reservists being discharged at barracks and going to swell the crowd of beggars who, with threats or blessings, violently demanded the milk of human kindness at every corner.'[16] But Henry was bound for the vast Russian countryside and Tolstoy, 'the most shattering of all living thinkers'.[17] His interpreter refused to travel beyond Tula (about 100 miles from Moscow). Ten days earlier nineteen people had been shot there. With a boy, a horse and a small sledge Henry journeyed on through the snow. Eventually a wintry sun appeared, illuminating the silver birch trees. Lines of whitened plain opened up ahead and 'Then indeed I beheld the beauty of Russia.'

Reaching Count Tolstoy's estate, Henry saw him standing erect, dressed like a Russian peasant. His grey hair was long and he wore a look of 'profound thought & great benevolence & simplicity'. It is not surprising that Tolstoy was one of Henry's heroes. The man who was cultivating his own reputation as a rebel saw here 'the greatest rebel in the world'. Not usually one to adulate novels, Henry appreciated that in Tolstoy's work 'the passion of humanity and the zeal of prophets are united to the highest imaginative power'. He was writing *The End of an Age* and told Henry that Russia was witnessing neither a riot nor even a revolution. It was the end of an era: 'the age of Empires is passing away'. Aged seventy-seven, this 'great prophet of the soul' was 'like a still pool, outside the whirling current of his people's movement'.

Henry returned to the vortex. Not much smaller than the capital, Moscow had initially displayed less revolutionary fervour than had St Petersburg. But now there was a dramatic shift. Officers

> began murdering in the name of the Tsar. Barricades were piled across the streets in the name of the people. The air crashed and whined with bullets and shells, and the snow was reddened with the blood of men and women.[18]

A student was killed outside Henry's hotel. He watched the procession at the Kremlin on St Nicholas's Day. The fervently patriotic organization the Black Hundred or Union of Russian People had issued a manifesto about exterminating Jews and foreigners. Moscow was fortified in fear. 'Our Special Correspondent' saw the ominous lining up of the forces of good and evil: 'In the pitchy streets, lurking in the darkness are bands of the "Black Hundred" who sate their lust for blood in the name of the Tsar.' A *Daily Chronicle* leader called his description 'worthy of any reign of terror'.[19] Patriots marched, fleeing at the cry that the students were coming.

Henry wished to visit the Caucasus. He boarded a train, anticipating four days and nights travelling. He went nowhere. After tactical differences between Bolsheviks and Mensheviks, on the instructions of the Moscow Soviet a general political strike was announced starting at noon, to be transformed into an armed uprising. Gas and electricity were cut off and shops, other businesses and banks closed. Two days later the first clash between soldiers and revolutionaries was triggered during a railway union meeting at the Fiedler Academy. A period of bloodshed ensued. On his very first day in Russia, Henry had noted that factories were building up their own defensive militias. Now Social Democrat militiamen were being instructed in guerrilla warfare. Muscovites erected barricades from whatever was at hand. Henry saw 130 in one morning. He explained to readers that they prevented cavalry entering side streets, slowed troops down and hindered visibility.[20] He aroused suspicion from revolutionists when he tried photographing a barricade but, after having a revolver pressed into his side, got away with simply surrendering his film.

We do not have Henry's usual diurnal account for the days between 23 December (10 December in the Russian calendar) and the end of the year. Pages were torn out of his diary perhaps because it was too dangerous to keep such an account with him. Men and women were shot in the streets around him. His hotel chef went to see what was going on outside and was shot through the heart. Another bullet passed through the hotel window. A boy in school uniform was splayed across the snow, his mouth a dark red hole. Henry and a local woman wrapped him in a tablecloth and carried him to an ambulance-room. But it was too late. In a back yard run by insurgents, under an open shed, Henry found 'a pitiful row of the dead lying on the stones'. Some were shattered by shellfire, others killed by rifles 'so merciful when it strikes the brain or heart'. 'Between the stones of that yard', he wrote, 'for the first time I saw men's blood trickling as in a gutter.'[21]

By Christmas Day Henry sensed that 'the highest moment of revolutionary success lay behind us'. Gradually, over the following days 'the feeling of disaster grew'. Soldiers continued their 'slow and perilous advance from street to street'.[22] Revolutionists officially ended street fighting. Business people returned to work. Henry made a vivid comparison:

Think of the feelings of our own City men if suddenly the morning train which for years they had caught successfully, stopped running and shells rained from Holborn Viaduct to Aldgate Pump! With what common sense they would welcome the restoration of any tyranny, with what scorn decry the fallen sentimentalists who had cared for freedom! So in Moscow, returning law and order met a greasy smile, and many extolled the Governor-General and officers for the vigour of their action.[23]

He was not, however, in tune with the majority of the British press, anxiously voicing their concern about the implications of popular revolution for the rest of Europe. The *Fortnightly Review* had depicted the general strike as 'the most portentous and terrible instrument ever employed by political agitation', while *The Times* applauded the arrest of the St Petersburg Soviet and the suppression of the Moscow Rising.[24]

Briefly and bravely the Presnensky mill district held out but troops with reinforcements from St Petersburg were soon shelling and shooting. The first day of Henry's New Year was spent there under eighteen degrees of frost. The last of the men had just surrendered. The leaders were bayoneted. The group executions lasted for over a week. As Henry might have put it, Russia's two foremost cities had some tale to tell: from Days of Liberty in St Petersburg to the brutal reprisals as authority was restored in Moscow, urban Russians witnessed the best and worst of times.

Yet, despite playing such a novel and crucial role in 1905, they were in the minority numerically. Over 70 per cent of the population lived in the countryside. And there was agrarian unrest among the peasants for whom emancipation had not brought prosperity. They tended to focus their attacks on landlords. Indeed, 1905 had shown just how discontented were peasants, industrial workers, students, liberals and national minorities. Throughout the Empire, disturbances reverberated. The battleship *Potemkin* mutiny demonstrated the disaffection of the navy, but keeping the army under control was an even bigger problem. 'Will the Line obey their officers and not hesitate to shoot?' was, Henry stressed, a vital question, ultimately crucial to the restoration of authority.[25] The government survived since disturbances did not occur simultaneously. But although autocracy was restored, the impact of Marxism, the glimpse of liberty and the nature of the subsequent repression ensured that nothing could ever be the same again – for both upholders and detractors of the system.

Keen to travel further afield, Henry made a twenty-eight-hour train journey to Kiev, now under martial law. He was shocked by the poverty of country people whose grain fed so many far-away foreigners. He travelled over the steppes to Odessa on the Black Sea. Roughly half of its population was Jewish so it was a target for pogroms. The October Manifesto had been followed by a three-day slaughtering of Jews. Synagogues and shops were plundered, leaving a trail of devastation, abject fear and closed schools. Henry's article on Odessa invited sympathy for the large Jewish population with its lack of rights. It condemned persecution and the recent violence. Yet it also revealed a refusal to appreciate the power of faith and why defiance remained so crucial to the Jews.[26]

Back in St Petersburg for the anniversary of Bloody Sunday, Henry found that so many had been incarcerated or sent into exile that there was just a one-day stoppage. He suggested that the uncanny silence of the streets that day signified not the restoration of order but evidence of the revolution's continued power. He believed that the Strike Committee could still count on the loyalty of working people.[27] Attending a 'concert' (mainly recitations with pointed parables) held by the Committee of the Working People to raise funds for workmen's dining rooms, Henry was deeply impressed by the audience's common faith. Unable to understand, he watched all the more intently. He later commented that 'There is a brotherliness among the Russian people that I have not found equalled in any other race.'[28] He was attracted by 'the touch of danger' and how different it was from 'the correct chill of a London audience, whose chief thought is to get home in time for bed'. He left soon after midnight, halfway through the performance.

He witnessed a different fervour on the tiny island of Kronstadt. Henry and the American correspondent Robert Crozier Long crossed the frozen shallows of the Gulf of Finland by sledge in a raging storm to see the man said to influence the Tsar: Father John of Kronstadt. They found him in a 'superior doss-house' where he dispensed – at a price – beds and miracles. To Henry's embarrassment and the envy of adoring women seeking the little priest's attention, Father John went on tiptoe and ruffled his hair. Henry saw Father John as an illustration of how reactionaries emerge from isolation, dogma and sycophancy.

At the end of January, Henry visited the Baltic Provinces. Only 2 per cent of the size of the Russian Empire and with less than 4 per cent of its population, they and Finland were distinguished by their degree of modernization, ethnic diversity and opposition to Russification.[29] Henry reached Riga at sunrise. He passed from beautiful fir forests and heaths to brutal scenes. As he left the railway station he glimpsed twenty-five bound men lying in a row on the sand dunes where they had been shot. From his hotel he saw groups of Latvians marched off daily to be shot. Russian troops summarily executed people of all ages. A schoolmaster was hanged on a telephone post for allowing a public meeting in his school. Two girls were flogged with rods for stitching a red flag. An estimated 1,170 were killed in the Baltic region between December 1905 and May 1906. Many were banished to Siberia. The Tsar praised Major Orlov for a thorough job.[30] Henry deplored both the brutality and the ongoing assault on an ancient language and culture.

Poles also suffered from Russification. Although contributing a disproportionately high percentage of the Empire's industrial output, the Russo-Japanese War had been disastrous for their economy. Within four days of Bloody Sunday there had been major strikes with political and economic demands taking the country to the brink of civil war. Henry found Warsaw under martial law with at least eighteen political parties vying for influence. He secured an interview with General Martynov, the city's governor. In print he used inverted commas as though he were quoting him. But the interview was not recorded in his diary and the original exchange was in French. The phrasing in the *Chronicle* is not identical to the version of the conversation used later in Henry's memoirs. Moreover, the Warsaw material for the paper was actually completed after his return home.[31] But by using reported speech, Henry conveys something of Martynov's obduracy. He appears to damn himself through his very frankness and categorical pronouncements. He dismissed Poles as full of 'crazy notions', expressing contempt for both Socialists and Nationalists. He denied the need for any special rights in any part of the Empire, believing too many concessions had been made to Finland. Martynov later described Henry as 'a terrible revolutionist'.[32]

Finland's future was indeed worrying. The Tsar had commanded two army corps to mobilize on its frontier, poised for invasion. Returning to England, Henry protested against European loans to Russia. The sweeping Liberal victory had meant that he now had friends in high places. Vaughan Nash and Arthur Ponsonby had become private secretaries to Prime Minister Campbell-Bannerman. Henry consulted them and then tackled King Edward VII personally about the Finnish situation. Vaughan Nash lent a top hat and off Henry went to knock at the door of Buckingham Palace. The episode receives scant attention in Henry's diary but he later turned it into a farcical tale, possibly influenced by Evelyn, veteran writer of fairy stories.[33] Greeted by a liveried 'paragon of princedom such as would delight a child in a fairy tale', henceforth referred to as 'the gorgeous apparition', and 'Gulping down my astonished awe', Henry asked 'is the King at home, please?' After wending their way down endless corridors they reached 'a comfortable sort of study' where an equerry ran to and fro, conveying messages with Henry in one room and His Majesty in another. The closest Henry got to the monarch was hearing, behind a hidden door, 'the guttural notes of the voice that rocked the Empire'. The purpose, though, was serious. Henry requested that the King write a personal letter to the Tsar, suggesting that if he wished to conclude the proposed agreement then 'the invasion of Finland with two Russian army corps would be a bad beginning'. When the equerry trotted back, Henry was informed that the King could make no such promise, as it would interfere with the affairs of a friendly Power. About two weeks later the Russian forces withdrew from the Finnish frontier.

Attending a large meeting of supporters of the labour movement, Henry was struck by 'the sense of security & the laughter' compared to the deadly serious Russian gatherings. After the Russian 'concert' he had written:

To have a cause like that, to dwell with danger for the sake of it every day and night, to confront continually an enemy vital, pitiless, almost omnipotent, and execrable beyond words – what other life can compare to that, not only in courage and love of every human faculty?[34]

This says much about Henry's idealism, fuelled as it was by a harsh reality he had personally witnessed. It made life in Britain seem tame and blinkered. But it helps explain why he would soon throw himself into a struggle at home which, to many, was known simply as the Cause: women's suffrage. It also suggests something of the alienation and frustration Henry must have felt when fellow journalists on the paper (including the editor) 'cared not the least about Russia'. He complained that only one of them bothered to read his badly displayed articles.[35]

There was, however, another opportunity to turn articles into a book for Harper's. Henry put his volume together quickly, adding factual and linking material, over two dozen of his own photographs and powerful cartoons. Early in 1906 Charles M. Doughty's study of pre-history, *The Dawn in Britain*, was published. Using the allusive language of midnight despair succeeded by dawn and hope popular in revolutionary rhetoric, Henry entitled his book *The Dawn in Russia*. It contained a nod to Wordsworth: he wrote that the Days of Liberty 'must indeed have been very heaven' for those young and Russian.[36]

It appeared in June to good reviews.[37] The veteran radical Felix Volkhovsky (a leading figure in the Society of Friends of Russian Freedom) thought it read better than many novels: 'Few authors have so brilliant a style, such an inexhaustible stock of humour – now grim, now good-natured, but always to the point.' Although spotting a few factual errors, his review was headed 'The Real Russia'. Here was a book to be read in Britain, translated into Russian and circulated as widely as possible.[38] Kropotkin told Henry that Russians must be thankful for an admirable account, both true and beautifully told.[39]

Two final chapters had been added at the last moment. Henry had completed his manuscript in Russia in May 1906 when he was covering the opening of the first Duma for Alfred Spender's *Westminster Gazette*. In print he expressed uncertainty about the prospects for freedom though admitted privately to 'a feeling of hope in the air' and 'a good deal of real confidence' in the Duma. His account from the gallery in the Coronation Hall of the Winter Palace lacks the deferential tone that often accompanies accounts of pomp and ceremony. On one side were nobility and officials: 'Pale, bald, and fat, they stood there like a hideous masquerade of senile children, hardly able to realize the possibility of change. Opposite thronged the people – young, thin, alert, and sunburnt, with brown and hairy heads, dressed like common mankind, and straining for the future chance.'[40] But when the Tsar spoke, 'With every sentence the hopes of the new age faded.'[41] Nevertheless, despite missed opportunities such as an amnesty for prisoners, the presence of peasant and urban proletariat members made it 'democratic beyond anything that our

House of Commons has yet imagined'.[42] Henry also saw the election of President Muromtsev of the Constitutional Democrats (the majority party in the Duma) at the Potemkin Palace and reported on the first meeting of the State Council and on the Duma's first sitting, almost twelve hours long.

After a delay due to rumours that something terrible would happen at the Duma, Henry came home. In July, aware that his Russian friends were suspicious of any efforts appearing to endorse their government, he protested against his own government's plans for a visit by the British fleet to Kronstadt. The Foreign Secretary argued that it was a harmless public relations exercise to promote understanding with the Russian people. But the Russian government itself decided against the exercise.

A week later the Duma was dissolved.[43] What followed involved Henry in Anglo-Russian affairs beyond the realm of the special correspondent. It was he who smuggled into Russia a British Memorial addressed to the Russian people, expressing 'sympathy and respect'. Henry conveyed it personally to Sergei Muromtsev, ex-president of the Duma. The original intention was for presentation by a British deputation.[44] Journalists writing for the *Tribune* (a Liberal paper started in 1905 which Henry had been approached to join) were the main instigators, notably its foreign editor G. H. Perris, David Soskice and Brailsford. It was initially called the Memorial to the Duma Committee. Henry was part of this group from the outset, and on his suggestion its name was changed in August 1906 to the Anglo-Russian Friendship Committee to mirror a committee of the same name in St Petersburg. The Memorial stressed the importance of representative government and personal liberty as essential prerequisites for national progress and prosperity. It applauded the 'heroism' of Russian sacrifices for freedom and anticipated 'the complete triumph of liberty' in Russia and cementing ties between nations as part of the goal for European peace. The men behind these words worked hard raising public awareness and disseminating information. By September they had collected about 10,000 signatures, including those of 365 MPs.[45] Professor P. N. Miliukov, president of the St Petersburg Anglo-Russian Friendship Committee, visited London and Henry spoke at his welcoming dinner.

When the British committee debated the deputation's composition, Henry was in Dorset visiting Thomas Hardy. Donald, the *Daily Chronicle* editor, suggested himself or Henry. The visit was planned for mid-October with three MPs, a trade unionist, the barrister Frederick Pethick Lawrence, Aylmer Maude (a fluent Russian speaker), Massingham and Henry. MacCallum Scott (its secretary) would precede them to St Petersburg. However, reactionaries and opponents of Russian liberals were determined to discredit the venture. The Russian ambassador in London dismissed them as 'un tas de littérateurs et des naïfs' (a bunch of intellectuals and innocents). Within Russia the official press attacked the deputation as unwarranted foreign interference. The Black Hundred threatened violence once it arrived. Muromtsev was about to stand trial for sedition. The influential Russian expert Sir Donald Mackenzie Wallace, who had the ear of King Edward, had been in St Petersburg since July.[46] He had applauded the Duma's dissolution and, as the *Times* correspondent, was responsible for a shift in its tone. It had earlier published the Memorial but now helped orchestrate disapproval. Wallace informed the King that if the deputation got 'gently hustled by the reactionary demonstrators' he would not be very sorry since 'I consider that Englishmen have no right to interfere obtrusively in Russian party politics.'[47]

Five days before the deputation was due to arrive, the Foreign Secretary learned from the British Embassy in St Petersburg that it was exciting interest and controversy 'out of proportion to its importance'.[48] Russians were not accustomed to the idea that 'that which is not forbidden by a Government has not its encouragement'. An anonymous letter to the British Embassy threatened 'scandal'. British residents were anxious and feared a demonstration by the Black Hundred. At home even papers like the *Westminster Gazette* now reflected government caution and opposed the visit. On 9 October Henry recorded great anxiety at the *Chronicle* office. He predicted that the deputation's collapse was imminent. Two days later the British Friendship Committee met and Donald proposed abandoning the plan. Foreign Office pressure and worry about British people exposing their Russian friends to danger resulted in a compromise: a private presentation.[49] Brailsford could not go because his court case had left him without a passport. Henry was about to visit the Caucasus and it was agreed that he would do the honours.[50]

He sailed on 14 October, accompanied by Aylmer Maude, his fiftieth birthday all but forgotten in the rush. They travelled via Hamburg, Copenhagen, Stockholm and Helsingfors (Helsinki), landing at St Petersburg to avoid border encounters. And 'the address from mankind', described in a *Daily News* leader as 'probably the most significant and influentially-signed document ever prepared in this country' was, all the while, 'stuffed up my waistcoat'.[51] After an appointment with the British ambassador, Henry explained to the St Petersburg Anglo-Russian Friendship Committee why the deputation had not gone ahead. The 'perilous parchment' was delivered at a dinner. In a mixture of English, French and German, Henry outlined what Britain might learn from Russia in terms of higher ideals. His diary suggests that Muromtsev did not really wish to receive the document. Henry later wrote that it then 'duly disappeared into space'.[52] However, MacCallum Scott argued that it was appreciated outside official circles and that the opposition to it had laid bare the wire-pulling of the reactionary government machinery.[53] In retrospect Henry argued that it was a pity the deputation had not gone ahead. He even made the somewhat improbable counter-factual claim that, had they gone ahead with their original plan and been 'torn from limb to limb':

> Our fate might have averted that agreement with the Tsardom which gave Germany the excuse of fear – fear of 'encirclement' on east, west and the sea. It might even have averted the Great War itself, and by our scattered limbs many millions of lives might have been saved, and the world spared its present load of incalculable misery.[54]

Perhaps an inflated notion of what might have happened helped deflect attention from the fact that, although at one point promising much, the event was something of a damp squib.

After a brief interlude in Moscow, Henry's next assignment took him by train to the far south, over plains and steppes and along the banks of the Don. A young Tartar conveyed him by horse and cart over the mountains to Georgia. During this three-day journey (see Map 2) he saw a wild bear standing on his hind legs in the snow. Always enchanted by mountains, he found the Caucasus range extending for about 900 miles 'unimaginably glorious'. Alien languages enhanced the sense of being in another world. As with the Romantics, part of the appeal for Henry was that such faraway places appeared to represent the antithesis of the civilized world as he knew it: 'It was peace, but a different peace from the Swiss Alps or the French – a savage peace, full of uncertainty.'[55]

Henry found Tiflis (Tbilisi) in a state of 'simmering terror', reeling from Russian repression. Schoolboys had been bayoneted, there had been massacres in the market place and 'Wherever you walk you meet men and women hurried off between fixed bayonets to the guard house, and there they disappear.'[56] Henry was not on his own here. He travelled with the Georgian Prince Varlaam Cherkesov and his Dutch-born wife, Frieda.[57] He also spent the best part of a week in Tiflis with Nannie Dryhurst and went with her to Batumi (Batoum) on the Black Sea where she began her voyage home.[58] Passionately committed to supporting small subject nations, she was in Georgia as a member of the Georgian Relief Committee, recently formed in London. She had learned the Georgian language and was supplying aid and fact-finding to raise awareness at home of the plight of Georgian women who had petitioned Britain for help.

Russia had annexed Georgia in 1801. Just over a century later the defeat of the Russian army by the Japanese sparked passive resistance against Russian officials, most evident, Henry discovered, in the province of Guria where the communes refused rent and taxes to Russia and made their own laws. Long-cherished hopes for freedom were raised in 1905, only to be followed by retribution. Stationed in the ancient city of Kutais, Russian troops slaughtered Georgians; 'from end to end the country smoked'.[59] Over 120 villages and a number of towns were plundered and

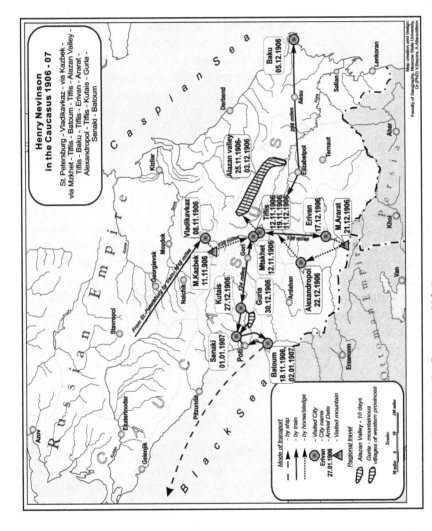

Map 2 Henry Nevinson in the Caucasus, 1906-7.

burned, women raped and men executed or imprisoned without trial. Henry saw villagers attempting to rebuild their communities.

In 1908 Henry published another series of articles for *Harper's Monthly Magazine*. They focused on the different geographical regions of the Caucasus. Harper's discouraged polemical and political statements so the articles, all amply illustrated, began as sharply observed travel pieces. 'A Valley of Caucasus' opens with Henry crammed into a cart (a more dignified diligence in the diary!) with 'a Russian soldier, an Armenian swindler, a Georgian prince and princess and the driver'. He describes the vineyards of the Alazan valley – much of Georgia's wine went to France as 'body' for Burgundy and Bordeaux – and talks of bridal processions in bullock carts and how ancient noble families seem like Homeric figures. His diary was less romantic: 'oh the boredom of these long days in incomprehensible company' as the language barrier took its toll. Towards the end of the magazine article he shifts key. His welcome, he argues, was not just as a stranger but because he was 'an enemy to Russia's tyranny'. The people were regarded simply as a source of taxes. Vast numbers of Russian troops were on the alert. In the Alazan valley tensions were slowly rising as all were aware of massacres close by. Henry met one child whose name meant 'Down with Nicholas'.[60]

Henry also wrote about religious and ethnic differences. 'The Fire of the Caucasus' describes Baku on the western shores of the Caspian Sea, the source of roughly half the world's oil.[61] It had become a twilight world of gambling, serious drinking and extortion. The week before Henry arrived, a Russian manager in the oilfields had been disembowelled for reducing his staff. The title of the final article, 'The Burden of the Caucasus', suggests Henry's serious message. After stressing the Georgian passion for knowledge and equality, Henry urged students of government and economics to take note of the Gurian co-operative experiment, contrasting this happy time with subsequent destruction and pillage. His final words, written in London early in 1907, were optimistic, arguing that the development of the Russian Revolution would transform Russia and all Europe. In that better future, Georgia would stand 'conspicuous as a gallant nationality of peculiar interest and brilliance'.[62]

Writing in the *Daily Chronicle* under the cynical title of 'Holy Russia', Henry stressed the superiority of the Georgian people, 'a singularly noble and intellectual race'.[63] The spring also saw Henry's first signed piece in the *Nation*. With the second International Peace Conference at The Hague approaching, it was on subject races denied the rights independent nations enjoyed in war and peace.[64] Henry and Brailsford sat on the new Nationalities and Subject Races (Joint) Committee. Its memorandum to the Prime Minister suggested that claims based on the Hague Convention of 1899 be included as part of the regulations to be adopted for subject races. In June, Henry attended the conference's formal opening at The Hague.[65] He could discern no real interest in peace, disliked the pomp and ceremony and was angry at the way diplomats treated journalists: 'Had to hang about all afternoon outside plenary sessions feeling horribly like a reporter.' The Georgian petition was rejected as being outside its scope.

The atmosphere at the International Congress of Subject Races in August, also at The Hague, was radically different, with delegates from fourteen organizations, including the Anti-Slavery Society, Friends of Russian Freedom and the Georgian Relief Committee. In the absence of Anatole France, Henry presided, leading a general discussion on the rights of rebels to a belligerent position. Nannie Dryhurst tackled Cossack savagery in Georgia. Henry became chairman of the international Nationalities and Subject Races Committee and Nannie its secretary.[66]

That autumn Henry's disillusionment and differences with the Liberals came to a head. Incensed by the Anglo-Russian Agreement handing Northern Persia to Russia, he finally announced in the press that this 'severs our allegiance to the Liberal Party as at present constituted'.[67] Arguing that the Persians had been betrayed 'to an overwhelming tyranny' and exposing the 'cant of Hague Conventions' and any pretence of international right, he was at his most cynical: 'Remembering the fate of Persia, let every people form themselves into an armed camp, regardless of progress.'

Earlier that year Henry had observed, locked in heated debate in north London, a number of those destined to be remembered in world history. Denied permission to meet in Sweden, Denmark and Finland, the Fifth Congress of the Russian Social Democratic Party had finally settled on the Brotherhood Church in Islington. Lenin, Trotsky, Gorky, Rosa Luxemburg and Stalin all attended. Henry was there on 23 May but for once displayed a singular lack of prescience, simply noting a 'rather chaotic mixture of men, women, pies & orange peel'![68] He met Maxim Gorky at the home of Dr Hagberg Wright, the Russophile running the London Library, noting his 'sad grey eyes', nervous gestures and 'rare but beautiful smile'. Henry helped Kropotkin and Hagberg Wright to raise money for the rescue of Maria Spiridonova. Shocked as a young woman by the persecution of Russian peasants, she had joined the Social Revolutionary Party. At twenty-one she was an assassin. She was now suffering from maltreatment in a Siberian prison. Although £500 was raised for her release, she refused to leave.[69]

Henry attended meetings of both the Friends of Russian Freedom and the more cautious Parliamentary Russian Committee though he personally felt the latter to be 'a quite hopeless affair, refusing to do anything'. By 1909 he and Brailsford were working under Gardiner at the *Daily News*, chafing under pressure to conform. A fellow editor commiserated with Gardiner: 'What a pair to drive tandem!'[70] In July, Gardiner cut and altered Henry's leader on the Tsar's proposed visit to England: 'All day I was mad with rage & could only think of resigning.' Two days later he spoke against the visit at a Trafalgar Square demonstration. The next day his leader attacked the naval build-up. Brailsford threatened to resign should Gardiner interfere. Gardiner then suggested that the leader was possibly too mild!

Concern about Russian autocracy also led him to protest against Edward VII's proposed visit to the Baltic to greet the Tsar and his government in Reval (Tallin): 'one of the most serious & shameful errors of our time'. He rebuked the *Manchester Guardian* for supporting it and was criticized in a leader.[71] He also canvassed numerous literary and political figures to sign a Memorial against 'an offence against human nature', the entente with Russia.[72]

He remained interested in Finland's fate. When Tsar Alexander I had become Grand Duke in 1809, Finland's constitutional rights were supposed to be honoured. But from the end of the nineteenth century Finland's loyalty was increasingly strained. The tyranny of Governor-General Bobrikov led to his assassination. There was a week-long general strike in 1905 but the Grand Duchy remained comparatively calm. It was therefore the one part of the Russian Empire to obtain concessions towards national autonomy. The October Manifesto promised a Diet elected by universal suffrage. Yet in June 1910 a packed Russian Duma removed all matters of imperial concern from the jurisdiction of the Finnish Diet. This made Finland's autonomy farcical. Henry penned a powerful middle for the *Nation* about Russia's treatment of Finland and Europe's shameful silence.[73] 'The Murder of a Nation' begins obliquely, like many of Henry's think pieces. It comments on the seriousness with which the murder of an individual is regarded by society and then contrasts this with Russia's callous indifference to the murder of an entire nation.

Henry and other journalists were invited by leaders of the Diet to visit Finland. For over a week in September 1910 they toured the country. Henry's extended letters to the *Nation* stressed the value placed on education and patriotism. Opposition to Russification united very different political parties, from the Swedish Party to the Socialists. The desire to extend the Russian Empire westwards, combined with Finland's strategic position so close to St Petersburg and concern about German ambitions in the Baltic, placed the Grand Duchy in a perilous position. Most importantly for Henry, the threat posed to Russia by Finland's 'widely educated, liberty-loving, and self-governing people upon the very frontier of its tyranny' meant that 'knowledge and the freedom without which knowledge is paralysed stand awaiting execution'.[74] At a Young Finns (advanced Liberals) dinner, Henry spoke 'rather fully' on the true purpose of the visit, stressing the value of self-government.[75]

Finland was a model and a travesty of democracy. Like Georgia, here was a subject nation that truly appreciated learning and freedom: 'To cross the frontier from Russia into Finland has always been like a passage from prison into open air.'[76] Henry and his friend Joseph Clayton, who was also on this tour, were embroiled in the British struggle for women's suffrage. The Finns were the first Europeans to enfranchise women, as Henry made clear in speeches at home. Finnish women over twenty-four had the vote. They were represented in a Diet that elected members by proportional representation and protected minorities and in no other country was 'such equal opportunity for every kind of knowledge, livelihood & work given to women'. This Diet was 'the most democratic assembly that had ever existed'. It was about to assemble for the first time in full yet 'perhaps for the last time in freedom'.[77]

At midday on 16 September, Henry was once more witness to a historic moment. The Diet met at a palace in Helsingfors. It was declared open in the Russian language. Henry contrasted the figures of Governor-General Seyn (formerly Bobrikov's agent) and the new President, the Young Finn, Per Svinhufoud: 'Violence and justice, despotism and democracy, Imperialism and nationality, might and right were thus brought to confront each other face to face.'[78] Three proposals were to be laid before the Diet: demanding the election of four Duma members and two for the Imperial Council, an increase in the contribution for imperial defence and the granting of special rights to Russians in the country. Contrary to the constitution, these demands had not been signed by the Tsar as Grand Duke of Finland but only by Prime Minister Stolypin and the Russian Council of Ministers. Defiance was anticipated since they intensified Russian influence and specifically infringed Finnish rights. Henry and the others assembled there heard the President utter just one sentence of acknowledgement. Then the ceremony ended. A month later, Stolypin dissolved the Diet for refusing to comply with Russian demands.

Seven years later the Russian Revolution took place. Henry initially welcomed it. 'Never has a revolution been so happy in its opportunity' was how he began 'The Dayspring in Russia'.[79] In the midst of war 'The astonishing Revolution in Russia has inspired the whole world with new and glorious hope.'[80] He addressed the vast Albert Hall meeting held on 31 March 1917 to 'congratulate the Russian people on their freedom and to demand a similar freedom for the people of this country'.[81] Ten thousand attended. Five thousand had to be turned away. Speakers included George Lansbury, Israel Zangwill and Maude Royden. Henry paid tribute to the sacrifices of 1905–6, to those who died on the barricades and 'under the hang-rope that they called Stolypin's necktie'. He named exiles such as Kropotkin and women activists like Ekaterina Breshkovskaya, Vera Zasulich and

Spiridonova and drew attention to 'that great cloud of witnesses, unnamed, unknown, unremembered'. He called on the audience to rise and stand as was the Russian habit (at the start of meetings a few seconds of silence was observed in memory of sacrifices) and later claimed that he was one of the first to introduce this custom into England.[82]

In honour of the March 1917 Revolution, the 1917 Club was born with Henry and Hobson its moving spirits. Its home was in Gerrard Street in Soho. It enabled people to talk freely in wartime without contravening the Defence of the Realm Act (DORA). Henry, MacDonald and Forster were all presidents. It provided a space for the discussion of progressive ideas, its lunches and discussions attended by figures such as Brailsford, Rose Macaulay, Sir Charles Trevelyan, Charles Laughton, Evelyn Sharp and Virginia and Leonard Woolf. A group of communists monopolized the long table, forming almost a club within a club. In 1924 when Henry was president, the club and elected committee failed to see eye to eye and all but one of the latter resigned. Henry was known to harbour 'an inconvenient sympathy for Poland and a passionate concern for Georgia' and when, in 1931, a Russian trade bank official spoke about the Five Year Plan Henry made clear, to the annoyance of some, the 'cruelty of executions & suppression of all freedom now'.[83] The following year the club closed. Blending into its surroundings it became a strip-tease club.

Henry had been the only correspondent the Soviet minister Litvinov would see in Copenhagen in 1919. Interviewing him for the *Daily Herald*, Henry received assurances that no military pressure 'should be brought' against Georgians, Letts (Latvians) or Ukrainians and that 'secession would be allowed to all'. After the Revolution the Georgians had combined with the Tartars and Armenians to declare the Independent Republic of Transcaucasia. Traditional loyalties rapidly put paid to such an alliance. By May 1918 the Georgians had their own republic (Wardrop, whom Henry met in 1905, was its British High Commissioner). A few months after meeting Litvinov, Soviet Russia ratified the Georgian Republic by treaty. But Henry remained uneasy, warning in February 1920 that the whole of Transcaucasia might soon be reclaimed.[84] In March 1921 over 10,000 Russian troops invaded and occupied Georgia. By 1924 the Soviet government had become for Henry 'almost as cruel in its tyranny as was the old Tsardom which I did all in my power to oppose for so many years'. Such a perspective was partly shaped by hideous accounts of Georgia's woes under the Bolsheviks.

With the exception of Greece and Ireland, Georgia was, for this much-travelled correspondent, 'the most beautiful country I have ever seen'.[85] Battling for freedom, Georgia stood for the unfree, that which must be challenged. It represented another aspect of that disintegration of empires and bid for nationhood that Henry was able to witness. Georgia also had a personal significance. It symbolized Henry's long-standing relationship with the woman who championed its people: Nannie Dryhurst. Not long after visiting Georgia, Henry wrote 'For freedom we know, is a thing that we have to conquer afresh for ourselves every day, like love.'[86]

CHAPTER FIVE

The Romantic Rebel

Suffrage, Sex and Family

'We cannot denounce torture in Russia and support it in England, nor can we advocate democratic principles in the name of a party which confines them to a single sex.' Thus ended a letter in *The Times* on 5 October 1909 by H. N. Brailsford and Henry W. Nevinson of the *Daily News*. Condemning the Liberal government's refusal to recognize imprisoned suffragettes as political prisoners, they deplored the new measure of forcibly feeding suffrage hunger strikers. News of this had broken eleven days earlier and in a leader their editor had excused this 'abomination'. Not wishing to be associated with such a position, the journalists announced their resignations. They also denounced the government's 'blind contempt' for women's suffrage, especially Prime Minister Asquith's 'obstinate refusal' to listen even to the law-abiding suffragist majority.

The term 'suffragette' had been coined by the *Daily Mail* as a term of derision. But the followers of Mrs Pankhurst's Women's Social and Political Union (WSPU) neatly appropriated it, turning a diminutive into such a strong word that it has misleadingly become modern short-hand for all suffrage support. Henry attended his first WSPU meeting with Evelyn Sharp on 12 February 1907. The next day they marched in a suffrage procession. Henry experienced the frustration of being 'policed': 'My language to a policeman who attacked me & ES was "something horrible".'

Men are better known as opponents than as supporters of women's suffrage. Yet recent research reveals numerous male sympathizers for the law-abiding National Union of Women's Suffrage Societies (NUWSS) headed by Millicent Fawcett and over a thousand members of male support groups. Henry was one of the forty founders of the largest such society, the Men's League for Women's Suffrage.[1] Formed in March 1907, it saw itself as a parallel organization to the NUWSS and supported votes for women on the same terms as for men. Henry sat on its executive committee for two years and edited twenty issues of its monthly paper. He was involved in many different forms of publicity for the League. At one large men-only gathering in July 1909 he spoke about Russian prisoners. It was they who had inspired British women to adopt hunger strikes. On another occasion he paraded in a top hat with a sandwich board.

Impatient with the somewhat legalistic League (chaired by a barrister), he helped found the more militant Men's Political Union for Women's Enfranchisement (MPU) in 1910 and became its chairman. He penned their pamphlet 'The Case of Mr. William Ball', the sad tale of a working man imprisoned for breaking a Home Office window and whose force-feeding led him to the lunatic asylum. But there were times when Henry sought to curb the impetuous members of the MPU. If the League seemed preoccupied with procedure, the MPU was too fond of embarrassing pranks. He intervened when they planned to throw bags of flour over government ministers. Yet he was not above boisterous intervention himself.

He came close to losing his job in 1908 when the Chancellor of the Exchequer, Lloyd George, addressed a meeting of Liberal women at the Albert Hall. The stewards used considerable force in throwing out suffragettes who interrupted proceedings so Henry cried out 'Shame' and mocked Lloyd George's past treatment of suffrage protesters. 'Oh, Mr Nevinson, I wonder at a man of your education behaving like this' was the Chancellor's reply. Mr Nevinson retorted that he would behave himself if the government treated the women decently. After a chase through the hall, he was thrown out. Unfortunately his editor, Gardiner, a supporter of adult rather than women's suffrage, was part of the platform party. On reaching home Henry found a note 'sacking me'. He cycled round to Gardiner's home and mollified him but was suspended for a week. Brailsford and three others on the *Daily News* threatened to resign over the treatment of their colleague. Henry was reinstated but disquiet over Brailsford's formal complaint found him, in turn, threatening resignation should the latter be unfairly dismissed. During these months Henry frequently complained of editorial interference. He had a 'portentous row' with Gardiner over the Children's Act, stressing the absurdity of such legislation being framed by men. Gardiner complained to Henry that he and Brailsford 'were always galloping out in the front of every battle'. His annoyance may have been tinged with relief when, prompted by Brailsford (who composed the protest letter), the intemperate two resigned.

Leaving the paper assumed more significance than Henry's fourteen months on its staff. It provoked a personal letter of sympathy from Mrs Pankhurst and has long been cited in suffrage histories as an example of the sacrifice principled men might make.[2] It was a courageous move since both men earned their livelihoods from writing. Henry had earned £500 a year for four articles weekly and also did stints as a special and war correspondent. He missed the night shifts and the challenge of regular deadlines. Neither he nor Brailsford secured regular work on a daily from this time on though Henry's reputation grew as a champion of causes. His enforced Albert Hall exit, like a number of his stories, got embellished. The *Daily Telegraph* reported that he had floored a steward with a mighty blow and a later account by the war correspondent Philip Gibbs had Henry jumping from the stage box and fighting 'half a dozen stewards at once'.[3]

Women's suffrage now occupied much of his spare time. Why? A cynical response might be that editors were no longer interested in him. He had a reputation as a volatile journalist, not keen to conform. Aided by admirers, he had built up an image of himself as a sturdy champion of freedom wherever in the world it might be threatened. In 1909 his *Essays in Freedom* appeared. What more obvious step than to espouse this on his own doorstep?

His support was also connected to his interest in Greek civilization and a belief in natural justice and fair play though he professed to be more motivated by actual examples of the denial of freedom than abstract principles. Committed to championing small nations and the oppressed, he described women as 'the largest subject race in the world'.[4] Like other suffrage writers and radicals, he drew inspiration from Italian nationalism. The section on suffrage in his autobiography begins with a quote from Mazzini. Disappointment with the illiberal Liberals also played a part. His Introduction to a pamphlet on the treatment of British political prisoners denounced forcible feeding: 'If these things had happened in Italy or Russia, or had been perpetuated by Conservatives, with what noble indignation the heart of the Liberal Party would have palpitated!'[5]

The struggle for women's suffrage was not new but with the beginning of the twentieth century it acquired greater urgency. Although large sections of the male working class remained unenfranchised and the campaign for men's voting rights had been protracted and contested, still not one single woman could vote. Like a number of progressive men, despite his age and essential Victorianism, Henry cast himself as a new man of the new century, part of the intelligentsia espousing advanced causes and envisaging a better world for all. He and other pro-suffrage men believed they could make a difference. They justified their intervention in a cause palpably not their own by arguing that, precisely because they already had the vote, they had no personal axe to grind. As men of influence in Parliament, the press, academia, commerce, the professions or other areas of power dominated by a male elite, they could get opinions heard. As a journalist Henry was also attracted to Edwardian suffrage meetings since the movement was rapidly colonizing newspaper space. Suffrage activists were superb self-publicists, delighting in the propaganda value of spectacle. But there was also a personal dimension which gave Henry an important connection to women's suffrage: his involvement with Evelyn Sharp.

In order to understand how and why Evelyn influenced Henry, we need to consider his family life over these years. A disjunction between private morality and public politics was nothing new in British society even though generally frowned upon. Yet there was a particular irony in Henry's position since gender relations lay at the heart of the women's suffrage campaign. He was a passionate romantic involved in multiple relationships and committed to the women's movement. He trod a thin, equivocal line.

Henry made an important contribution to the winning of women's suffrage, particularly through its less glamorous and less publicized side of negotiations during the First World War. But, like a number of pro-suffrage male supporters, there was a gap between his public utterances and his personal practice. He was inclined to represent his affairs with women as inevitable given his romantic nature. His private behaviour is not easily squared with his public pronouncements and he did not seriously critique gender relations. Yet, compared to many men born in the mid-nineteenth century who also inhabited the largely male worlds of high politics, national newspapers, clubs, the military and travel in the Empire, he was remarkably sensitive and attuned to women's perceptions. He also knew what not to say. Claiming that men could 'never bring the same personal & overwhelming conviction into the movement as women' helped win appreciation from both men and women. His lovers were invariably feminists who recognized that he was much more supportive than were most men they knew. And although they disagreed on most matters, women's suffrage was one subject where Henry and Margaret respected each other.

Henry, Margaret and their small daughter had lived in Hampstead since the summer of 1887. They had personal and familial connections here and it was a home for artistic and progressive thinkers. In 1901 Henry was one of its 166 male authors and editors.[6] With reasonable transport to the West End and City by railway and underground, it nevertheless maintained the feel of a village. At the turn of the century Hampstead became a metropolitan borough, though its Heath disguised its position as one of the capital's largest suburbs. It boasted the lowest level of poverty in London as a whole. Opting for a good location rather than comfort, the Nevinsons rented Scarr Cottage in John Street (later renamed Keats Grove). The white stucco cottage was built on the old River Fleet. It lacked foundations so was extremely damp. Bath water had to be boiled on top of the stove and carried in cans up two floors. There was neither gas nor electric lighting. The outside cistern frequently froze. On their first night rain came through the roof of one bedroom and a bedstead leg went through the floor into the larder below. The Nevinsons lived there for almost nine years. It was an especially difficult time for Margaret. Her mother died the year after the move. When Richard was born in August 1889, Margaret was dangerously ill and depressed with puerperal fever. She found the constant demands of small children trying and, unlike Henry, lacked the time to fulfil her literary ambitions.

A legacy left to Margaret enabled the family to move in June 1896 to a brand new house at 44 Savernake Road, running parallel to the railway line in south east Hampstead. Close to Gospel Oak, it was, in Hampstead terms, literally on the wrong side of the (railway) track. Charles Booth delineated it as a 'comfortable' district, housing the lower middle class, as opposed to the fashionable, 'well-to-do' area around Parliament Hill.[7] Close to the signal box for Hampstead Heath station, it was very noisy. Yet the pleasant redbrick houses with gardens were not crowded together, a flat roof afforded views across Highgate and Parliament Hill Fields and there was a bathroom with modern plumbing.

A new home could not, however, camouflage the problems facing the Nevinson marriage. Unravelling the complexities of marriages of any period is fraught with difficulties. Seeking to uncover and understand such emotions raises issues of prurience and privacy as well as sensitivity to an era of different mores and morals. Nevertheless, Henry's remarkable diary is invaluable here. It provides insight into world events and the workings of politics, journalism and the arts. It also reveals his personal musings, showing how his personal life affected his writings and work. The diary affords a glimpse into an aspect of masculinity not often documented. A highly sensual man, Henry appears to express his love, anger and frustration with refreshing and remarkable candour for a Victorian.

We are, nevertheless, dependent on what *he* has chosen to reveal and hide. Even with caveats and qualifications, we are only privy to one side of a complex equation. Margaret's voice is, at best, muted. Although many women kept journals where they might unburden themselves, unlike her refreshingly confessional husband we have no diary giving Margaret's side of the story. Admittedly the writers of surviving diaries can posthumously be made accountable for their thoughts whereas those without this 'evidence' are exculpated from such responsibility. But we have here very unbalanced sources. Most of what we can learn about Margaret's views is refracted through Henry's (and their son's) biased perspectives or hinted at in her later published writings. We have a partial tale of marriage, itself a fluid, unstable construct. Indeed, even the 'Significant Others' in Henry's life are just that. In the diary he is cast as Significant: they are Other.

Compton Mackenzie wrote that Henry 'looked and was a paladin'.[8] He had a soldierly bearing. He was cultured and courteous yet rebellious. He travelled to faraway and dangerous places. A touch of shyness, an ability to listen to others and an appreciation of women's rights and of intelligent women ensured that many found him irresistible. A self-confessed incurable romantic, Henry wrote of Goethe that 'to women he was singularly attractive, and there was hardly a week in his life when he was not in love'.[9] He might have been writing about himself. And he aged gracefully, his appeal enhanced by the stories that had grown around him.

Unknown to most, 'The chief inspiration' of Henry's life[10] was neither Margaret nor his devoted second wife, Evelyn Sharp. It was the woman he had joined in Georgia with the distinctly unromantic name of Nannie Dryhurst.[11] Her real name was Hannah Ann(e) Robinson but she changed it to Nannie Florence (her sisters called her Nannie and she had a friend called Florence who died young). Henry's 'inexplicable passion'[12] for Ireland has been commented upon. This and some of his other commitments become comprehensible when seen alongside his passionate affair with Dublin-born Mrs Dryhurst.

She was the daughter of Alexander Robinson, a dyer, and Emily Robinson (née Egan). According to her death certificate she had been born, like Henry, in 1856 and in 1906 she described herself as a woman of fifty. The 1891 census, however, shows her as several years younger.[13] Her birthday was 17 June, a date cherished by Henry for many a year. After her father's death in the mid-1870s she was a governess in Ireland and then London, where she tended Nellie Tenison, an Irish doctor's daughter. But her letters hint at an attempted or actual seduction by the doctor and she returned to Dublin quite suddenly. Tenison was the Dryhurst family's doctor, which is probably how she met Alfred Robert Dryhurst, known as Roy, to whom she became engaged in 1882. He had an administrative post at the British Museum. Although Nannie's letters to Roy suggest something of her passionate nature, she briefly sought in the spring of 1883 to extricate herself from what had largely become an epistolary relationship. But in August 1884 (four months after Henry and Margaret's marriage) they married in Dublin. A year later their daughter Norah was born in London and, three years later, Sylvia.

Henry and Nannie probably first met on 11 February 1892 and per-haps became lovers on 26 December. Boxing Day was certainly revered as a significant date thereafter. By this time the Dryhursts were living round the corner from Henry at 11 Downshire Hill. This wisteria-clad home was one of two houses owned by Roy's brother, Arthur George Dryhurst. He also owned houses in John Street so might have introduced the two families. Nannie was a writer and linguist. She spoke Irish, German and French and was an accomplished translator. She and Roy translated from French *Researches in the History of Economics* (1889) by Ernest Ny. An accomplished artist, she also painted Christmas cards to order. Long before she met Henry she was devouring the works of his literary heroes Carlyle, Heine and Goethe.

Henry's diary is crammed with coded references to her. In 1893 when the surviving volumes start, she is mentioned by name. The Dryhurst

7 Nannie Dryhurst in 1884.

and Nevinson families play cricket on Hampstead Heath with the four children. Margaret and the Dryhursts hear Henry lecture on Carlyle at Toynbee Hall. Henry and Roy often travel together to work at the British Museum (the former in the Reading Room). Henry refers to some spirited discussions with Nannie. They have 'a terrific duel' on the Irish question, he 'maintaining our honour to protect the unhappy Ulster minority, however uncultured, bigoted & blind'. She made her position clear, sympathizing with 'every atrocity & outrage agst [*sic*] the brutal Saxon'. She hoped to see 'the whole oppressive stock swept into the sea'. Her commitment made him 'wish I was Irish myself that I might fight at her side'. Henry's language is charged with sexual innuendo: 'she was magnificent in wrath, longing to drink hot blood – slitting into me with scorn & irony & hatred, urging any & every weapon like a noble leopard in the chase'.

His diary makes it evident that home was not where his heart was. Home was depicted rather as the source of woes. Staying amongst 'silvered woods' with Nannie during 'one of the great interludes' was contrasted with domestic life: 'horrible wrangling & ill-temper at home all day from Richard's illness & Phil's opposition & an unhappy woman's unhappiness'. There were many barbed references to domestic quarrels over the following decade. Margaret returns from a trip to Abersoch 'like a nagging ceaseless blast of ill temper'. Margaret was usually called M in the diary but in 1901 she was even denied an initial: the

> usual abuse & contempt at home from the woman who lives here
> & spends all her time speaking evil of me to her friends & the
> children. It is strange how difficult it is to be indifferent to the
> opinion even of one's bitterest & most intimate enemies.

Nannie ceased to be named directly for a different reason. Henry's diary became much more personal about their relationship. From January 1895 he began reproducing sections from her love letters. She seems to have initially signed herself as Evelyn, perhaps because she knew they were destined for a diary. There is a terrible irony here: this was the name of the other woman at the centre of Henry's life. He now referred to Nannie as 'my beloved lady' or used the letters E or EW for her, possibly initials denoting Irish words.[14]

Reporting on military affairs provided an excuse to get away. After covering army manoeuvres in Wiltshire he 'explored the inmost & most delicate recesses of joy'. In August 1896 'whilst field-days thundered' he was in 'arcady' – the frequent use of Arcadia to describe meetings with Nannie gives a personal twist to the opening of Henry's autobiography: 'I was not born in Arcadia.' His writing becomes truncated and euphemistic and he deliberately inverts the conventional notion of what is seen as sinful:

> Gathered plums, green & purple. Meeting arr. [*sic*] in carriage
> Vision of golden hair long evening under trees. Countless stories
> . . . the rose thrown in at window, the wild rose and wild hair . . .
> the lily head just bent towards the man twice in sleep . . . we do not
> say goodbye. Gallop like hell and by a new road back to the severed
> old life of sin & half hearted deeds.

A number of his poems are about Nannie. 'Sitting at a Play' suggests the pain and pleasure of seeing her at public gatherings and is based on an actual incident at a concert.[15] From the gallery he looks down on his lover sitting demurely at another's side and thinks about the shock the audience would get if they could see the images inside her head:

> A summer scene, a moonlit night,
> A garden, a sweet-scented rose,

A cottage glimmering in the moon,
A door not shut too tight
And two that enter by the door,
And stand so close embraced they cast
One shadow on the moonlit floor.

Henry may have been dismissive of most fiction but his diary supplies all the ingredients for a romantic novel. At the British Museum, long the site of writers' assignations, the lovers met 'among those great dark pillars in darkening air'. A few words were exchanged; then they parted 'as though indifferent'. Nannie taught an evening class in English literature at a Highbury board school and they often met near there or in Hampstead at the home of their friends the Podmores. Eleanore Bramwell (originally from Perth and called Scotia in Henry's diary) had married Frank Podmore in 1891. She was an expert on Scottish folklore and Celtic literature and he a leading figure in psychical research who gave the Fabian Society its name. Their home in Well Walk was a centre for those involved in Left politics.

Nannie's letters imply that her marriage was not a happy one, though Henry would have been mortified to know that she and Roy were mistaken for honeymooners by the guard on the train taking them to Rome in 1895. Her diary of this tour did, however, include cryptic references to letters and mentioned Xenophon, the Greek warrior who also wrote about war and whose name she sometimes used for Henry. Dryhurst family descendants stress that Nannie and Roy were not well suited. Both enjoyed music, were atheists and challenged the status quo. Yet he was more conventional and conservative than was his wife in style and politics.[16] One granddaughter has described him as 'a pedant with a supreme gift for saying the wrong thing'. He hated modernization within the home, often sitting behind a curtain when there were visitors. He earned the nickname of 'Grumpy Grandpa'.

But he was living in the knowledge that his wife was seeing Henry. Years later, after both Nannie and Henry had died, Roy told his daughter Sylvia the poignant tale of how he found out for sure. Returning home one day from work rather earlier than usual, he walked up Downshire Hill behind Henry, who had noticed him. Henry walked on, past the Dryhurst home, but his little dog turned automatically in to the gateway. Roy's suspicions were confirmed. He went through his wife's desk, found Henry's love letters and 'The result was a tremendous ruction, separate bedrooms and divided charge of the Dryhurst daughters.' He took responsibility for Norah's education, giving her a conventional schooling. Sylvia was sent by Nannie to a new, experimental school. She became a poet and married the journalist Robert Lynd. From time to time an 'ancient & lying scandal' circulated in Hampstead that Sylvia was Henry's daughter.[17] In 1940 Philippa Nevinson mentioned it to her cousin.[18] But, as Henry's diary shows, he had not met Sylvia's mother when she was born.

Although disdainful of convention, Nannie was concerned about the situation as a mother. In 1897 she wrote 'if we yielded to ourselves we cd {*sic*} look all the world in the face except those 4 young lives'. Yet even with her words included in Henry's diaries, we cannot discern the silences and what he chose not to transcribe from her letters. Neither can we get a real sense of her side of the conversations. Unlike Margaret, Nannie was slight and graceful. The writer of rural life George Sturt visited her in 1889, finding a 'Surprisingly young looking' woman with her hair in a coiled plait, high cheekbones and dark eyes.[19] Family photographs and a painting show her as youthful yet poised. For the Fabian Sidney Olivier, she was 'a person, with whom, when I first knew her – and probably at any time – it was impossible either not to fall in love, or to conceive of signifying the same in the usual manner'.[20] She seems to have been more assured in her political beliefs and judgements than Henry. Sturt described her as 'the most intellectual lady that I have ever spoken with – or rather, that has ever spoken with me; for she did most of the talking . . . without any affectation or cleverness: agreeably serious: its subject-matter very varied.'

At Christmas time 1901 Henry received (through Mabel and Oswald Cox, friends acting as intermediaries) one of Nannie's many letters:

> This week I wanted you more than ever in my life before – what I like best next to seeing & touching you is the few passionate words you write me in those dark cold grey hours, hours that are also dear to me because you sometimes come in my dreams then touch my mouth & breasts – never has man been more loved by woman than you by me.

Henry often described their secret trysts as 'fairyland', evoking Yeats's 'The Wanderings of Oisin'. Nannie dubbed herself 'your secret rose', blending their romance, poetry and Ireland. Henry published in April 1897 one of his most powerful poems. Called 'The Rose', it appeared in the final volume of *The Yellow Book*. It is about Stephen (perhaps a reference to Boxing Day), medieval clerk of Oxford:

> Stephen swore, as God knows well,
> Just to touch that topmost bud,
> He would give his soul to hell –
> Soul and body, bones and blood.[21]

That summer Henry visited Ireland for the first time. This, his literary work for the *Daily Chronicle* and Nannie's influence turned him towards W. B. Yeats. The first of Henry's articles on the Celtic Revival appeared in the *Chronicle* the following January. Just over a year later Henry met Yeats at the Podmores. His initial estimation was measured:

'as good a typical young poet as could come out of Ireland.' He soon revised his opinion. As Schuchard puts it, 'Yeats would have no greater champion in the London press.'[22] Henry credited Yeats with inaugurating a new era in Anglo-Irish poetry and his review of the 1899 *Poems* (the second English edition of the 1895 collection) had a profound influence on the future poet laureate John Masefield.[23] Nannie read Henry's work in draft, making suggestions for improvements. In February 1903, for example, one of his Irish articles received 'all her keen judgment & correction'. There was a powerful surge of Irish cultural nationalism in London at this time and Henry and Nannie attended many Irish literary and political meetings. She was also secretary of the Purcell Operatic Society run by her neighbours, the musician Martin Shaw and Gordon Craig, whom Henry helped promote as a stage director. Craig's mother, the legendary Ellen Terry, once declared: 'All men are fools about women!' Pointing at Henry, she added that he was 'a terrible fool about one!'[24]

Nannie and Roy were members of the Fabian Society. Margaret was also influenced by Fabian ideas for a while, frequenting the Fellowship of the New Life in Bloomsbury which saw the route to social improvement in the betterment of individuals from within themselves. The Fabians, believing in the primacy of political commitment through incremental means, broke away. Henry had little patience with such groups. In 1893 he noted them 'all sitting round with the fixed smile they always assume for [Bernard] Shaw'. His anti-statism and Nannie's influence led him instead to try anarchist meetings.

Nannie became a leading light in London's anarchist circles, one of several remarkable women connected with *Freedom*, the first British anarchist-socialist periodical. Nannie edited the propaganda column and on several occasions ran the paper. She wrote regularly for it and Henry made occasional contributions. British anarchists were primarily concerned with theoretical issues rather than direct action. However, in the early 1890s, the exposure of anarchist bomb-makers in Walsall and the Greenwich Park bomb began to suggest otherwise, prompting the term 'outrage' for anarchist and Fenian activity. Nannie was undeterred, remaining as committed to anarchism and Irish nationalism as the newly founded Special Branch was dedicated to exposing both. Very active in the Freedom Group from 1888 to 1906, she belonged to the anarchist communist wing of British anarchism.[25]

Henry attended some of their discussions and fund-raising events. He also visited the anarchist-communist farm at Benton in north east England. In the early 1890s he and Nannie helped in what must have been an uphill task, instructing 'little Anarchs in the elements of drill and orderly behaviour' at their International School at 19 Fitzroy Street, London. Over eighty children, mainly the children of Russian, Polish and Italian émigrés, attended. Louise Michel, dressed in black in memory of the Paris Commune, was in charge. She also attempted, not very successfully, to teach French to Henry. Teaching was child-centred: the child decided what to study in a bid to 'avoid the hideous poll-parrot system of the Board-schools'.[26] Although closed down after a couple of years, it was probably the first libertarian school in Britain.

The London-based anarchists were a very European group. It was Nannie who translated into English Kropotkin's book *The Great French Revolution*. Henry first met Kropotkin in 1891 at the Autonomie Club off Tottenham Court Road. Although later distancing himself from his views, he remained impressed by Edward Carpenter. Henry met this 'academic Carlyle' in 1887, later calling him 'a very beautiful and attractive person'.[27]

He was also horrified by society's treatment of Oscar Wilde after the revelations of homosexuality at his 1895 trials. A frequent theatregoer for pleasure and work (reviewing plays for the *Daily Chronicle*), he sat through *The Importance of Being Earnest* whilst 'the creator of it all' was in a cell 'fallen never to rise again. And for a sin Socrates smiled at and Plato & Aristotle used in defining love.' It was not often that Henry focused on this aspect of Hellenism but the trials marked a significant shift in public attitudes towards sexual orientation. Henry was particularly incensed by the hypocrisy of theatre managers who erased Wilde's name from their playbills yet still made money from his brains. His diary suggests some personal unease about Carpenter and his homosexual friends but a desire to be tolerant. Ruminating on same-sex attraction after visiting them, he admitted that 'certainly in boyhood I was capable of this feeling'. He immediately qualified this, adding that even then (in boarding school) he would have felt far 'deeper & more passionate, affection for a girl, if one had been with me: and since then it has not troubled me at all'. He stressed that 'All my passion & true friendship has gone to women' though he liked men and had 'the need of a world of men'.

In the summer of 1904 Henry immersed himself in Havelock Ellis's lengthy study of sexual character, *Man and Woman* (1894). He noted that the description that seemed to most fit his own disposition – 'the sanguine but variable mind, the energy, the love of fame, the love of beautiful women, the sexual passions, the disregard of common morality' – was one that ends in paralysis. His one redeeming feature seemed to be his love of athletic games. This study presents a bifurcated, complementary representation of the nature of men and women, arguing that motherhood is the apogee of woman's existence. Margaret's recollections of motherhood do not fit such descriptions. In the 1920s, in a remarkably frank statement, she confessed to finding it 'a terrible thing to be a mother'.[28] She later invested much of her time and emotion in supporting Richard's career, a gesture not much appreciated by the self-absorbed artist.

Margaret was deeply hurt and disillusioned by Henry's behaviour. Quite when she became aware of his affair with Nannie is not clear but it may have been between mid-1893 and early 1895, a period for which no diary survives. When Margaret died, Henry wrote of his 'overwhelming passion for a woman which broke her heart'.[29] Early in 1901 he had been seen with Nannie in the lane and 'abused as a devil & all manner for what to me is as innocent & natural as sunshine or breath'. Margaret seems to have resolved in these years to map out her life as independently as possible whilst remaining married. She was deeply religious and much of her energy went into Anglo-Catholicism. She enjoyed travelling abroad and became one of those, often unsung, women who dedicated considerable time and energy to local government.

She was an elected school manager for a quarter of a century, working first in the East End under the London School Board and then, in the late 1890s, transferring to the Haverstock Hill and Fleet Road Group. Although in the poorer end of Hampstead, the Fleet Road School was known as the best elementary school in London. Margaret was one of its twelve hard-working managers. In August 1904 she was elected a Poor Law Guardian for Hampstead. Despite some local opposition, she topped the poll, serving for nearly eighteen years. Women had been entitled to be Poor Law Guardians since 1875 but not until the property qualification was abolished in 1894 did their numbers grow. Hampstead had been one of the first boards to include women but Margaret's position was unusual. Although a middle-class married Hampstead lady without paid employment, she had lived and worked in a deprived area and now represented Hampstead's poorest ward (Kilburn). The Hampstead Minute Book from September 1904 until the end of 1921 reveals her dedication. She played an active part in over fifty meetings a year, chaired sub-committees and used her familiarity with the workhouse and infirmary to write fiction, drama and campaigning articles about the problems facing impoverished women. Her play 'In the Workhouse' challenged a married man's legal right to decree that his wife be detained in the workhouse against her will. It helped change the antediluvian law.

In 1920 Margaret became a pioneer Justice of the Peace. She had lectured on the need for women magistrates and now sat on the Hampstead Bench as the first woman in London to adjudicate at Criminal Petty Sessions. She had long found comradeship and challenges in the women's movement, particularly through women's suffrage. She was on the committee of the Hampstead branch of the NUWSS and then joined the new WSPU. After its split in 1907 she was a founder member of the Women's Freedom League (WFL), participated in demonstrations and debates, was a witty speaker and wrote pamphlets. She was a branch treasurer for the WFL, national treasurer of the Women Writers' Suffrage

League and active in the Church League for Women's Suffrage and Cymric Suffrage Union.

Both Henry and Margaret participated in the passive resistance tactics encouraged by the WFL. Margaret was a tax resister (as later was Evelyn) and Henry refused to complete the 1911 census form. In the same year Philippa Nevinson married the architect Sidney B. R. Caulfield at the Chapel Royal, Savoy. The ceremony was conducted 'in accordance with Suffragist principles'. The Revd Hugh Chapman, a member of the Men's League, officiated and the word 'obey' was omitted.

In the late 1890s Henry wrote that his wedding anniversary reminded him only of 'a day to be blotted out'. Yet despite a mutually unhappy marriage, the couple never divorced. When Margaret died in 1932 they had been married for forty-eight years. Since 1901 they had lived at 4 Downside Crescent, a modern redbrick, semi-detached house just off the fashionable Haverstock Hill. We do not know whether they discussed divorce or legal separation. But social attitudes to divorce were markedly different to today's even though the future of marriage was keenly debated in the late 1880s and 1890s in progressive London circles. 'New Woman' novels, short stories, plays, newspapers and feminist groups all considered the marriage question. But Margaret would have needed to prove aggravated rather than 'simple' adultery to divorce Henry. Gendered laws meant that offences like cruelty or desertion had to be cited as additional grounds for a woman to obtain a divorce rather than a judicial separation. Not until the Matrimonial Causes Act of 1923 (when Margaret was sixty-five) did wives gain the right to divorce on the same grounds as men.

Margaret's story 'Pros and Cons' (1922) was dedicated to the Divorce Reform League and posits its arguments against those of a canon in considering the 'hourly torture' of living with an unfaithful husband.[30] The wife in the story is thirty-three (about the age Margaret would have been when Henry and Nannie met) and has seen her husband with his lover by the Embankment. The canon suggests forbearance, arguing that men are naturally less pure than women and that she must not allow passion and emotion to ruin her life. Margaret and Henry appear to have reached an agreement, possibly influenced by Margaret's concern about the impact of an open separation on her family (her brother Lloyd became Canon of Peterborough). Having stayed together when the children were young, they carried on living in the same house, largely occupying separate space. Henry's late shifts – Richard recalled him rarely being home before 3 or 4 a.m. – spells abroad, evening talks and independent socializing meant he was often absent.

When he was home there were frequent family arguments. Philippa, a talented pianist and singer, had gone to the Royal College of Music and Milan Conservatoire, a remarkable achievement for a young woman in the early 1900s. Yet she found it difficult to meet her father's high

8 The Nevinson family home in Hampstead.

standards and received less attention than her brother from both parents. Richard became increasingly quarrelsome. He was miserable at his public school (Uppingham). Margaret and Henry blamed each other for the decision to send him there.[31]

In many respects Henry behaved as though he were not married. Domestic life connoted the mundane for him: after returning from Macedonia he lamented the 'misery of getting up like an ordinary man'. Like other war reporters, then and now, adjusting from the extremities and contamination of war was never easy.[32] Frequenting gentlemen's clubs and reporting from near and remote corners of the Empire, he seemed to embody the late Victorian man's retreat from domesticity. Yet he wanted to be seen as a modern man. There are even diary references to him cleaning the house when Margaret was away.

Henry once wrote 'oh how I waste my life in loneliness & futility & commonplace, just because I was married too soon & all wrong'. He was, however, twenty-seven when he married although the extremities of joy and anguish he wrote about suggest a lovesick teenager's journal. Not only is the expression of such emotions rarely associated with mature Victorian men but, more importantly for the historian, it is also unusual to see documented so frankly a respected Victorian man's private sentiments.

Henry's coverage of the Spanish–American War illustrates this. In 1898 Henry was sent, not to Cuba as he had hoped, but to Spain. It meant three months away from Nannie: a time 'haunted with loneliness & passionate longing as I always shall be unless another is with me'. He travelled south to Andalucia, the orange blossom evoking memories of Greece. Far from 'the burning heart of my life', Henry was wretched whenever the mail failed to produce a letter from Nannie. Seeking the location of the Spanish fleet, he was mistaken for an American and shadowed wherever he went. Crossing to Africa, he and Wilfred Pollock of the *Daily Mail* were arrested at Ceuta after examining its fortifications. Fortunately Henry had first visited the Governor of Gibraltar so they were rapidly released.

By early June Henry was eagerly waiting to return home. Then came 'A day to be blotted out in black for ever'. He went out into 'a bright world singing with sweet promise & kindness & delight' only to receive a Cook's telegram ordering him to remain until the arrival of the American fleet. In a telling analogy he wrote that he felt like a man 'struck by a shell who stares at his heart's blood running out'. He lay on his bed and 'cried & howled like a child'. He urged Massingham to change his plans and on 2 July arrived home.

Prepared to admit in writing how he cared for a woman and how much this affected him, Henry's travel plans and journalism were affected by what the Greeks called 'mania'. Much as he loved the challenge of travel, he was often lonely. Working in the Black Country, he recorded a night of 'wild desire reaching the furthest limit of torment'. The next morning:

> a spirit message came. 'We think together. When you return you will find that there will be much to write . . . What touches me touches you . . . the mere idea of your existence generally serves to illuminate the whole earth for me . . . How I love you no words can tell.'

Sometimes he despaired of this volatile state, knowing how it threatened peace of mind. For years Henry and Nannie wrote to each other about the pain of being apart. In 1908 she wrote to India, telling Henry that without him 'my soul freezes & my body crumbles'. His exposure to danger, the partings and the distance all added to the intensity. When he sailed to South Africa in 1899, Nannie's farewell letter recalled 'Seven years of all the glory of the earth & sky . . . if anything happens to you,

you know I shall join you in the world of shades as quickly as possible . . . If we had only met twenty years ago.'

Only hours after his wife died in 1932, Henry was writing about their 'mistaken' engagement and 'dismal marriage'.[33] Part of his justification for their growing apart he attributed to natural differences. Margaret was 'by nature & tradition catholic & conservative, always inclined to contradict me on every point & all occasions'. He conceded that she was 'eloquent in the Welsh manner' and 'often humorous and full of observant stories' though melancholic and pessimistic. He complained that she never welcomed him from his travels, was jealous of his success and cared for nobody but Richard. Henry thrived on intimate friendships but she liked 'few men & fewer women' (though her many years in the WFL seem to belie this).

This is a remarkable diatribe given its timing. It is also a poignant expression of the tragic state of this marriage. It is revealing too for the way it circles around Henry even allowing for the fact that he had been reared when Victorian patriarchal relations were at their height. Nowhere do we get a sense of what Margaret's needs might have been. A little later a letter from a Canadian woman friend reproved Henry for his treatment of Margaret. He conceded that he might seem outwardly callous but fell back on what he called 'my natural inability to express emotions & affection'.[34] Given his evident ability to be generous with both, where and when it suited him, it seems that, even if not fooling others, he was good at deceiving himself.

The title of Margaret's autobiography is *Life's Fitful Fever*, a quotation from *Macbeth* where Duncan is in his grave and not even 'Malice domestic' can touch him. Henry and Margaret were now approaching seventy. Daily life was less turbulent than it had been but they never had a companionate marriage. Her stories in *Fragments of Life* (1922) throb with bitterness and loneliness. With little narrative and much polemic, she warns that 'the wives of literary men must get used to being forgotten'. In one story a woman explains how she forgave and then continued to endure her husband's affairs since 'I had my son, you see I could not leave him'. Nothing, we are told, hurt like that first betrayal.[35]

Henry's marital difficulties are not far from the surface in some of his prose writing of the *fin de siècle*, most notably in his contribution to the debate surrounding the posthumous dissection of the marriage of Thomas and Jane Carlyle.[36] These protracted reflections include comments on the rarity of long marriages without disaster or disillusionment. Suggesting that the Carlyles were the exception rather than rule, he implied that men of letters were exempt from ordinary responsibilities and 'safe', stable marriages.

Margaret does not feature in Henry's fiction but Nannie is woven into it with allusions and coded references. Reading *Between the Acts* she told him 'there are so many of my sayings wh. [*sic*] you have remembered

9 Portrait of Evelyn Sharp by E. A. Walton.

& embodied in the book it seems indeed like a child of our making'. But it is *The Plea of Pan* that most clearly radiates Nannie's influence. Its fourth story about 'Verticordia' or Venus, who transfigures the heart, is a hymn to passion. Henry, like Margaret, introduces a canon to represent morality and religion (their various writings are best read contrapuntally). But here the sympathy is with the lovers 'continually driven to rise above the past, seeing that day by day love had to be conquered afresh, like a persistent enemy'.[37] It was Nannie who, in 1895, had told Henry that 'The lover's assurance of the beloved's love hardly lasts a minute. Next morning all has to be won again.'

Nannie might have been assured by the fact that she was the passion of Henry's life. But she was not his sole amour. When he sailed to Angola in 1904 he wrote to 'The Three & Phil'. If his love life had been complicated before, it was now remarkable.

Evelyn Sharp had skated into Henry's life at the very end of 1901. The venue was the Prince's Rink in Knightsbridge where the Ottawa Skating Club met twice weekly. Evelyn was a member and on 30 December she literally bumped into Henry Nevinson. He found her and her companion (the journalist Mrs Hamilton Fyfe of *The Times*) 'delightful'. Henry and Evelyn had not met previously, though as a novelist and freelance journalist she wrote occasionally for his Literary Page in the *Daily Chronicle*. They met again at the rink in February where she talked 'very prettily'. The following month he was invited to her 'gathering of wits – a gallant thing for a young girl' – at her flat at Mount Carmel Chambers, Duke's Lane, Kensington. He came away with his brain 'whirling'.

At thirty-two Evelyn Jane Sharp was hardly a young girl. She had been born at Denmark Hill, south London on 4 August 1869, the ninth of eleven children and youngest of the four girls.[38] The third-eldest child was the folk song and dance expert, Cecil Sharp. A few months after Evelyn's birth her father left his slate firm and he, his wife Jane and eight youngsters travelled round France and Germany for a year (one child dying en route). Evelyn's beloved family nurse came too. She was pouring out tea in a side room while Henry enjoyed 'Excellent converse with Mrs Fyfe & Miss Sharp' in Kensington in 1902.

Returning to London, the Sharps rented a house in Cornwall Gardens before buying an old Buckinghamshire manor in the picturesque village of Weston Turville. Evelyn's father assumed the role of squire. Her mother was the quintessential Victorian lady. Evelyn was not. Neither was she content to play the part of dutiful daughter. She wrote a novel and taught local lads. A few short stories were published in journals and she passed university local examinations before escaping to London where she taught by day and wrote at night. John Lane's Bodley Head press then published her first novel, *At the Relton Arms*, in 1895. The first of six short stories also appeared in the infamous periodical *The Yellow Book*. Evelyn was now part of its bohemian set, with friends such as the writer Netta Syrett and Henry and Aline Harland. They may have helped Henry's brain to whirl at Evelyn's party. Yet although in many ways a New Woman of the 1890s, Evelyn was more accomplished at children's stories than adult fiction. Collections such as *Wymps and Other Fairy Tales* (1896) appealed to children's imaginations, to what she called 'the marvellous in their minds'.[39] And as she became influenced by feminism, so she increasingly subverted the genre. She has witches who are positive forces and princesses who seize the initiative and are the impetus for change. Her determination to treat children, especially girls, as creative, intelligent beings was seen in her school stories. Long before Harry Potter was created, she spotted the appeal of magic and of using boarding school as a setting for suspense and adventure. When Henry met Evelyn she had already published six books.

Stephen Gwynn MP recalled 'an absurdly boyish figure' with large, expressive brown eyes.[40] The timid Kenneth Grahame was known to be in love with her. Though fond of him, Evelyn kept her distance. With Henry it was different. They did not see much of each other in 1902 when Henry was preoccupied with Africa and Nannie but this began to change the next year. Indeed, when the final volume of Henry's autobiography was published, he wrote in Evelyn's copy: 'To Evelyn Sharp, truest of friends. from HWN [*sic*]. 1903–1928.[41] In July, Henry and a group of friends dined out. The party included Evelyn, Nannie and Scotia. On 19 September, Henry cycled to Evelyn's flat. She was 'both pretty and wise – exquisite in every way she seemed, with eyes singularly brilliant. I stayed unwitting'. She told him 'The first time I saw you I knew you wanted something you have never got.' Henry's diary records leaving suddenly and regretting it. Later this occasion would be seen as an anniversary. He comforted her when her father died and 'Stayed long conversing on heaven & earth & the daedal stars. I found her secret & she mine.'

Meanwhile, Nannie wrote Henry a very 'weary and despairing letter'. Evelyn's comparative youth and infectious enthusiasm seem to have been a welcome respite from the seesawing of emotions generated by the complicated relationship with Nannie. Evelyn was soon admitting that Henry had 'bewitched me for all time' and nicknamed him 'the magician'. He called her 'The Wymp' after her mischievous fictional creatures. Soon he would refer to her in the diary as D. E or EW already denoted Nannie so he needed a distinguishing symbol. Evelyn and Henry had talked about the daedal stars. Daedal is short for Daedalus, creator of the Cretan labyrinth. Henry might have used the fact that the diarist John *Evelyn* adopted the word to refer to a labyrinth. Henry developed his own labyrinth to prevent possible readers deciphering his references. Alternatively, he may have been representing Evelyn as the Roman moon-goddess Diana, patroness of chastity and hunting and subsequently identified with the Greek Artemis. Or he could have been alluding to a novel he had read at the time, George Meredith's *Diana of the Crossways*. Based on a disputed incident in the life of Caroline Norton, champion of women's rights, its eponymous heroine is a writer. References to Evelyn are further complicated by Henry using D for private meetings but Evelyn Sharp or ES at other times.

During a lecture tour Henry received a letter from Evelyn admitting that 'if you had gone away for a whole year just now I sh. [*sic*] have given up all hope & wanted to die. You do make beautiful heavenly interludes that keep me going.' Unusually this was attributed. More often sections of letters reproduced in his diary from lovers and admirers were anonymous. Occasionally it is difficult to tell who was writing, though a close reading of the style, approach and allusions usually makes it clear. Early in 1904 Henry learned that Evelyn had been attracted to him long before he had realized. She admitted that she could kill herself 'more easily than I could promise not to love you any more – if it all ended now you wd [*sic*] still have put that smile into my heart'.

But in April Noel and Jane Brailsford returned from Macedonia, Jane severely weakened by typhus. Henry visited, 'all quivering with strange sorrows & memories & hopes'. Henry had first met her the previous year in Macedonia where she had set up a small hospital in the ravaged town of Ochrida (Ohrid) by the famous deep lake of 'brilliant blue'.[42] In the tenth century Ohrid became the headquarters for a Tsar. Much more recently it had been the centre of national opposition to the Turk. For Henry it was immortalized as the place he met Jane. She therefore became O in his diary.

Jane Brailsford (née Malloch) was in her late twenties, Scottish and an early Fabian. She had studied Greek under Gilbert Murray for whom she apparently 'harboured a passionate attachment'. After initially refusing him, she married Noel Brailsford. She told Henry that she would not wear a wedding ring as it was a sign of bondage. Jane, with blue-grey eyes and dark hair, was, like so many women Henry was attracted to, highly intelligent, beautiful and a feminist. He was smitten and they parted 'with lingering touch'. He saw her now for the first time since their Macedonian meeting, standing behind her husband, 'in blue, silky thinnish dress, smocked at neck and waist, pale, thin'. His accounts of Jane invariably describe her appearance: 'I never saw anything so flower-like, so plaintively beautiful & yet so full of spirit & power.' Henry and her husband attended meetings together, 'discussing everything except the thing in our hearts'. Over the following months Henry frequently visited them in Brunswick Square. Jane and Henry flirted. Henry was in turn elated and frustrated by the way she tantalized him. 'She was most sweet', he wrote, 'with dove's eyes, but full of dangers', summing up the attraction and anguish he courted. He found her fickle and volatile and sometimes 'a mocking spirit lay on her'. But he kept coming back for more. She wrote to him about their feelings:

> my struggle to resist my own desire . . . you are not made of stone – well I am not an iceberg. I am a 'wild animal' yes but with a brain – and because of that I see how degrading it was for both of us . . . a mere body I will not be to anyone. You might surely find in me something more than a physical excitement. Have once before been regarded like that by a man & I took it as a proof of his inferiority.

At the theatre with the Brailsfords, he and Jane talked of Ochrida: 'Towards the end a change came between us & we drew into the intimate lines of the friendship we had known & thought of all we had suffered together & of that dark staircase in the high & savage house.' Leaving, he encountered both Nannie and Evelyn.

There were some similarities to the relationship with Nannie, who was also married, creative and fiercely independent. Yet Henry's obsession with Jane was more of an infatuation than a love affair and complicated not only by his other relationships but also by respect for Brailsford. At first sight Henry appeared the more attractive and confident of the two. He was, though, full of self-doubt and jealous. He also admired (and was a little envious of) Brailsford's intellect. But part of Jane's appeal was her inaccessibility.

This was illustrated during The Hague Peace Conference. Henry's frustration with the event was compounded by Jane's treatment there. She would encourage his advances one day, only to spurn him the next. The attraction seems to have been mutual but Jane was wary of a sexual relationship. This challenge made her even more appealing. She told Henry that he had no right to pleasure without responsibility. In his diary Henry indulged in some unconvincing protestation and verbal hair-splitting: 'but it is not pleasure I want. It is the delight of recognition, of intimacy, and close relation of mind & body.'

Evelyn appeared to be more straightforward. And Henry appreciated her sense of humour. After writing from Russia that he was wearing 'revolutionary goloshes', she replied in jest and in earnest: 'I cd [*sic*] love you in anything but goloshes & I do love you, terribly, madly.' And although Henry aided Jane's suffrage activities, it was Evelyn who became his real comrade in this struggle. Indeed here, too, Jane was not prepared to accept Henry's perspectives without making clear her own. In October 1909 she and a small group of WSPU activists had made a stand against forcible feeding. They travelled to Newcastle upon Tyne where Lloyd George was speaking at a theatre. Having concealed a hatchet in a bouquet of flowers, Jane struck a barricade. Henry had known about her plans for this symbolic act. When she refused to be bound over to keep the peace, she received a month's Second Division imprisonment. Henry wrote indignant letters to the Home Office and an article for the *English Review*. The names of Jane Brailsford and Lady Constance Lytton ensured that they were not force-fed and they were released after three days.

Henry's article criticized talk about woman's weakness being her strength. It also ridiculed male tube travellers who 'spring up to offer their seats to pretty and well-dressed women, but remain profoundly occupied with the politics of their paper while a worn-out and draggled creature with a baby and a roll of butter sways from the straps against their knees'.[43] But he stressed that the vote would not and could not make women the same as men: 'You might as well say that a poplar is the same as a church because it is equally high.' Far from being a problem, difference was a plank in the argument *for* the women's vote: 'It is just because they are different that the votes of men cannot represent them.' Jane, however, had reservations about Henry's conception of difference. She challenged his claim that, although it was bad for men to be forcibly fed, it was unendurable for women.

Suffrage marked a fatal rift with Nannie. Before leaving London for the opening of the Russian Duma in 1906, Henry made a 'sudden & stupid confession' which he immediately regretted. He probably told Nannie about Evelyn. Nannie now told him not to try to dominate her any more. She hoped they could be good friends but pointedly commented that she would 'try to widen my mind with many interests as you do'. Arguing with other correspondents about Duma tickets, Henry reflected on his past, admitting that 'I shall not give up the new, & that is the saddest part.' Meanwhile Evelyn was writing passionate letters: 'Oh I am so glad I love some one who cd [*sic*] never make me feel ashamed of what I have given him so freely.' Yet she seems to have been aware of what she had taken on with Henry. During his next Russian trip she wrote that he showed 'all the ingenuity of the traditional sailor in establishing women all along your route'. He was on his way to meet Nannie in Georgia. Their joint work for small nations gave them a legitimate public connection. Nevertheless, Nannie's son-in-law has recalled how, at the end of a subject races conference in 1910, Nannie muttered as they took refreshments with Henry, 'You need not say anything about this at Number 11 [Downshire Hill].'[44]

Nannie did not feature much in Henry's diary in the years that suffrage militancy gathered pace, but on the last day of August 1912 Nannie, Henry and her daughter Norah met for dinner before seeing the play *Hindle Wakes*. At the end of the meal, Norah began talking about the militants and the Dublin prisoners. The suffragettes Mary Leigh and Gladys Evans had been sentenced to five years' penal servitude for setting fire to a box in Dublin's Theatre Royal. In the *Nation*, Henry had described the sentence as 'monstrous', arguing that the government had provoked rebellion by deception and ill treatment, dragged Liberal principles in the dirt and insulted women by introducing manhood suffrage instead of the women's suffrage measures sought in the Conciliation Bills. He had, though, added 'We Liberals reply that force is no remedy; that our measures must be remedial.'[45] Nannie took issue with this: 'there was a storm of rage & passionate dispute'. She left in the middle of the play, effectively walking out of Henry's life. His conciliatory notes had no effect. In a deliberately harsh letter the following January, using words dear to him, Nannie said she had 'never been so happy mentally' as the last few months 'for I have been absolutely free, & liberty is the sweetest thing on earth'. Henry read this 'motionless & numb . . . So there the event of my life ends.'

But if suffrage was the catalyst for the final rupture with Nannie, it brought Henry and Evelyn closer together. A supporter since 1906, she was secretary of the Kensington branch of the WSPU from 1910 and, like Henry, wrote regularly about it for the Liberal press.[46] After its editors the Pethick-Lawrences were imprisoned in 1912, Evelyn in practice took over the WSPU newspaper, *Votes for Women*. Henry helped her. They often spoke at the same meetings but Henry was convinced that Evelyn was more effective, displaying an effortless eloquence he could never match. He told an old friend that 'Above all she is a supreme rebel against injustice, possessing the martyr's indignant rage but illuminated with wit' and with 'one of the most beautiful minds I know – always going at full gallop'.[47] She wrote a collection of suffrage stories called *Rebel Women*.[48]

In November 1911 Evelyn was arrested after breaking a window in the War Office and spent fourteen days in Holloway. Suffrage prisoners were now allowed some privileges (though not recognized as political offenders) but Evelyn complained that all were infantilized. Henry sent 'Dear Miss Sharp' a carefully worded letter: 'No one can say how we all miss you. Day and night we long for Saturday to come.'[49] Reflecting on the events of 1911, Henry singled out 'the renewal of militancy and ES in prison'. In 1913 Evelyn and Henry joined a delegation to the House of Commons to protest against new legislation nicknamed the Cat and Mouse Act. This enabled the release of advanced hunger strikers from prison on licence and their subsequent re-arrest once deemed fit enough. Unable to see the Home Secretary, Evelyn was forcibly ejected after trying to address MPs. Refusing to leave, she, Emmeline Pethick Lawrence and Lady Sybil Smith were arrested. Henry was 'flung out down the steps' only to see Evelyn led away 'deadly white with indignation'. She spent the night in a police cell. After a night of 'blind terror' Henry attended Bow Street Court. Sentenced to fourteen days, the women were suddenly released after four (Lady Sybil Smith was the daughter of the Countess of Antrim and had seven children). Henry bought red roses and muscat. There was 'The perfect happiness again'. But Evelyn was nauseous and weak.

Henry did not go to prison. He was struck by a policeman on the back of the neck and was briefly unconscious in November 1910 during 'The battle of Downing Street'. Mrs Pankhurst, with Henry proudly walking alongside her, had led a 200-strong deputation to Downing Street that had clashed with the police lines. But he was not one of the 124 arrested. Early in 1913 he thought he might be arrested at an MPU parliamentary protest and, despite having earlier warned members against aggression, seemed disappointed when he was left 'listless at home instead of vital in gaol'! A deputation to the Prime Minister to protest against the Cat and Mouse Act organized by Mrs D. A. Thomas did, however, lead to arrest in February 1914. Refused permission to see Asquith, Henry and a few others addressed the crowd from the statue of Richard the Lionheart.

Francis Meynell recalled Henry, 'the most famed radical journalist of his day', mounting the plinth.[50] A policeman seized his ankles and tipped him off. Henry and five others were arrested and marched to Scotland Yard. He was let out on bail that evening but made sure that his account for *Votes for Women* was composed in a cell.

Preparing to emulate Evelyn, he packed a bag ready for a fortnight in gaol. Henry spoke for five minutes at Bow Street the next morning, declaring that:

> This was the proudest event in a long & varied career in which I had tried to do the State some service and it was a dangerous condition when men & women regarded prison as their greatest honour: he cd [*sic*] imprison me but cd not imprison the cause [Evelyn had used the same words in court] or the indignant protest of men's hearts.

He anticipated Pentonville and becoming the subject of news rather than its conveyer but was simply bound over for six months. After a couple of hours in custody, the stipendiary magistrate (whom Henry had known in the 1890s) scolded the protesters individually in an empty court during the lunch recess before ignominiously discharging them. As Henry put it, 'you can't go to prison if the law keeps you out'! The authorities were well aware of the publicity they would have unleashed in imprisoning the wife of an immensely rich coal owner and former Liberal MP, one of her relatives and four famous men, three of whom were writers. And what might the wily war correspondent have written?

Henry was by now very critical of WSPU tactics, particularly Christabel's decision to stay abroad. At the end of 1913 a new phase began when Henry and Evelyn helped found a new mixed-sex suffrage society, the United Suffragists (US).[51] Henry was its first chairman. The Pethick Lawrences handed *Votes for Women* to the new society. Evelyn was its editor. The US played a crucial, somewhat unsung, role in the women's victory of 1918. It worked hard throughout the war. Through such societies and the protracted, tortuous negotiations with the government via the National Council for Adult Suffrage which Henry chaired, eventually early in 1918 the Representation of the People Act granted the national vote to women over thirty fulfilling householder or other criteria.[52] Women's suffrage did matter to him. When the Royal Assent was announced in Parliament on 6 February, only three stalwarts were left in the central lobby to hear the news: the US secretary Bertha Brewster, Evelyn Sharp and Henry Nevinson.[53] In his autobiography Henry described this date as one of the two happiest days of his life.[54]

CHAPTER SIX

The Indian Spirit

'He seems to be a dangerous sort of young gentleman and I really think we shall have to send him home to you if we hear much more of his eloquence!' wrote Lord Minto, Viceroy of India, to John Morley, Secretary of State for India, in December 1907.[1] The threateningly eloquent 'young' man was the fifty-one-year-old Henry Nevinson. On the day Minto penned these words Henry was speaking in Eastern Bengal. He had been in India for the British press since October, investigating 'unrest'. Having journeyed in the Portuguese and Russian Empires he had now come to the most prized part of the British Empire. And, as Minto's words suggest, controversy was his companion. Indeed, the name of Henry W. Nevinson was associated with a 'journalism of attachment'[2] which both disturbed and challenged.

Henry's brief was to 'discover the causes of the present discontent and to report, without prejudice, the opinions of leading Indians as well as officials'[3] for the *Manchester Guardian*, Conservative *Glasgow Herald* and *Daily Chronicle*. He also sent the *Nation* five 'Letters from Abroad'. C. P. Scott of the *Guardian* had suggested that the tour might 'touch on some of the fundamental questions' such as the economic condition of cultivators and 'the growth of something like national or at least race self-consciousness'.[4]

Henry did his homework, reading books on India and visiting experts such as Sir William Wedderburn, who chaired the British Committee of the Indian National Congress (INC). In two days this veteran of the Indian Civil Service 'taught my ignorance as much in detail and in principle as it could bear'.[5] He talked to Vaughan Nash, who had written about the famine districts, and Britain's first Asian MP, Dadabhai Naoroji. Sir Henry Cotton, former Chief Commissioner of Assam and leader of the Congress lobby in the House of Commons, helped him, as did Sister Nivedita (Margaret Noble), disciple of Swami Vivekananda. She ran a school in Calcutta that Henry later visited.

On 25 September Henry met Lord Morley at the India Office. He was greeted with 'rather plaintive though fatherly benignity'. Morley was acutely aware of the power of the press in 'the Raj equation' and the value of informally influencing journalists.[6] He had heard that Henry was an 'impressionist', taking his own line, and asked him to be vigilant and report privately to him. He should see 'the big men on the English side'. Morley wished the Extremists to know that they 'had no support in any English party'. He also complained ('pathetically' in Henry's view) that 'people gave no credit for a long past of Liberalism'. Deploying what Henry later described as 'an extraordinary platitude' for a man who had spent nearly two years as Secretary of State for India, he remarked that east was east and west was west. Henry thought he 'looked like a mummified relic of the Gladstonian age who had somehow contrived to keep a glimmer of life in his mummy clothes'.[7]

The timing was unfortunate. That day the Anglo-Russian Agreement over Persia was signed. Asked by Morley for his opinion, Henry immediately denounced it. The next day Henry's letter in the *Westminster Gazette* spelt out his anger at Liberal betrayal and dismissed as 'diplomatic twaddle' the claims about respecting Persia's integrity and independence. Morley had glimpsed Henry's spirit. He told Minto that he had offered 'some excellent advice' but feared that it would 'probably share the usual fate of that cheap commodity!'[8] Nevertheless, he asked Minto to extend 'some trifle of civility'. He described Henry as 'a cleverish writer, though belonging to a rather flighty company of young men'. Henry would retain some residual respect for Morley.[9] He saw him as a fine biographer and former idealist whose hands were tied. But Morley's opinion of Henry soon plummeted.

Henry left on 4 October 1907. Nannie was at Tilbury. He had seen Jane and Evelyn the previous day. Jane had told him 'not to come but was expecting me' (which aptly sums up their relationship) whereas the parting from Evelyn was one of 'infinitely long sorrow'. Recently she had admitted her desperate longing for a child. At Marseilles Henry read her birthday greetings. Commenting on her recent literary success,[10] she added 'O my dear I would give it all up to have you back & belong to you openly & fairly.'

Henry reached Bombay (Mumbai) three weeks later. Keir Hardie, on a world tour, had just left. His visit had provoked crude press claims that he was inciting rebellion.[11] Henry learned that his speeches had been 'shamelessly distorted'. At a cotton mill he was delighted to be asked if he were the Labour leader.[12] It was no coincidence that Henry, Hardie, MacDonald and the Webbs were investigating conditions in India.[13] British progressives were engaged in debates about how India could achieve Home Rule. How might Indian civil society best be nurtured? What might sustained British control, albeit with a caring face, signify in the light of recent expressions of Indian nationalism? Yet the world these politicians and writers encountered in India was one for which familiar definitions of acceptable radical and democratic behaviour were inadequate. Western methods could not simply be grafted on to India.

British radicals could not fully appreciate the varying needs of localities and spiritual dimensions of daily life. They found themselves in a curious, indeterminate position. Seen as critics of empire by the British establishment, they were also alienated from the complexities of nationalism in India as indigenous politicians deployed whatever mode of politics seemed expedient at a particular moment.

Morley's predecessor, Lord Curzon, had divided Bengal into two in 1905. It had been India's largest province with over 78 million people, almost a third of whom were Muslims. Partition created a new Bengal, within which was the old province's capital, Calcutta. Only about 16 per cent of its 55 million or so inhabitants were Muslims. With the former provinces of Bihar and Orissa incorporated, Bengali-speakers, despite the province's name, were now in a minority. To its east, distinguished largely by faith, was the new, smaller and predominantly Muslim province of Eastern Bengal and Assam. Dacca became its capital. Reform was overdue and partition may have fulfilled British administrative and economic needs but the division of Bengal, cutting right through the heart of the Bengali-speaking areas, spoke for itself. Bengalis saw Calcutta (the country's capital) as the centre of their culture, trade and legal affairs. A day of fasting and prayer marked the day that partition came into force. It was also evident that Britain was encouraging Muslim strength to counteract the educated and increasingly nationalistic Hindu Bengalis. An All-India Muslim League was formed. Curzon had fomented the unrest he had so desired to curb.

There were boycotts of imported British goods for Indian goods or Swadeshi ('belonging to our own country'). Such ideas had been advocated since the mid-nineteenth century but the Swadeshi movement was effectively prompted into action by partition. It spread rapidly outwards from Eastern Bengal and Calcutta, many seeing the encouragement of indigenous goods as a beacon for a new era of prosperity. By 1906 imported cotton fabric had fallen by 40 per cent. At a Swadeshi co-operative store in Bombay, Henry purchased a turban for Sylvia Dryhurst, and in Madras he was presented with Swadeshi goods by the *Indian Review*.[14] He watched a Swadeshi meeting on the beach, noting its popularity among ordinary people. He suggested that it was 'necessarily a women's movement, because women wear most of the cotton and do most of the housekeeping'.[15] It rapidly spread beyond cotton to cover native cigarettes, toys and other goods and was extended to boycotting British government and legal systems, becoming passive resistance with economic, educational, judicial and administrative dimensions.

For Extremists like Aurobindo Ghose, Swadeshi was the prerequisite for the ultimate goal, Swaraj (self-rule), a free national government with no foreign control. Yet, although united in disparaging the methods of the Moderates, there were differences within this camp. The Extremist Bal Gangadhar Tilak, leader of the nationalist New Party (formed in

1906), envisaged Indian administrative control stopping short of severing British connections. They sought, he told Henry, 'to attract the attention of England to our wrongs by diverting trade and obstructing the Government'. Henry contrasted what he saw as the unpalatable fanaticism of Aurobindo Ghose and Bengali nationalists with the shrewd political judgement of Tilak and Poona Extremists, possibly underestimating how Ghose 'thought of a series of methods to be adopted, successively or in unison, according to circumstance'.[16]

Repression and the suspension of civil rights followed disturbances and riots. Henry found that students could be arrested simply for singing the Bengali song 'Bande Mataram' ('Hail to the Motherland'). The chapter on India in his memoirs opens with its words. He joined crowds on the beach at sunset to celebrate the release of the Punjabis Ajit Singh and Lajpat Rai (deported without trial on the eve of the fiftieth anniversary of the failed revolution of 1857 or Indian Mutiny). Relishing being the sole European there, Henry heard a little boy sing 'Bande Mataram' in Tamil. Although it was a meeting of Extremists, Henry stressed that they were more restrained than a Trafalgar Square crowd.

At Poona (Pune) he fund that plague had driven much of the population into health camps. At the offices of Tilak's newspaper *Mahratta*, to his embarrassment, the printers garlanded him. Decked in orange marigolds and lavishly sprinkled with scent, he focused on something suitably manly: rowing at Oxford! In fact Oxford graduates accounted for more than half of the Indian Civil Service, with many of its elite from Christ Church. On graduating Henry had even fleetingly toyed with the idea of joining the Indian Staff Corps or Ceylon Civil Service. He now found his Oxford contacts useful.

It was in the Poona district that he interviewed the leaders of Indian politics: Tilak and Gokhale, highly educated Chitpavan Brahmins. He met the Moderate Gopal Krishna Gokhale, former INC president, with his Servants of India Society.[17] It was the festival of Diwali. Henry was pleased to see a copy of *The Dawn in Russia* in the society's library. Gokhale possessed 'Courage underlying a sweet reasonableness',[18] which Henry found humbling. His gradualist approach envisaged India evolving as a self-governing member of a commonwealth. When Gokhale died in 1915, the Calcutta *Statesman* paid tribute to 'the greatest leader that India has ever produced – perhaps her greatest man'.[19] Henry's admiration grew over the years for 'the greatest statesman I have ever intimately known'.[20]

The meeting with Tilak was, fittingly, at a more dramatic setting: the Singarh fortress, south west of Poona. The published interview is reminiscent of Henry's account of meeting Cretan rebels in 1897: 'So I left him, standing upon this mountain top, surrounded by the ruins of empires, while the familiar British soldiers flash their helio from the rocks close by.'[21] Henry noted, however, the quiet manner and self-command of this Extremist who was also a Sanskrit scholar. Henry believed that the Moderates and Extremists differed in method rather than purpose. Sir George Clarke, the new 'well disposed & thoughtful' Governor of Bombay, informed him that Tilak was irreconcilable and doing harm. Henry's first article bluntly stated that Anglo-Indians did not draw distinctions between the political groupings: 'They claim them all as swine.'[22]

Fascinated by the nationalist seer Aurobindo Ghose, 'the best Bengali mind I have met', Henry saw him as the voice of the future. The ability to secure meetings and even establish long-term friendships with some of India's political leaders is testimony to Henry's networking and socializing as well as careful preparation and application. Historians have perhaps not paid sufficient attention to the all-important letter of introduction. Henry may have annoyed Morley but not before he had secured the necessary written support that opened doors and had knock-on effects. He was also adept at recognizing who might best aid him within the societies he examined. He soon had Gokhale writing to Madras, urging that Henry be introduced to leading Congress members and given:

> opportunities to know our views of the situation. It will be a great advantage to our cause that a gentleman of his broad sympathies and influential connection with the British press should examine for himself the character of the stories that have been recently circulating in England about the state of things in India.[23]

Ever conscious of the value of support from the famous, Henry would call on public figures, from Thomas Hardy to Gokhale, to validate causes other than their own. Wearing his women's suffrage hat, for example, he asked Gokhale if he could use his name in a list of distinguished men demanding First Division treatment for these British political prisoners.

Henry's articles on India ranged widely. As Map 3 shows, he covered vast distances. The extensive railway network helped. On the train to Delhi he found an archaeologist with an intriguing gadget: 'a contrivance called a Thermos for keeping things hot or cold'. Travelling by train, pony and even elephant, he wrote about the problems of rural India: the 'ryotwari' (peasant tenantry) system in Madras and the Bombay presidency, floods in Orissa and the effects of famine. He was especially shocked by the starving figures that threw themselves at him, rubbing their foreheads on his boots. But in an article (that he was particularly proud of) in the *Nation*, after deriding Indian deference and British insensitivity, he warned that throughout India a new national consciousness was awakening. It heralded 'a revival of dignity, a resolve no longer to take insults lying down' or to 'lick the hand that strikes, or rub the forehead in the dust before any human being, simply because he has a

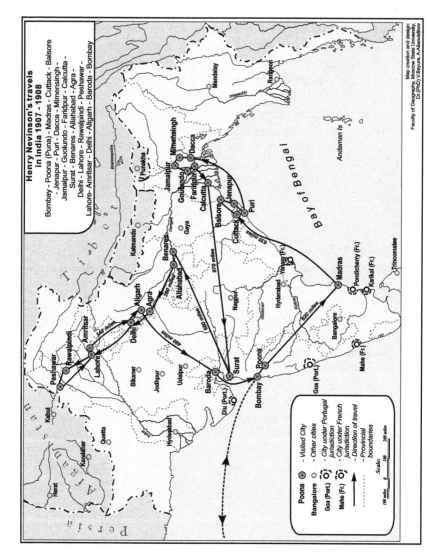

Map 3 Henry Nevinson's travels in India, 1907–8.

red face and a helmet'.[24] Written after he had visited the popular ancient Temple of Juggernath (Juggernaut) at Puri in the Gulf of Bengal, it reads rather like a sermon and probably had its origins in the speech he made at an open-air meeting of about 4,000 at Cuttack in Orissa. Most speeches were in Uriya though some used English. Henry recorded that he spoke:

> I think better than I have ever spoken before – the realities of the flood, the good heart of voluntary help compared to official, the weakness of Indians in over-politeness & taking things lying down: spoke of Juggernath too & the ideals of equality & freedom, and of Indian devotion to spiritual causes.

He interviewed Sir Andrew Fraser, Governor-General of Bengal, finding him 'friendly & polite'. He might have used different words had he known what Fraser would say to Morley. A month later Morley wrote to Minto about Henry, no longer portraying him as the 'cleverish writer'. Morley was embarrassed that he had ever authorized 'a certain *Nevinson*' to leave his name on his commendation at Government House: 'From what I read of his utterances, and from what Fraser tells me, he appears to be turning out a pure donkey. So I must apologise to you, if he used my name . . . the donkey tribe is numerous, and not without artful powers of disguising their long ears, until the bray reveals them.'[25] Morley liked the donkey analogy. He had described Sir Henry Cotton as 'a donkey and a perverse one'.[26]

Henry was being watched. Since 1904 central and provincial criminal intelligence departments had become experienced in political surveillance. Henry first featured in the weekly reports of the director of criminal intelligence on 19 October 1907 in a file on the 'Doings of Mr. H. W. Nevinson in India'. The following month he addressed members of the Mahajana Sabha Club in Madras.[27] He was reported to have approved of the national movement, stating that he 'did not believe it was possible for a nationality so different as the English to contemplate remaining for all time the supreme leaders of another nationality so different as the "Indian" '. He apparently apologized for the Liberal government and Morley's conduct, suggesting that he was misled by 'lying telegrams' and 'very probably by official information' as well as 'his own crew'. Intelligence had copies of Henry's interviews with the *Hindu* and *Madras Standard* where he provided further ammunition for those seeing him as inflammatory. He argued that Indians often appeared too polite and submissive and should assert themselves more, especially in claiming municipal and political rights.[28]

In an increasingly repressive climate, a new Seditious Meetings Act empowered local governments to designate areas where a week's notice had to be given for all public meetings and private gatherings of over twenty. District magistrates or commissioners of police could prohibit such meetings or direct police to attend. Henry was especially critical of the spy system. At Serajganj in Eastern Bengal he suddenly turned on the man who had been shadowing him, hidden under a black shawl and umbrella: 'I gave him many strong words' and 'watched the poor hired worm grovel away'. In Peshawar a spy attempted to bribe his servant to reveal their destination. Most worrying was 'the indignant contempt which our Government thus stores up against itself'.[29] Not surprisingly, Anglo-Indian newspapers criticized him. The *Bombay Advocate* warned: 'We have seen this Mr. Nevinson. Outwardly he has the appearance of a gentleman, but at heart he is no better than a Socialist!'[30]

Hardie had told the Indian press that Henry was held in the highest esteem in Britain and that Indian people could expect 'disinterested and valuable advice from such an ardent lover of British justice, freedom and truth'.[31] Both men condemned police corruption. Despite their Western mind-set, they were interested in the plight of subject nations and more internationalist than many of their British counterparts. Perhaps most importantly, their articles in the progressive press and subsequent publications helped inform the public from radically different perspectives from those generally promulgated by the British Raj. They disseminated ideas and debates too often restricted to the British Committee of the INC and small parliamentary pro-India group. And they were aided by improved internal and international communications. Telegraphs now reached London within a few hours.[32]

Rioting in Calcutta had been connected with Hardie's visit and there had been calls, ultimately unheeded, for deportation. Like Henry, he used strong language but (contrary to press opinions) did not argue for the immediate withdrawal of the British from India. By early February 1908 Minto was telling King Edward VII that Hardie had been one of the best of the British radicals:

> For misguided as he was, he gave ample evidence in his conversations with the Viceroy and others, that he was honest in his intentions and quite ready to hear the other side. On the other hand, a certain Mr. Nevinson, who has been here on behalf of some English newspapers, has given vent to utterances calculated to cause endless bad feeling against British rule, but which unfortunately there would appear to be no legal power to deal with.[33]

Returning to Bombay, Henry found the Assistant Commissioner far from pleased to see him. He was told that 'the wrath of the Anglo-Indians knew no bounds. They had clamoured for my deportation.' When, in 1909, the crusading journalist W. T. Stead told Morley that he proposed going to India, Morley declared that it would do no harm now that Nevinson had gone. Henry noted (probably with pride) Morley's remark that 'he had always thought Stead violent & extreme till he met me'.[34]

So, what exactly was concerning the authorities? For a start, Henry was in India for almost four months. He listened and watched, just like the spies. He was not a political figurehead like Hardie. But whereas the latter's visit lasted only a few weeks, Henry had the time and the experience to seek out and interview people, from newspaper editors (including an old Salopian in Allahabad) to principals of educational institutions and political and religious thinkers. He also met figures such as the influential Dacca Muslim, Nawab Salimulla, though his representation of the Nawab assumes a benchmark of values and civilization that is distinctly white, Western and Christian.[35] Yet, according to a governess to the progressive Maharajah and Maharani of the Native State of Baroda, the latter had declared that they had 'never been treated with such perfect equality & sympathy before' by a British person. Not long after returning home, however, Henry shocked himself with his angry reaction when he was pushed aside by an Indian at a London reception. However, in the early twentieth century his very self-awareness must have seemed refreshing to Indians.

Henry was known to be outspoken. Theodore Morison, former principal of the Anglo-Oriental College at Aligarh and a member of India's Council, remarked on 'what a bombshell they had thrown into India' by sending him there. The principal of the Cambridge Mission near Delhi was, Henry found, 'a little afraid of my violent reputation'. His articles were often more like speeches than reports and he was unequivocal about the increasingly cavalier treatment of native Indians and the spread of 'the infection of arrogance'.[36]

Henry's fraternizing, especially meetings with students and political leaders, concerned the authorities. He joined crowds of eager men on the riverbanks as the sun rose and followed politicians in torchlight processions. A confidential report from the Chief Secretary to the Government of Eastern Bengal and Assam to Morley on the political situation in the province between mid-December 1907 and mid-January 1908 noted that Henry had met various government officials in the Dacca district but 'paid but small attention' to their information. In Eastern Bengal he was:

> accompanied throughout by gentlemen who have distinguished themselves by opposition to the measures of Government, and he was met at the various railway stations by bodies of students and pleaders, who made him the centre of processions and congratulatory meetings and kept him carefully aloof from most Indians who could have given him an *unbiassed view* [my emphasis] of the present situation.[37]

It was claimed that he did not obtain 'any very accurate understanding' of the state of affairs in Eastern Bengal. 'His meetings and processions' had not caused great harm but he 'fanned the agitation by excitement and noise'.[38]

Henry's diary inevitably puts a different gloss on such events. His descriptions challenge the idea that they were 'his' meetings, suggesting that he merely contributed to gatherings largely organized by and for Indians. At Faridpur he was welcomed by a huge crowd and led through the town in a carriage decked with garlands and flags. He recorded talking to a 'rather chilly' pro-partition magistrate before attending a meeting of several thousand men and boys under a huge awning. His published prose does not mention that he was a speaker but his diary describes him sitting on a little platform and talking on 'my mission, false reports, spirit of nationality, Swadeshi boycott, necessity of self-help, & good in disguise of Partition'. All apparently went well. He was garlanded and photographed. There was a long torchlight procession before he left.

A few days later, just before Henry was due to speak at a large Calcutta meeting, Edward Buck, a Reuters agent, wired his London office:

> Growing feeling here Government should prevent mischievous persons like Keir Hardie and Nevinson making speeches which only calculated inflame Native feeling continue unrest. Nevinson's advice to Cuttack audience to stand up to British been followed by harangue Fardipur [*sic*] where accompanied by A. Mazamdur noted agitator he denounced certain recent telegrams to English press as hateful lies condemned partition absolutely denied sedition ever existed India – Consequence Nevinson treated popular hero friend oppressed Bengalis who formed ridiculous ideas influence English travellers . . .[39]

Buck was the government correspondent and on close terms with Minto. He told Minto's secretary that he was reconsidering the situation. After the 'Keir Hardie affair' it had been thought that 'perhaps to ignore Nevinson entirely might be the wisest plan' for the highly influential news agency. Now he was 'not at all sure that I was right, or that the Government of India can afford to let these irresponsible firebrands wander about as they are doing'. They were sowing seeds of discord 'from which no one can tell what the crop might be'.[40]

Henry met newspaper editors in Calcutta. He was especially impressed by Surendranath Banerjea, former INC president and editor of one of the leading dailies, the *Bengalee*: 'Except for Mr. Gladstone, I have heard no speakers use the grand and rhetorical style of English with more assurance and success.'[41] They went together to the meeting of several thousand white-robed, bareheaded Bengalis in College Square. According to the intelligence report, its purpose was to demonstrate the reasonable nature of Bengali public meetings to Henry and the Indophile Liberal MP Dr Vickerman Rutherford (who was unable to attend). In his memoirs Henry told how Banerjea spoke about the impending Congress 'with a magnificence of phrase, and continuity of expression'.[42] He added

'Then I spoke, and the meeting ended.' But his diary reveals that he spoke about sedition, the need for independence and the mistake of looking to the government for everything. He deplored the use of detectives, opening letters and stopping telegrams, ending with 'the crisis & parting of the ways, one to hostility & revolution, the other to generous & open-hearted agreement'.

The speech provoked a 'Storm in the papers'. Unfortunately, Henry had a breakfast appointment with Sir Andrew Fraser, the Lieutenant-Governor. His autobiography suggests that the welcoming atmosphere changed once the morning papers arrived and Fraser read about Henry in the press. Henry's diary simply mentions a one-and-a-half-hour discussion of Indian politics in Fraser's study and parting 'in good temper on both sides'. The weekly intelligence report gave an account of Henry's speech. According to this, Henry complained that he was denied copies of the *Manchester Guardian* and denounced the telegrams of Indian news transmitted to England. Such 'abominable crimes' were 'deliberate attempts to stir up race against race so as to enable the Government to issue repressive measures with the consent of the people at home for a supposed danger which did not exist'. He praised efforts to develop 'self-reliance and manliness' – an interesting conjunction – as one of 'the most important and admirable signs' he had seen of the national movement in India. And he declared that there was 'no glory in ruling over a flock of sheep and there was no glory in being one of a flock of sheep'.[43] Indians should 'stand up and show their independence to the white man both socially and politically'. Fraser sent Henry an account of the speech in an angry letter, warning that he could not 'expect to pick up sedition like blackberries'. Henry dismissed the account as 'garbled'.

Henry met another Lieutenant-Governor, Sir John Hewett, at Agra, describing him as 'very open'. The next day he attended a meeting of about 120 educated men and heard about 'the other side of Hewett'. He admitted, however, that he was more popular than were most administrators. Henry spoke to the Agra men in a 'conversational way', discussing the Congress split, the aims and merits of Moderates and Extremists, what they shared and whether government concession could restore confidence. He deplored government espionage and interception of letters 'ruinous to our honour though it may detect bits of sedition not worth that cost'.

Henry may have been a nuisance to the British Raj, but his eyewitness account of the unprecedented fiasco at the 1907 Congress is certainly valuable for historians. The INC met annually in December for three days. Formed in 1885, this umbrella organization was the most important all-India body, bringing together the vast country's disparate political viewpoints. It discussed and planned the way forward, meeting at different locations which themselves had a huge impact on its deliberations, participants being chosen or selecting themselves from a wide range of local groups. The years 1905 to 1910 were critical in the INC's history and Henry recorded one of its most dramatic moments when the twenty-third INC disintegrated in chaos at Surat on the Gulf of Cambay.

The scene had already been set. At Benares in 1905 a clash between the different factions was narrowly avoided. Crisis was averted at Calcutta the following year by inviting Naoroji from England to preside. The 1907 Congress had been planned for Nagpur in the Central Provinces and, according to intelligence reports, Henry had intended to be there.[44] When the reception committee met in November – just as Henry was talking to Tilak – the Moderates opted for the experienced jurist Dr Rash Behari Ghose as president. Extremists retaliated with their choice of Tilak. He, in turn, suggested Lajpat Rai as a compromise but the latter refused. Dr Ghose became president-elect. The location was changed to Surat, north of the Moderate stronghold Bombay, a further bone of contention for the Extremists.

On the eve of its opening Mr Allen, the collector of Dacca, was shot (but survived). Henry heard the news on Christmas Day on his forty-four-hour train journey back to the west coast. He thought it made Congress's task 'infinitely more difficult, perhaps hopeless & brings discredit on all I have attempted'. His illustrious fellow passengers included Dr Ghose and Banerjea. Henry's diary claims that he 'Induced Dr. Ghose to insert a passage in his opening speech expressing regret & horror' at the attempted assassination of Mr Allen.

Henry and Dr Rutherford were caught up in the welcome awaiting the dignitaries at Surat. It took two hours to travel by carriage from the station to the Congress camp. Henry noted that Gokhale seemed chilly and distant, hardly surprising given the problems he faced. The Extremists had just held their own first Indian Nationalist Conference at Haripur on the outskirts of Surat and remained in this separate camp. The conference had passed resolutions on total boycott and complete independence. Two distinct views had emerged about Congress. Tilak's supporters rejected any intention to cause a split. Aurobindo Ghose's followers wanted to take it over or, failing that, to wreck it.

Proceedings began on 26 December with 1,200 delegates and about 10,000 spectators[45] gathered at the pandal (pavilion) on the banks of the Tapti. Henry described the fraught atmosphere, rife with rumours and suspicions. The reception committee had already elected Dr Ghose, after recommendation by all bar one of the provincial Congress committees. Yet when it came to the ritual proposing of the new president, there were cries of dissent. As soon as Banerjea began to second the proposal, 'the storm burst'. Arms, scarves, sticks and umbrellas were brandished. Banerjea sprang on to a table and all stood, 'shouting for order, shouting for tumult'.[46] In under an hour the unthinkable had happened: the meeting had been suspended and broken into 'excited groups'. It was depressing but also a journalist's delight. Henry was assured by Tilak and other Extremists that it had all been a mistake and unexpected. Henry's telegraph to the British press stressed that 'the situation is critical, and the division of the Congress into separate groups is probable'.[47]

Proceedings resumed the next day. Unfortunately, the original text of the delayed presidential address, complete with criticism of the Extremists which, according to Henry, Dr Ghose had decided to omit, had been printed in some newspapers. Henry's autobiography explains that he was invited to sit among the Congress leaders at a table stretching the length of the high-raised platform. Tilak, however, pointedly chose to sit with the delegates and sent a note to the chairman of the reception committee indicating that he wanted to speak on the election of the president. He later stressed that the note included his wish to move an amendment for a proposal for another special delegate conference. The chairman, however, claimed that this amendment was for an adjournment of Congress itself.

Banerjea resumed his speech, followed by the Moderate lawyer Motilal Nehru. It was proposed that Dr Ghose take the chair as president and the motion was carried. Ghose got no further than his opening sentence of thanks. Tilak, who had been waiting to be called, suddenly appeared on the platform in front of Ghose's chair, insisting on his right to move his amendment and refusing to accept Ghose's authority. He declared that Ghose had not been elected and that he would appeal to the delegates. He turned to face the audience, his arms folded. Ghose attempted to read his speech but was drowned out by shouts. Incensed Moderates sprang up shouting. 'Ingeminating peace, if ever a man ingeminated', Gokhale shielded Tilak.[48] Tilak stated that only violence could move him. Then:

> Suddenly something flew through the air – a shoe! – a Mahratta shoe! Reddish leather, pointed toe, sole studded with lead. It struck Surenda Nath [Banerjea] on the cheek; it cannoned off upon Sir Pherozeshah Mehta [a wealthy, influential Parsi Moderate]. It flew, it fell, and as at a given signal, white waves of turbaned men surged up the escarpment of the platform. Leaping, climbing, hissing the breath of fury, brandishing long sticks, they came ... I caught glimpses of the Indian National Congress dissolving in chaos.[49]

Tilak was taken to safety but pandemonium reigned. Henry, seasoned observer of conflict across continents, leapt on a chair for a better view and watched as other

> Chairs, useless now except as missiles, flew through the air like shells discharged at a venture; long sticks clashed and shivered; blood flowed from broken heads. Group rushed upon group, delegate upon delegate. Breathing slaughter, they glared for victims. It was hard to tell friend from foe. Ten thousand men, all crowded together among ten thousand chairs ...

Henry's diary was less dramatic and polished: 'Somehow the fighting was never quite serious' though a good many were hurt. A *Times of India* reporter was kicked in the testicles, Ghose was 'wild with rage' at Tilak's appearance on the platform and Banerjea and Mehta were 'proud of being hit'.[50] There was 'a sort of wave of fighting sticks rolled up on the platform'. Two opponents, seized with murderous intent, attacked each other, one cracking his stick over the other's head, unravelling his turban. Police arrived. Within an hour order was restored. 'Strewn with broken chairs, sticks, and rags of raiment', the pavilion stood empty 'as a banquet-hall deserted'.[51] Henry telegraphed 280 words to the *Manchester Guardian*. On 28 December readers were told how the 'Indian Congress Breaks Up Amid Wild Disorder. Free Fight: Many Injured'. The leader praised Henry.

After a sleepless night he found 860 Moderates gathered at a meeting chaired by Dr Ghose. They signed an agreement to preserve peace and promote constitutional reform and took the name of the All-India Conference.[52] The general feeling, according to Henry, was that the split would have been avoidable but for Dr Ghose's impatience. Bombay Moderates had, Henry argued, been determined to oust the Extremists and follow cautious lines.[53] In the courtyard of a private house he witnessed about 400 Extremists at a meeting chaired by the other Ghose (Aurobindo) 'with his desperate grave face'. Tilak acknowledged that Congress was a valuable institution but stressed that '*a new spirit* [my emphasis] had entered Indian affairs'. Unless the INC became permeated with this new spirit 'it had better die – it was dead already'.[54] Henry dined with the rival 'Bombay set' and had a long talk with Gokhale. The next day he left for the calmer waters of the Ganges.[55]

Henry's account of the Surat Congress opens with the rapturous greetings of the Moderate leaders of the Congress movement and their entourage as they travelled to Surat. Borrowing from Robert Browning, it begins 'It was roses, roses all the way.' It ends with the angry declamations of both sides ringing out as they departed, closing with the words 'It had been roses, roses all the way.' As at Ladysmith and the Russian Duma, Henry had once more been present at a seminal event in a nation's modern development. His story of Surat is especially useful because the world's media had not foreseen this drama. Henry had quite literally had a privileged position and was helped by his prior acquaintance with a number of the key players. Both sides published their own versions of events soon after the split. Years later, Aurobindo Ghose admitted that, without consulting Tilak, he had given the order that led to the breaking up of the Congress. This was not known at the time and speculation was rife. So an eyewitness account from an outside observer free from faction fighting was invaluable. As Tripathi explains, Henry had 'picturesquely captured for us' the descent into chaos in that crowded Congress.[56]

Henry wanted to prolong his visit but his paymasters would not extend his engagement. He saw Gokhale once more before leaving. He expressed regret that Henry had informed the British press that the Moderates were bent on excluding the Extremists. Henry arrived home on 1 March. Five days later he signed a contract with Harper's for a book to be called 'India in Unrest'. The title was eventually changed to that of a magazine article he had written called *The New Spirit in India*, a recognized euphemism for unrest. In his first budget speech in 1906 Morley had mentioned that everyone was complaining of a 'new spirit in India'.[57] When the artist William Rothenstein went to Benares in 1910, Henry wrote a letter of introduction to Gokhale explaining that his friend wished to avoid English people and officials and possessed 'a genuine interest in the Indian spirit'.[58] Rothenstein found that the Nevinson name got him 'into all Indian homes' but that this name was 'detested by Anglo-Indians, being always coupled with Keir Hardie's'.

Apart from *Nation* articles, Henry was once more without regular paid work and lamenting 'these hateful evenings in the suburbs'. He worked on his book, admitting that he had 'never approached any subject with more overwhelming distaste & uncertainty'. He completed the manuscript in Dolgellau in between cycling and walking. Published in the autumn, it was over 350 pages long. A detailed introduction recounted India's recent historical and political background. It lacked Henry's customary verve but served a purpose. Slightly amended versions of his press articles followed and a personal assessment of the new spirit and way forward.

It was deliberately different in tone from J. D. Rees's carefully titled *The Real India*. Henry had loathed this book. A former high-ranking civil servant and translator in India, Rees supported partition, presented Bengalis as excitable, dismissed most Indian reformers as agitators, argued that the INC should be brought under regulation and concluded that 'we must make up our minds that India cannot be governed upon democratic lines'.[59] Although Rees had not directly mentioned Henry's articles, he claimed to portray a true picture, unlike some accounts that he believed were 'frankly seditious and disloyal'. He and other Anglo-Indians were critical of the 'casual visitor' who did not live in the country, required translators and pontificated. 'A Poona Resident' took Henry to task for his claims about the financial hardships of the 'ryots', though the veteran Indophile Sir William Wedderburn replied, upholding Henry's facts and figures.[60] *India*, the official organ of the British Committee of the INC, compared the 'malignant distortions' of Rees's book with Henry's study based on 'intimate acquaintance with most of the prominent leaders'. Henry was emphatically not the 'bungalow club' kind of visitor. It was hoped that Morley and his circle would read him since 'There has seldom been a book on India better worth buying, better worth reading, and better worth keeping.'[61]

Henry's critique was measured. His defence of Indians was largely a plea for equal treatment of educated Indians or, to be more precise, high-ranking, intellectual Hindus. The Indians he knew were mainly male, professional and political or spiritual leaders.[62] Moreover, despite the image of radicalism and danger that preceded and followed him, his remedies for unrest were far from extreme.[63] He believed that it was probably to Britain's advantage to retain military and administrative command in India. Withdrawing prematurely would 'degrade our national life with a cowardly sense of failure'. It would open the way for other powers, notably Russia, Germany and Japan. India would be far worse off under the Russian Empire. Henry suggested to Sister Nivedita that Russia could walk through India if Britain withdrew suddenly. Incandescent, she 'took me for the enemy . . . as though I had said I wished to keep India enslaved for ever, & it was rather painful'.

Henry particularly objected to educated Indians being treated with 'an habitual contumely'.[64] He laid great store by the influence of what he called the 'English feeling for justice'. He did not identify himself with Asquith's Liberal Party but still espoused the values of a radical Liberal and argued that it was to the Liberal Party that India should appeal for the advancement of her rights.[65] At a Caxton Hall reception to welcome Hardie home from his world tour, Henry argued that the danger for Britain was neither India nor sedition, or even loss of empire, so much as the potential loss of liberty and justice.

But 'Till India is sufficiently advanced in arms, unity & knowledge to hold her own' it was 'probably to our advantage to retain it' as well as being for the good of the country and its people. In also arguing that the new spirit should not be ignored, Henry was placing a particular gloss on the term. He was not so much implying its usual association with indigenous unrest as suggesting that civilizing, beneficent influences were pointing towards a rebirth, influences that could, in large part, be attributed to British rule.

Henry represented the Curzon era and recent suppression of personal liberty and freedom of speech as cutting across what was otherwise a broadly sensible evolutionary policy towards India. For example, excluding fully qualified Indians from public positions was retrogressive, out of line with the policy espoused in Victoria's 1858 Proclamation for India, which had talked about the obligations of duty. Racism was an abrogation of the tact and sensitivity required for governing. There is a hint of the parent–teenager relationship, with its implication that the parent ultimately knows best and the gradual emergence of an adult modelled upon the values of those who have provided unobtrusive, yet clear, guidelines. Critical of British bureaucracy and warning that it should neither ignore nor stifle the new spirit, it was assumed that guidance was still needed.

As for the future, Henry compared the tempting line of most resistance with the line of less resistance. The latter was 'probably the way of wisdom'. Such a course required 'sweet reasonableness'. He drew attention to Lajpat Rai, still a Moderate despite 'the outrage upon his own freedom and the very basis of our liberties'. He brought together the elements of Congress politics that Henry admired: he had made personal sacrifices yet retained wise moderation and dignity. Henry and other British radicals may have admired the Extremists' sentiments but could not empathize with their distinctly non-Western methods such as caste boycotts. Henry respected Tilak as a symbolic rebel but he was disturbed to hear that he was alleged to have campaigned against mandatory government-sponsored inoculation against plague and worried that Tilak's messages to his supporters were not the same as those he received.[66] Surat helped shift his thinking further.

Henry's conclusion outlined his plan for change.[67] Bengal should be restored as a province, a presidency under one governor with residence in both Calcutta and Dacca. There should be at least one Indian on each of the executive councils and an enlargement of the Viceroy's and other legislative councils by changes in their voting system. Half of their members should be elected. Police reform was needed and an expansion of primary education crucial. Remedial measures must be accompanied by fundamental shifts in attitude: 'a change that would transform our people's arrogance towards natives'. But, Henry warned, the crisis was too acute for a change of heart to occur of its own accord:

> Upon our immediate action will depend the terms under which we must maintain our position in India: whether we are to hold the new spirit fairly on our side, and to co-operate with it for the progress of the country in enlightenment and self-government; or whether we are to have our rule confronted by impenetrable resentment, and our best efforts thwarted by indifference or suspicion.[68]

Unrest held out 'a promise of the highest possibilities'.

This alignment with the Moderates and emphasis on Britain retaining, for the time being, the ultimate supremacy in government and war, albeit with a reforming, modernizing and sensitive touch, does not sit easily with the image of Henry Nevinson, fighter for freedom. Henry had a track record in supporting nationalist claims and described Aurobindo Ghose, 'the man who inspired official circles with the greatest alarm', as someone 'to whom I was most naturally attracted'.[69] In his valedictory 'Farewell to India' he had asked whether a more inspiring and significant name than Moderate might be found for a party with 'so many of the noblest, wisest, and most self-devoted leaders' in India.[70] Yet, although a name change might have saved Henry's radical reputation, it would hardly have solved the complex divisions *and* links between parties, let alone the cultural distance of the British from Indian politicians and their methods.

The final words in Henry's book are about freedom though not in the way Indian Extremists would have conceived it. Britain, known for a love of freedom, is exhorted to welcome in India the spirit of freedom and nationality 'which we have done so much to create' and to have the strength to 'advance with it hand-in-hand for the furtherance of India's welfare as a self-respecting country'. If, however, suppression were to deteriorate still further into persecution, atrocities would follow.

Henry's book opts for the gradualism of Gokhale and the Moderates, the conclusion appearing less radical than the earlier image he had cultivated.[71] His diary had referred to the 'endless whimpering' of the Moderate leaders after Surat. Attending a dinner in his honour at Lahore in January 1908 he had spoken of 'my bent to Extremism & its dangers & signs of awakened nationality & unity in Asia'. Critical of a culture of deference, he had 'astonished & hurt' the college principal Aswini Kumar Dutt by suggesting that he should have refused to obey the Governor-General when he bullied Dutt and his companions into withdrawing their Swadeshi appeal to the villages. Henry told the Indian press that the people were 'always too much inclined to submit to insolence with reverential astonishment'.[72] Those who grew up in the heyday of the British Empire found it difficult to resist giving advice.

The cautious tone of Henry's conclusion needs contextualizing. Henry was well aware that it might not be appropriate or wise to repeat in print what was uttered in the heady atmosphere of a meeting. There was also a distinction between the demands on a correspondent sending copy home for a newspaper and the less ephemeral, more personal situation of composing a book for posterity. Henry's audience in India had been those whose present and future he was discussing. The mapping of imperial Indian society in his newspaper articles emanated directly from the country itself whereas the book, though largely drawing upon these articles, was written in Hampstead and north Wales. It was primarily aimed at British readers even though Henry wanted Indians to appreciate it. Whereas in India the rebel rouser had been attracted to the Extremists (though not always their non-Western methods), in the longer term the more familiar politics of the Moderates prevailed in his thinking. Most importantly, the book's sentiments were geared to the political climate of 1908. It needs reading as a deliberate strategy in response to proposed government reforms.

When Henry was writing his book, Morley was developing a scheme of reforms for India. Reforms had been mooted since mid-1906 but the new Indian Councils Act was passed in 1908. Morley appears to have been the driving force behind what are called the Morley–Minto reforms even though they were announced in Calcutta and Minto claimed them as his own.[73] Behind the scenes stood Gokhale. He had come to London in the spring of 1906 and had lengthy discussions with Morley who appreciated the vivid manner in which he presented India's problems.

On 10 May 1908 Henry joined other pro-Indians and Indians at Charing Cross to welcome Gokhale back to London. The next day he worked on his book. Over the following weeks he held meetings with Gokhale who told Henry that he had heard 'hopeful things' about Morley but feared as to his power. He thought 'the violent party' could not now be checked but would 'run on for some years'. In September he gave Henry 'very secret & important' information. Yet this seasoned politician would have had his own reasons for 'confiding' in a British journalist, even one he respected. He told Henry that Morley looked set to present a 'great scheme of reforms': an Indian majority on legislative councils, local government without officialdom, Indian members on executive councils and even a modification of partition and release of Tilak. Change indeed was imminent, though Tilak, imprisoned for sedition since July, would not be released until 1914. Yet, despite the changing climate, Gokhale was not sanguine about the prospects for peace, fearing, as Henry put it, that nothing would now stop violence among young Bengalis such as Aurobindo Ghose 'because they love to die for their country'.

That final warning in Henry's book therefore needs to be read in the light of Gokhale's influence, particularly his presence in London in May for delicate reform negotiations with Morley and the India Office. The element of political expediency is revealed in a letter Henry wrote to Gokhale: 'I agree with you that we must support Morley's reforms for all they are worth – for even more than they are worth perhaps.'[74] Despite the growing constitutional crisis over the House of Lords and Henry's antipathy towards Asquith, he wanted the government to cling to office so that Indian reforms were not jeopardized.

Sir William Wedderburn praised the book and its author:

For the last ten years and more, in regions wild and remote, in South and Central Africa, in Georgia, Macedonia, and the Caucasus, wherever there has been a storm centre, a struggle for freedom, or oppression of the weak by the strong, there has Mr. Nevinson been found, a recording witness of the truth – calm, open-minded, and fearless.[75]

Not all, of course, saw Henry as 'open-minded'. Neither was he without criticism from Indians. Virendranath Chattopadhyaya (Chatto), who became one of the most important leaders of the Indian independence movement in Europe, acknowledged that it was 'excellent and thoughtful'. But, Chatto argued, there was a newer spirit than the one he outlined. Henry's new spirit merely asked for more freedom and self-government along colonial lines. The newer spirit 'does not think of asking for anything'. Mendicancy should be replaced by self-reliance. Absolute severance was demanded: an unqualified 'libertas' in place of 'imperium'. Henry's concept of a new spirit might be a bridge but the newer spirit did not *ask* for a book but sought 'to write its own eventful chapters in the pages of history'.[76]

Nevertheless, Henry provided the standard British account of the historic Surat Congress. As recently as 1988 it was described as 'one of the best pieces of contemporary writing on this important period in India's political development'.[77] As for his suggestions for reform, the 1909 legislation did reinstate Bengal as a united province. There were also modest political changes. The number of Indians eligible for election to legislative bodies was slightly increased and budgets and other matters could be questioned. The official majority in the provincial legislatures was abandoned and most non-official members were to be elected either directly or indirectly through recognized interest groups. The end of Henry's book is best understood in the light of the negotiations leading to these changes.

Yet, despite this cautious tone, Henry was irrevocably linked with troublemakers. In November 1908 a Royal Proclamation marked the fiftieth anniversary of the Crown's direct assumption of control over India. Morley told Minto that it was received with much approval 'though Mr. Nevinson and one or two others of that breed, have dropped a little peevish criticism'.[78]

Henry sustained his interest in Indian affairs for the rest of his life. Aged eighty-four he wrote a sketch of Gokhale that was translated into Hindustani and broadcast in India.[79] He also became acquainted with a new generation of Indian leaders. In Allahabad he had been the guest of Motilal Nehru. In 1936 Henry provided supper at home for his son, India's future Prime Minister. He described Jawaharlal Nehru as gentle and highly educated. He avoided talking about politics but spoke of his love of animals.[80] Another gentle man was the poet and philosopher Rabindranath Tagore, whom Henry first met in London in 1912, the year before he won the Nobel Prize. Returning to London nine years later, Tagore wrote that 'one of the finest men' he had met in England was H. W. Nevinson: 'I felt that man's soul was alive in this country, which had produced such a man as that!'[81] Henry Nevinson may not have impressed Minto and Morley but he did make an impact on influential Indians. His 'eloquence' alarmed but it also charmed.

CHAPTER SEVEN

From the Balkans to World War

Henry was in Germany when the First World War began. Archduke Franz Ferdinand, heir to the Austro-Hungarian Empire, and his wife, the Duchess of Hohenberg, had been assassinated at Sarajevo on 28 June 1914. When Austria declared war on Serbia, the *Daily News* wanted Henry to go to Vienna. He demurred, arguing that he was unlikely to be able to get there and that the place to be was Berlin. So to Berlin he went on 31 July. Four days later, on 4 August, Evelyn's birthday, Britain went to war with Germany. What Henry called 'the flash of fire' from Bosnia followed his lengthy and intense, albeit intermittent, involvement in Balkan affairs. Looking at these years highlights the importance of this region to Henry. It also reminds us of its significance for modern Balkan and world history.

In August 1903, Henry had commented in his diary: 'Balkans blazing now'.[1] He saw Macedonia as 'the chief point of interest in European affairs'.[2] He badly wanted to be there and was prepared for 'a very small salary rather than miss it'.[3] But the papers did not seem interested. Opportunity came, however, through a different route. Henry was paid £180 to report on devastation in Macedonia for the new British-based Macedonian Relief Committee (MRC).[4] It was his first assignment independent of the press. Setting off on 18 October 1903, he wrote 'I start the world afresh again.'

It is usually at times of extreme crisis that Western Europe considers the Balkans. One such time was 1903, provoking intense debate from outside about what was best for these peoples of different races and religions. The Macedonian lands were, as Goldsworthy puts it, 'a microcosm of all the complexities of the Balkans', a toponymic delight.[5] Under Ottoman rule, Macedonia was divided into three 'vilâyets' (provinces): Salonica, Monastir and Kossovo (Kosovo). Neighbouring Greece, Serbia and Bulgaria had their own ambitions and plans for nationalizing, so watched them carefully. Rival Balkan nationalities set up organizations within Macedonia. The egregious Abdul Hamid II routinely persecuted its Christian inhabitants. Early in 1903 Russia and Austria intervened with plans for reform but Serbia rejected them. In August, the Macedonians, organized by the Internal Macedonian Revolutionary Committee, rose against the Turks. The rising lasted two months. Ruthless reprisals followed with massacres and villages destroyed. Over 4,500 civilians and almost 1,000 guerrillas died.

Russia and Austria introduced further reforms. They reminded Henry of benevolent uncles scrutinizing a wicked stepfather's treatment of his charges. Despite positive moves, including funds for rebuilding devastated villages, Ottoman power remained intact. Memories of the 'Bulgarian Atrocities' of Gladstone's era and Disraeli's restoration of Turkish rule in Macedonia in the 1878 Treaty of Berlin helped prompt British Liberals to form the Balkan Committee. The brainchild of Noel Buxton (whom Henry had met at the Playing Fields Association), it sought to publicize and influence British policy in the Balkans and to investigate the revolt against the Turks.[6] It attracted leading Anglicans and Nonconformists anxious about oppressed Christians, politicians, scholars and journalists. Buxton was chairman, James Bryce its president.[7] Henry was actively involved from September 1903. Membership of the MRC overlapped with the Balkan Committee.

By 21 October Henry was in Salonika (Thessaloniki) and 'all the sense & smell of the dear East is upon me'. It was here that he met Noel and Jane Brailsford who were relief agents for the MRC. Travelling together to Monastir (Bitola) they met the infamous Hussein Hilmi Pasha, the seemingly omnipotent Inspector-General, with 'the face of a tired but unflinching eagle'. Henry conceded that 'There was something attractive and even superb about the man' yet he came away 'without having gained anything at all'.[8] He then saw what Hilmi, ensconced in his official residence, never faced. In the mid-1920s, after witnessing many brutal scenes, Henry still felt 'a rage of pity and disgust' when recalling the burned-out villages and their inhabitants.[9] Leaving the Brailsfords he went south with the Englishman Henry B. Harris, an Austrian priest, Albanian interpreter and a cavalry escort. About 150 villages had been destroyed in Monastir province alone. Nearly 100,000 people were destitute. Henry visited nineteen ruined villages. Communities of 200–300 people had, at best, a handful of houses left standing. Some places were totally deserted. In others, people lived in makeshift straw huts. The Sultan's house-building grants (raised by forced 'gifts' from Christians) were meagre and spurned by many. Relief was a sham. 'So they stand, loitering among the skeletons of their homes or looking out upon the fields which they cannot cultivate.' Brigands levied taxes on Christian villages. Winter was imminent. Henry was told that 'It would be better for us to walk into the sea and drown.'[10]

And in the background were purple mountains, brilliant red maples and yellow poplars, the stunning beauty of the Balkan landscape. Yet 'I never saw people so unhappy and despairing.' It was not far, as the crow flies, from the terrain Henry covered in 1897. Back in Monastir (after his romantic encounter with Jane Brailsford in Ochrida[11]) society seemed 'absurdly over civilised & fatted'.

Once home, Henry wrote his MRC report, attended meetings and composed articles for the press. In a leader in the *Speaker* (its editor Hammond was a Balkan Committee member) he ridiculed Europe waiting 'in clownish stupidity' for reforms.[12] In line with Balkan Committee policy he urged 'the courage to follow where plain justice leads' and the appointment of a Christian governor responsible to the six Great Powers. He prophesied that, unless reform came soon, the bloodshed and anarchy of Macedonia would 'find their climax in a war, which may possibly lead to a European conflagration'. His long letter in *The Times* stressed the need for at least £1,000 per village.[13]

His main activity was as a fund-raising speaker. He undertook a punishing routine 'as though I had been a travelling circus or a theatrical company', lecturing on Macedonia all over England.[14] He even spoke from a church pulpit in Halifax. Always a strict timekeeper, he gave illustrated talks that lasted forty minutes. Henry tried not to rely on rhetoric but knew the value of a good anecdote. He retained a slight trace of a regional accent, spoke clearly and seems to have been effective.[15] At Cambridge he 'quite conquered a set of undergrads. who had gathered to obstruct'. A talk at Bolton garnered £200. In a few months Henry and other speakers raised just under £3,500 for the MRC. This helped his reputation as a champion of lost causes though he was taking an official line rather than his preferred independent radical voice and was a little uncomfortable with the evangelical tone of his colleagues.

In 1908 junior officers in the Ottoman Empire overthrew the despotic Sultan. They called themselves the Committee for Unity and Progress but became known as the Young Turks. Misha Glenny suggests that their emergence was as momentous as the Russian Revolution of 1917.[16] Henry initially gave them a cautious welcome but became increasingly concerned that policy had not shifted fundamentally, particularly among their nationalist wing. The desire to Ottomanize, if not exterminate, subject races had not abated, as the presence of 60,000 troops in Albania in the spring and summer of 1911 demonstrated. Since 1909 Albanian disturbances against the Ottoman Empire had flared into open rebellion. A new Albanian Committee of the MRC sent Henry to Albania for six weeks in August 1911. The rising of the mountaineers of northern Albania had been crushed and about 10,000 people were thought to be destitute. Henry was to help organize relief.

From the Adriatic port of Trieste where he arranged with the British consul for maize, blankets and tarred felt, Henry sailed down the Dalmatian coast. It was just what he loved: travelling in what had once been Roman Illyria, with a challenge ahead. In the *Nation* he mocked the well-fed tourists on the coastal steamers, declaring the distant mountains '*so* romantic'.[17] His destination was Turkish Scutari where he joined fellow English relief workers: a schoolmaster, an engineer and the traveller and ethnographer Edith Durham. Now forty-eight, Edith Durham had been based in Albania since 1904. In his autobiography Henry commented that it had been the misfortune of the Balkans that 'every English person who knows anything at all about them has adopted one or other of the Balkan races for a favourite pet'.[18] Denied statehood and a proper education system, Albanians were the least known of the Balkan peoples in pre-war Western Europe. And they lacked championship by a Great Power. But Edith Durham dedicated herself to them.[19] Like Gertrude Bell who helped shape Iraq in the 1920s and became much better known in Baghdad than England, she is best remembered in Albania where streets were named after her. By the time Henry joined her she was known as 'Kraljica e Malesorëvit' (Queen of the Mountain People). He basked in reflected glory as he accompanied her, telling the Central Asian Society in 1916 that he was sometimes called the King of Albania.[20] He later told BBC listeners how, during the war, the word 'Durham' prompted Albanian protection and hospitality.[21]

Henry and Marko Shantoya (Edith's sixty-year-old German-speaking Albanian guide) travelled into the northern mountains. Barely 200 miles long and little over 70 miles wide, Albania had no railway and its mountains made it difficult to cross. Two-thirds of Albanians were Muslims, though there were Orthodox Christians in the south close to Greece and some Roman Catholics in the Italian-influenced north. The Catholics were the most likely to attract British support so Henry went north: 'I crawled and climbed and plunged about among glorious mountains day after day.' He slept on the slope of a field, in a chieftain's makeshift shelter and, with a cartridge box for a pillow, in a priest's deserted house.

The Foreign Office suddenly imposed a temporary ban on writing about the area for the press: 'a crushing blow' for fund-raising.[22] But aid work continued. Henry and Edith rode up the gorge east of Scutari to the central mountains of Shala and coastal plain beyond. They found starving villagers eating grass and distributed woefully inadequate supplies of quinine to fever-ridden Drin peasants. Edith regaled Henry with ancient Serbian ballads. They heard belatedly that, following the invasion of Tripoli, Turkey had declared war on Italy. The Turkish officer who told them added prophetically that it was 'the beginning of the end'.[23]

Henry was impressed by Edith's ability to remain calm and cheerful. When Turkish officials arrested them, she reduced the police to laughter by using her hands to create shadow animals on the wall. After another week of organizing relief from Scutari, Henry left by boat from Croatia, spending his fifty-fifth birthday off the Dalmatian coast. He returned to Venice, 'the strangest & most beautiful city of time', last seen when he was a student. The Doge's Palace, familiar from childhood when a picture of it hung in his bedroom, 'gave me a sudden thrill like meeting an ancient acquaintance, a little shrunk & crumbled'.

Home once more, Henry drafted a financial appeal, attended meetings on Albania and wrote for the press.[24] To his surprise, Edith sent him love letters, suggesting a rather different image from the one usually portrayed by scholars. In amongst denunciations of Turks and suffragettes was 'I am yours to take – or leave.' Henry was bemused, admitting that he found this 'very strange, causeless & incredible'. They had inevitably been in close proximity in remote regions. Henry's diary describes them sleeping in the same room but at a distance from each other and fully clothed. Throughout their travels she is called Miss Durham in his diaries. Yet her letters called him 'Sweet love' and admitted how much she loved him. Their parting had been as 'terrible as death'. Henry asked himself what she could see in him: 'What is it then that this strange hard creature loves?'

Men and women regarded Edith Durham as eccentric. People commented on her short hair, lack of stays, sensible waterproof Burberry skirt and golf cape. Henry publicly praised her physical and moral bravery. In Albania he had discerned both her superb 'courage & wit' and 'the essential feminine' beneath this, 'not so deeply hidden as people think'. It was this perception which seems to have made the difference. Edith told Henry that he was 'the only person' who ever credited her with 'feelings'. Soon she was suggesting that they meet in Rome. In June 1912 Henry explored the city with her. Not surprisingly, when Edith died in 1944, Evelyn wrote that she had always found her difficult.[25] However, this 'beautiful interlude of Rome' was not free from past or present. Henry kept thinking about Nannie's Roman tour. And when Evelyn wrote with news that the suffragette leaders were going on hunger strike, Henry commented in his diary, 'All joy in this visit is over.' Suffrage and the Balkans took precedence over holidays.

Change was imminent in the Balkans. Encouraged by Russia, which envisaged a Balkan alliance as useful against the Hapsburgs, Montenegro, Serbia, Bulgaria and Greece created the Balkan League. Quite apart from the desire of the Great Powers to maintain stability, inherent rivalries between states and their own competing nationalist ambitions meant that the alliance was flimsy. But the opportunity to capitalize on the Ottoman Empire being diverted and weakened by war with Italy led to the First Balkan War beginning in October 1912. The two short but devastating wars in the Balkans in 1912–13 can be seen as 'the first phase of the First World War'.[26]

Just before the First Balkan War started, Henry was strategically placed in Bulgaria. He was reporting for both the *Manchester Guardian* and *Daily Chronicle* (receiving £16 weekly in peace and £100 monthly in wartime). He had slight misgivings about his age, health and suffrage commitments but could not resist 'the most difficult & insane of my adventures, except, perhaps, Angola'. In the novel *The Miracle* (1908) Bulgaria declares war on Turkey. Its author, the correspondent Arthur Moore, first secretary to the MRC, had woven Henry into the story as Henry Anderson, champion of the underdog and lover of Greek poetry. Unofficially connected with a legion of British volunteers, Anderson explores worlds 'which the city clerk could never hope to enter' and maintains that 'compromise is the curse of progress'. Yet, although the Turkish army was routed and 'the dawn of freedom flushed the skies', Anderson is bayoneted.[27]

Having read of his fictional death, Henry boarded the Orient Express for Sofia. The direct annexation of Bosnia-Herzegovina by Austria-Hungary in 1908 had prompted Bulgaria's formal declaration of independence from the Ottoman Empire. Troops were being mobilized in Bulgaria and Serbia. On 9 October 1912 Montenegro declared war on Turkey. On the same day Henry and two other journalists interviewed Prime Minister Gueshoff. He appealed for British aid. Henry watched battalions march to the front and feared the worst.

Bulgaria was teeming with European and American correspondents: 'We were the strangest menage, not to say menagerie, ever seen since Noah's ark.'[28] Henry met again Bennett Burleigh, Lionel James and Frederic Villiers, familiar from the South African War, as well as Philip Gibbs. A far cry from his Great War image, Gibbs looked the type 'who never has anything to eat and always loses his luggage'.[29] Towering above everybody in local knowledge and his contribution to the founding of the Balkan League was James Bourchier, the *Times* correspondent in the Balkans. Henry knew him through the Balkan Committee. Strict censorship made it difficult to get telegraphs and letters out. Henry was frustrated by the *Chronicle*'s requests for fuller, more personal copy, though he appeared to enjoy greater freedom of movement than did some correspondents. Evelyn wrote to tell him that Bone (of the *Guardian*) had said 'If anybody can get news through, it will be Nevinson.'

A few days after war was declared Henry was one of sixty-eight correspondents sent east to Stara Zagôra for a week whilst the Bulgarians scored the first of their major victories against Turkish troops. They were then taken to Mustapha Pasha on the Turkish frontier. For three weeks Henry camped in an empty, cold house 'raging and fuming like the wintry river itself' with Percival Phillips of the *Daily Express* and a German correspondent. It was difficult to get to the front though he rode out across battlefields in search of action. Wires were delayed but the *Chronicle* still clamoured for news. In the evenings the journalists met in a restaurant where the Italian Futurist, Filippo Tommaso Marinetti, bombarded them with exuberant lectures and 'performance poetry' on the Siege of Adrianople.

Henry and Phillips were suddenly recalled home because the *Daily Mail* was scooping all the war news via the *Reichspost*. This Viennese

Figure 10 Henry Nevinson in the Balkans, 1912.

paper was getting stories from its correspondent at the front, Lieutenant Wagner. *The Times* voiced doubts about the veracity of these reports and, when the two correspondents dutifully returned to Sofia en route home, they found Wagner in the Hotel Bulgarie. Henry did some detective work, checking the hotel's register and asking questions. The Foreign Office suggested that he should not take the issue 'so tragically' but he was determined to expose Wagner. C. P. Scott had told Henry, 'We shall always know the truth from you.'[30]

Henry composed 'The Complete Wagnerite or How To Succeed as a War Correspondent'. To be successful, you had to emancipate yourself from the 'common trammels of time and place', and settle down in the best hotel in town to glean information from a safe and comfortable distance.[31] This prompted the *Reichspost* to claim that Herr Nevinson was part of a Jewish press ring. Its rival translated a letter from Henry ridiculing such misguided attacks and denouncing anti-Semitism. The *Reichspost* sued. In 'The Lie in War' (*Daily Chronicle*) Henry argued that the very nature of war conspired against the telling of truth. Circumstances meant that 'Hardly any combatant knows what is going on.' Modern technology aided the creation of the fake story and photograph with censors, editors and the public colluding. He warned that 'Wars are not made for the glory of newspapers, as some correspondents vainly think. They are made for victory, in the hope of maintaining or advancing the destiny of nations.'[32]

December saw an armistice and a conference in London. The previous month Albania had become an independent state with its own provisional government. Early in 1913, signing himself 'A correspondent who knows Albania well', Henry argued in *The Economist* that it was 'the duty of all who have weight and influence to insist that the Balkan peninsula shall be freed from the risk of unlimited butcheries and plunderings'.[33] War was resumed in February. The fall of Adrianople (Edirne) to the Bulgarians in March cheered Henry but Scutari was taken by Montenegro a month later. Serbia's desire to secure a free port on the Adriatic now threatened the heart of Albania. Here, Henry felt, was the 'danger-point of Europe'.[34] He persuaded the *Chronicle* to let him return to Albania in early June.[35] The First Balkan War had just ended. The Treaty of London had not, however, been ratified and, provoked by the Bulgarians attacking Serb forces, another stage in the bitter, protracted conflict was about to begin.

When Henry reached Scutari (now administered by the Great Powers) he found Edith giving advice to British officers. He travelled south with her and a missionary to Muslim and Orthodox populations. Edith was, he wrote, 'better protection than a cavalry escort'.[36] They listened to both Bey and Archbishop. At Durazzo they saw bedraggled, starving Turkish soldiers making their escape, a far cry from the image of the fearsome Turk and a symbol of the Ottoman Empire's expulsion from its European territories. Ochrida, 'this most holy place', was full of Serbian troops. It was Kosovo Day, the anniversary of the fall of the Serbian Empire when the Turks had established a dominance that persisted for over five centuries. In Albanian Kóritza they discovered that the Second Balkan War had started, with Serbia and Greece pitted against Bulgaria, which was invaded from all sides. The consequences of Bulgaria's rapid swing from victory to defeat were immense. The failure of its Macedonian claims resulted in Bulgaria taking the side of the Central Powers in 1915 and occupying Macedonia in two world wars.

Kóritza was occupied by Greek troops. The Greek bishop announced that 'the Englishman' would address a public meeting in support of Greece's position. But Henry kept out of the way, using the excuse of Greenwich Mean Time to explain why he and Edith arrived too late for him to speak. He was no longer championing all things Greek, visits to Albania and commitment to small nations having shifted his perspectives. His partisan position was evident in his articles on Kóritza entitled

'A Greek City or a Nationalist?' They prompted a heated exchange of letters, Henry particularly resenting the Hon. W. Pember Reeves's depiction of it as 'the best frontier town of Hellenic civilisation on the edge of barbarous Albania'.[37] Henry chose to see Albania as a lamb among wolves. The leaders of the pack (Austria and Hungary) were carefully watching the smaller wolves (Greeks, Serbians and Montenegrins) so that they did not get there first and devour the lambs themselves.[38] Albania's reputation for savagery was, he stressed, based on ignorance and Byronic romance.

Accompanied by Greek soldiers, Henry and Edith rode with a caravan of mules into the mountains. Leaving them behind at dawn, they rode on, camping in fir woods before telegraphing the Foreign Office from Berat. Edith's later account of this episode is rather more dramatic than Henry's:

> Along with Mr. H. W. Nevinson (the famous war correspondent) I rode three days over the mountains arriving at Berat early in the morning, and drafted a telegram to the Council of Ambassadors in London as a petition from the inhabitants of Korcha [Kóritza] saying they wished to remain Albanian and Korcha remains Albanian to this day as a result of that desperate ride.[39]

At Avlona (Vlonë), the new capital of Albania, they were received by the council of ministers and met the self-appointed president. Then they sailed north on a coastal steamer transporting asphalt for a French company. On his way home Henry stayed in Spalato (Split). This prompted a historical fantasy (with a little help from the eighteenth-century historian Edward Gibbon) centred on Diocletian's time.[40] Henry reached home on 17 July.

The following month the treaty of Bucharest handed most of Macedonia and all of Kosovo to Serbia, stoking internecine conflict. The Balkan Wars had exacerbated Austro-Hungarian hostility towards Montenegro and Serbia. They set in train conflict that created the preconditions for war on an unimagined scale, helping set the scene for the nationalist conflict which resurfaced at the end of the twentieth century. Just one year after the Second Balkan War ended, the First World War began.

From Berlin on 4 August 1914, Henry wrote in his diary: 'So the terrible end comes.' He had seen crowds gather in the streets singing patriotic songs. Turned out of the Hotel Bristol, he moved to the Adlon. After dining there alone he heard cries for the English correspondents to be brought out. The police arrived and, with two revolvers pressed to his head, Henry was dragged out through the back door as the crowd tried to break the windows. He and a Dutch journalist were taken by taxi to a police court, given official papers and then returned to the hotel. The correspondents, including Bill Deedes's uncle, Sir Wyndham Deedes, were invited to stay at the British Embassy. The Kaiser had given orders for Sir Edward Goschen and his staff to be taken to a station outside Berlin. The correspondents tagged along, escaping by train through northern Germany to Holland.

The *Daily News* now wanted Henry to accompany the British Expeditionary Force (BEF) and asked him to be ready to leave. He was. But nothing happened. When he visited the War Office he was informed that he and the other eleven correspondents on their official register would be sent out in a small party, each with limited baggage, a servant and a horse (replaced the following month by a motor car). But three days later Henry discovered that Kitchener had 'stamped on all correspondents & crushed our expedition'. So they 'took to running across to France and Flanders at the risk of being imprisoned or shot as spies'.[41]

Accredited war correspondents were not introduced to the Western Front until May 1915. At the end of July 1914 the press agreed with the War Office and Admiralty to a *voluntary* code of censorship about the reporting of troops and shipping which might threaten national security. The day after war was declared, H. H. Kitchener, First Earl of Khartoum, had been appointed Secretary of State for War and head of the War Office. His service in the Sudan and South Africa had shown that he was no friend of correspondents, whom he saw as thorns in the flesh of the military. Originating news in wartime was mainly the latter's responsibility. The government had already taken over by proclamation the network of telegraph, cable and wireless communications. On 7 August, at Churchill's instigation, the Press Bureau was created. Farrar argues that its creation eliminated the need for war correspondents at the front, its prime aim being 'to limit the power of the meddling war correspondent and provide the newspapers with a distraction'.[42] The press was also subject to DORA, approved by Parliament five days later.

Yet although the Press Bureau issued newspapers with directives on all aspects of the war, they were not forced to obey them and collectively were too powerful for government to control fully or repress.[43] But this was not how it must have seemed to correspondents like Henry who were as wary of Kitchener as he was of them. As hard news became increasingly scarce due to the very conditions of war, war correspondents could cast themselves as champions of freedom and heap blame on censorship. They were, however, at the mercy of editors' decisions and there were examples of papers publishing information voluntarily suppressed by others. In his diary Henry complained that the Bureau favoured *The Times* and the *Daily Mail*.

From 9 August the BEF was landing at Le Havre, Rouen and Boulogne. Although these movements were secret, rumours abounded. On 18 August it was announced that they were in positions in France. The following day Henry crossed to Boulogne and visited the St Martin and Marlborough camps, but three days later his paper instructed him to return immediately. He was impatient to see action. By early September he was complaining that all the other correspondents seemed to be 'waltzing about' close to Compiègne and the Somme whilst 'I sit, unknown & idle'! It was small compensation overseeing drill for the Women's Emergency Corps in a London warehouse.

He voiced his frustration in the *Nation*, accepting the BEF's initial need for secrecy but arguing that 'It seems a pity not to use us just because we are supposed to be good.' It was:

> Absolutely impossible to imagine men of this experience and quality giving away our country or making dangerous revelations or mistakes, even if they stood under no regulations at all. They simply would not do it. They would die rather. Everything is ready, and yet we are kept chafing here, week after week, while a war for the destiny of the world is being fought within a day's journey and others of our colleagues are allowed to go dashing about France in motors, almost up to the very front.[44]

Henry's own experience and age meant that fellow correspondents saw him as a senior figure. He and a few others, including the Ladysmith veteran Donohoe and Ashmead-Bartlett (*Daily Telegraph*), wrote to Kitchener demanding information and a departure date. In mid-October Henry went to Calais, travelling home a couple of days later with refugees. Such journeys were dangerous and not necessarily productive. Henry's ensuing article betrayed, he believed, no more about 'our position' than had the *Times* correspondent. But the censor thought otherwise.

On 20 October the Germans launched their offensive against Ypres (Ieper). For just over a month a series of engagements took place known as the First Battle of Ypres. The British army suffered a dramatic increase in casualties but the result was stalemate. Henry returned to Calais the day after the offensive began: 'the whole place swarms with correspondents & photographers'. He and Geoffrey Young, mountaineer and former master at Eton, moved into Belgium and visited Furnes where, in a priest's college, was a British hospital with a mobile column attached for fieldwork, run by the Scot Dr Hector Munro. Gibbs and Ashmead-Bartlett were based here. Henry accompanied an ambulance cart to Dixmude. It looked as though an earthquake had hit it. He and Lady Dorothy Feilding, one of four women in Munro's team and the first Englishwoman to win the Military Medal, helped take the wounded to hospital. The following day Henry went by ambulance to Nieuport. Its esplanade was strewn with bodies and 'by day and night the thunder of imminent destruction never ceased'.[45] Returning home, he wrote on the 'Realities of War'. But British editors were reluctant to portray war 'as it really is and always must be'. His account was deemed 'too horrible' for people to bear.[46]

Henry's son was now in his mid-twenties and making a name for himself in the London art world. Rheumatic fever had left Richard with a limp so he was not a prime candidate for active service. At the end of October Henry wrote to Munro, suggesting that father and son join him. The next day Henry got the chance to join a Quaker ambulance unit. In charge was the future Labour politician Philip Noel-Baker. Even crossing the Channel was dramatic. They rescued a torpedoed cruiser, the *Hermes*, saving most of the men. At Dunkirk they found about 3,000 wounded men, largely French and Belgians, tended by just a handful of helpers. Working in two long railway sheds beside the quay, nicknamed The Shambles, they lifted men on to stretchers to be taken by ambulance to a hospital ship.

Henry returned there in mid-November with Richard, who had done a short course at home in motor engineering. German prisoners lay on straw with 'suppurating, stinking and gangrened wounds'.[47] French and Belgian surgeons apparently spurned them and threatened to get the Quakers sent home. Henry was able to speak to the prisoners in German. Richard dressed the prisoners' wounds 'with some success' but his ambulance driving skills proved less impressive. Henry negotiated with the British consul to use an empty hotel at Malo-les-Bains as the unit's new headquarters. During the search for somewhere suitable, a few of them took an ambulance to Ypres. The 7th Division had been wiped out and whole battalions reduced to pitiful numbers. At dawn Henry glimpsed the beautiful walled city, so famed for its medieval cloth trade. Suddenly, huge shells crashed into the Gothic Halle des Drapiers and former Cathedral. In the midst of chaos:

> A random battalion, made up of mixed and scattered details, came marching through the south end of the square, singing 'Tipperary' as they came. I went with them out beyond the ancient walls and the moat that Marlborough knew, until we came to the batteries trying to conceal themselves among the trees. Forward along the road . . . that confused little body of Englishmen advanced, straight towards the line of smoke and fire – *morituri*. It was the saddest sight I have known – that early morning of November 3rd. The 'Ypres Salient' was being formed.[48]

In an unattributed middle, Henry suggested that the attack on Ypres saw the end of the Middle Ages, the 'War-God's broom' sweeping away the 'sweet, long-last enchantments'.[49] A speech by the French ambassador in London provided the text for another middle: 'In this murderous war . . . we remain true to our ideals of humanity and freedom.'[50] 'This Murderous War' begins innocently, evoking Flemish countryside, sluggish streams and a copse brilliant with autumnal colours. Then comes the contrast: 'The whole landscape is prettily wooded and that makes war more murderous.' Every paragraph ends with a bitter refrain, bombarding the reader with the fact that 'the thunder of cannon never stops'.

At the end of November Henry learned that Sir John French, Commander-in-Chief of the BEF, planned to send four correspondents to Ypres and Verdun for about ten days. Henry was to report for the *Daily News* in the next batch. He consoled himself by protesting about restrictions on freedom at home. He complained to the press about the 'shameful' case of prostitutes court-martialled in Cardiff for breaking the 7 p.m. curfew and opposed the suggestion that the separation allowances of soldiers' wives be monitored due to their increased frequenting of public houses. Returning to Dunkirk before Christmas, he delivered supplies to villages to the accompaniment of guns.

In the New Year the French general staff invited an international group of correspondents (British, American, Russian, Spanish and Romanian) to visit recent scenes of battle. Conducted by French officers, they travelled by train along the valley of the Marne and on to Nancy, and then motored up the Moselle valley. Given the honorary status of captains, they wore officers' uniforms with green armbands. The front-page headline in the *Daily News* of 29 January was 'On the German Frontier: Special Dispatches by H. W. Nevinson'. Henry began by describing the defeat of the barbarians near Nancy in the fourth century. Unlike Herr Wagner, time and place mattered dearly to him, though here he was using the past partly to circumvent the lack of eyewitness reportage. He told how, just across the river, Germans were waiting. It seemed deceptively calm. Luneville had been occupied in August when the Germans sought to cut their way into France just south of Nancy but then met a violent counterattack by the French, deflecting their attention to Nancy itself. After the fighting for the low hills known as the Coronet of Nancy, the German forces had withdrawn on 12 September. Henry's account of this action was retrospective though the devastation it had wrought remained and he declared it just as bad as the scenes he had witnessed in Macedonia and Albania. He also wrote about a French bayonet charge in fog and the capture of a position held by the Germans. Towards the end of the article he admitted that this had taken place almost five months earlier but so powerful is the writing (and the exact place names are only revealed at the end) that it reads as though he were with the brigade.

In January Henry was delighted to be dubbed 'the King of Correspondents' by his colleagues at a dinner in Paris. It was a sobriquet that stuck.[51] But it was only in March that he got to France courtesy of the War Office. His front-page article in the *Daily News* on 13 March announced 'With the British Army At Last'. Henry and three other correspondents were quartered at the General Headquarters at St Omer for just over a week, accompanied by officers. They travelled round the

French and Flemish country, attended lectures on mapping, discipline and munitions and visited a cadet school for officers. They were shown how war was organized and administered rather than how it was fought. Henry described the vast machinery that made fighting possible: how the army was fed and supplied, and the use of bathing factories and convalescence hospitals by the Royal Army Medical Corps (RAMC). But, although he did not wish to act the old war-horse and 'neigh lamentably over days that do not return', it was witnessing action and conveying the immediacy of this to readers that appealed. A writer was unlikely to be able to describe 'a Waterloo'. But, if he could make a reader now, or in the future, appreciate 'what was the truth of struggling for a bit of trench or storming a village street in the flat lands of North-East France', then 'he might perhaps have done some service'. For Henry, the devil lay in the detail.

On 10 March he recorded that guns were firing from the Neuve Chapelle district. He heard, but did not go near, the Battle of Neuve Chapelle. The bombardment had started early in the morning, taking the Germans by surprise. Victory came with a heavy price: more than 11,500 British men were killed, wounded, missing in action or taken prisoner and there were over 8,500 German casualties. Had there not been such serious action during this visit, the correspondents might have seen more. They had been told that they could not be near the front because motor cars on the road might delay the transportation of reinforcements for the firing line. Henry penned an article 'but heard at night it was cut to pieces'. This was a different world from the one in which war correspondents were *encouraged* 'to ride as hard as possible to the sound of guns'.[52] Now it was implied that they might impede developments. Pointedly polite – usually a signal of sarcasm – Henry wrote about their courteous welcome, adding that they would have liked 'to live with the army rather than pay a call or visit as a guest'.

In the 1920s Harold Spender reminisced about older war correspondents. He believed that they could not adapt to the new press restriction:

> Men like Nevinson were not going to go out to a field of war and find themselves shepherded by day and night, placed under the control of some military martinet ignorant of Press conditions, allowed to see fighting only by sufferance, and in place of sight and hearing compelled to fall back on the reports of wounded men and prisoners.[53]

Refusing to consent to these restrictions, they took 'the high view' that, unless the press was allowed 'at the seat of war as a real critic and spokesman of the public', it would be preferable not to be there. And so 'most of these men came home', younger men taking their place. In fact, some younger men were also unhappy with the situation. Gibbs, who was with the military staff and missing the action, wrote 'It was hard to have seen nothing so near the front . . . It would be good to see real business again and to thrill once more to the awful music of the guns.'[54] Spender's remarks implied more choice in the matter than was the case. And although Henry protested vociferously, censorship was hardly new to him.

He was, though, old for this job. In May 1915, when Gibbs and four other correspondents were finally selected as official war correspondents, Henry was fifty-eight.[55] In the eyes of the authorities, the chosen men (who initially included the novelist John Buchan) were more likely to be amenable to censorship rules than seasoned rebels like Henry. Indeed, Gibbs and his carefully selected colleagues had their loyalty and service rewarded after the war with the French Chevalier of the Legion of Honour and British knighthoods. Spender's account is also misleading because Henry's war was not over: far from it.

Five weeks after Henry's visit to St Omer, on 22 April 1915 the Second Battle of Ypres saw the first use of lethal poison gas.[56] Algerian soldiers were the most affected. Although banned by the 1907 Hague Convention, it became part of modern warfare. The British began using it at Loos in September. Henry wrote about some of the 'scientific contraptions by which death is now secured'.[57] War, he stated, was the killing of foreigners, sanctioned by the state. Writing in the third person in the *Nation*, he charted the change in the Berlin crowd once war was declared and 'the mania of the mob', suddenly seeing the Englishman as a spy.[58] 'Spy-Mania', whether abroad or attacking a German pork butcher long settled in Deptford, was 'the subtlest and most contagious of epidemics', feeding on xenophobia. In the mid-1920s he would denounce the official propaganda of the Great War and the 'cunningly invented and gluttonously swallowed' stories of atrocities by the Huns.[59]

Henry was troubled by the surge in 'patriot slush' on the outbreak of war and refused to join the writers' manifesto in favour of the war signed by fifty-three authors, including friends like Zangwill. It stated that, with Belgium in dire need, Britain had to fight rather than let 'the rights of small nations count for nothing before the threat of naked force'. Henry saw this as hypocritical given the blatant disregard of small nations like Persia and Finland. And as a suffragist he protested that 'it's no good pretending to champion liberty when half our population is excluded from it'. Long gone was his belief in the efficacy of national service. In 1911 he had delivered the Conway Memorial Lecture at South Place Institute, chaired by Hobson. Entitled 'Peace and War in the Balance', he had called the refusal of the Catalan reservists to fight in Morocco in 1909 'the greatest gain ever yet won for the cause of peace'[60] and speculated on the possible consequences of the working classes refusing to fight wars. How would they then be manned? An army recruited from 'kings, lords, Cabinet Ministers, Members of Parliament, speculators, contractors, and officials – the people who are the primary originators of our wars' would have considerable advantages, not least from the compensations provided from losses in battle!

When military conscription for single men began in January 1916, Henry denounced this 'new despotism', criticized the treatment of conscientious objectors (COs) and examined the tension between compulsion and conscience.[61] At one meeting of the No-Conscription Fellowship, formed by young men of military age, he controversially drew parallels between the treatment of COs by the military and of suffragettes by the civil authorities. He expressed his views in the press and spoke at the Parliamentary Committee on the treatment of COs. He attended the funeral of a Durham miner who had refused to serve and then died in prison from pneumonia. In 1916 Richard was refused a passport for Spain on the grounds that his father was presumed to be a CO. An indignant Henry rushed to the Passport Office to stress that his son was not responsible for his father's opinions. Nor were they, he explained, COs.

Henry's sentiments were allied to hatred of both officialdom and restrictions on freedom. He warned that liberties were being eroded under the plea of patriotism and efficiency and that 'all the old battles for freedom will have to be fought again lest officers and the police became the country's real governors'.[62] Influenced a little by the Quakers but rather more by Evelyn's opposition to war, Henry had become a passionate opponent of militarism. When he and Lansbury were labelled pacifists by the press, Central Hall, Westminster cancelled their 'Welcome' meeting hosted by the Daily Herald League, and another venue had to be found. Henry explained to a confused critic:

> I sh. [sic] have thought Christ a pacifist if episcopal authority were not against me; but certainly I was not. Experience of wars had taught me how hideous war is, & I longed all sane men to see this end, but no definition of pacifist applied to me, except in vague abuse or disagreement.

Yet even mild criticism of war seemed audacious when it emanated from a man whose very business was war. And because he was 'in the know', Henry was aware that his words attracted attention. At a time when, apart from serving in the forces, most people spent their lives in their own locality and foreign travel, let alone internationalist outlooks, seemed alien, he was aware just how important and problematic was the war correspondent's role:

> It seems to be a mental law that the power of imagination, like the sense of fear, varies inversely with the distance. The greater the distance, the less the imaginative interest in an event, and the slaughter of half a million Asiatics excites less feeling than a suicide at the back door.[63]

He wanted to make people at home appreciate the 'true hideousness' of war.[64] After addressing 200 soldiers in Sussex, some told him they wanted to resign: 'the horror was so brought home to them'. Accused of being unsparing, he replied 'any horror is better than allowing the nation to regard it [war] as "great sport" and "a splendid time"'.[65]

Henry and Richard Nevinson now appeared to be converging in their messages to the public about war, albeit through different media. War helped sustain both men. Before the war the complicated, symbiotic relationship between father and son had manifested itself in different ways. In creating C. R. W. Nevinson, Richard forged his own name and identity. Yet his father knew important figures in the art world, men such as William Rothenstein (who made several drawings of Henry), Frank Rutter and Muirhead Bone. They helped promote Richard's work. In today's parlance, Henry networked for all it was worth. He may have disapproved of the false hope generated when he discovered that Margaret was behind the sale of Richard's first painting but he was not averse to subterfuge to ensure that his son's work was displayed and publicized.[66] Richard was ambivalent about Henry's interventions. He desperately wanted to be fêted in his own right and (rather like Henry) loathed deference. One way of handling this was to disparage his father's values and to spurn, even as he sought, the connections they promised. In his autobiography Richard mentions trying journalism, diminishing his father's profession by adding that it 'seemed a great lark to me'.[67] Yet such bravado never quite rings true.

The Nevinsons are parodied in Gilbert Cannan's novel *Mendel: A Story of Youth* (1916).[68] Mendel, artistic son of Jewish immigrants, was based on the artist Mark Gertler, Richard's friend at the Slade School of Fine Art. Richard was Mitchell, full of 'frank conceit'. His father, 'that great man, a journalist who had been a correspondent in a dozen wars', was about to go to the Cocos Islands. He sought evidence of horrors abroad. His wife exposed them at home. They had 'a platform manner of speaking', blaming the government for all ills. Once it was removed, 'hey presto! Women would have votes, the slums would be pulled down, maternity would be endowed, prostitutes would be reformed, capital punishment abolished, the working classes properly housed.' Henry was furious. Yet, although misleading and cruel, it probably suggested something about how Richard was cast in his father's shadow.

Before the war Richard lived briefly in Paris and was influenced by Cubist and Futurist artists. But it was with the flamboyant Marinetti that his name became most closely linked. His parents met Marinetti first. Margaret reviewed his speech at London's Lyceum Club in 1910.[69] Henry was with him in Bulgaria. When Marinetti came to London a year later, he performed the Siege of Adrianople poem at a welcoming dinner organized by Richard and Wyndham Lewis. In May 1914, Marinetti dined at Downside Crescent. Henry found him 'quite tame &

sensible'. The following month, 'Vital English Art: A Futurist Manifesto', known as the English Futurist Manifesto, was issued jointly by Marinetti and Richard.

Marinetti's views cut across much that Henry held dear. He ridiculed Ruskin and rejected classical civilization and composers such as Beethoven whom Henry revered. He sought to replace contemplation with noise, and poetry as Henry knew and loved it with free verse. He called for the destruction of museums and libraries, opposed feminism and glorified war and militarism. Surely such a creed was anathema to Henry's sensibilities? It is a measure of Henry's support for his son that he wrote in favour of the Futurist claims. He also wished to cut across tradition for its own sake and recognized that this challenge helped to expose stultifying tendencies, the dead hand of the past and what should be obsolete. As a rebel, Henry empathized with elements of Marinetti's protest. So he focused on its novelty and excitement, either conveniently skirting over its more distasteful implications or subverting them to his own purpose. Since the Nevinson name was inextricably associated with the movement, Henry sought to make the message acceptable in order to help his son.

His 'Marinetti: Futurist' exposes the problems of the past by showing the importance of History for understanding the artist, thereby also implicitly undermining Marinetti's claims. Henry suggests that this Egyptian-born Italian lawyer's son, educated by Jesuits, was weighed down by History. He was 'born in the tomb of the world, the habitat of mummies, the ash-pit of seven thousand years, the home of unchanging arts which took twenty dynasties to die . . . swaddled by the Law and the Church, [to] reach manhood in a museum'. Was it surprising that he rebelled?[70]

Henry conceded that Marinetti's message was violent and insolent but understood that his audacity, imagination and *élan de vie* appealed.[71] And although he gradually distanced himself from Marinetti's sentiments, he acknowledged that his Siege poem captured the essence of war. Describing this, Henry created in turn one of *his* most powerful descriptions of what war was all about:

> The noise, the confusion, the surprise of death, the terror and courage, the grandeur and appalling littleness, the doom and chance, the shouting, curses, blood, stink, and agony – all were combined into one great emotion by that amazing succession of words, performed or enacted by the poet . . . Suddenly, the air full of the shriek and boom of bullets and shells; hammering of machine-guns, shouting of captains, crash of approaching cannon. And all the time one felt the deadly microbes crawling in the suppurating wounds, devouring the flesh, undermining the thin walls of the entrails. One felt the infinitely little, the pestilence that walks in darkness, at work

in the midst of gigantic turmoil, *making history* [my emphasis].That is the very essence of war. That is war's central emotion.[72]

The early years of the war were crucial in establishing Richard's fortunes and set in motion a shift in who was meant when the name Nevinson was uttered. By 1920 it was Nevinson junior who was most in demand. At an exhibition of Richard's work four women asked Henry if he were *the* Nevinson: 'one said she was glad I was not as she much preferred ordinary people'.[73] After becoming the chief nursing orderly at Malo-les-Bains, Richard had returned home early in 1915, purportedly for health reasons.[74] A month later 'Rich refused to return' to the Quaker unit. Their loss was art's gain. Richard's first war paintings had just been exhibited with the London Group at the Goupil Gallery. Richard's experiences were being translated into highly original depictions of the stultifying effects of war. From extolling modern machines, he had come to show how men were reduced to mechanical components, demonstrated in his depiction of French soldiers in *Returning to the Trenches*. As Richard Cork has argued, his new work, touched by the reality of warfare, displayed a sudden, startling maturity.[75]

Richard's reluctance to return to France was increased by his romance with the elegant garden designer Kathleen (Kas) Knowlman. Described, somewhat dismissively, by Henry as a 'sweet draper's daughter of Islington', her father had founded Knowlman Brothers, a department store in the Holloway Road.[76] On 1 November 1915 she married Richard. He was now an orderly with the RAMC at the Third London General Hospital. Immediately after his honeymoon Richard painted his 'breakthrough' picture, *La Mitrailleuse* (The Machine Gun).[77] Described by Sickert as 'the most authoritative and concentrated utterance of the war', it chillingly depicted gun and gunner as one.[78] First exhibited in March 1916, it was shown again in September at Richard's first, highly acclaimed one-man show at London's Leicester Galleries. An immensely proud Henry attended the opening, returning four more times. The usually reserved theatre critic William Archer alarmed himself and delighted Richard by weeping in public for the first time.[79]

As Walsh puts it, this exhibition 'made Richard's name as the painter of modern war, or, indeed the modern painter of war'.[80] Walsh also stresses that the credit for its organization and publicity should go to Henry for his hard work. It had been the idea of Henry's old friend Lewis Hind, and it was thanks to Henry that General Sir Ian Hamilton wrote the catalogue's Introduction. Henry had first met Hamilton in South Africa but it was their recent experiences in Gallipoli that bound them together. Here the challenges of war and writing were tested and melded for Henry once more in extreme circumstances.

CHAPTER EIGHT

From Our Own Correspondent

Gallipoli and the Western Front

It was in April 1915 that Henry was asked to go to the Dardanelles on behalf of the *Manchester Guardian* and other provincial newspapers.[1] The infamous landings took place in this month but it was not until July that he reached the Gallipoli peninsula. Dramatic episodes of bravery and tragedy were, however, by no means over.

The Commander-in-Chief, General Sir Ian Hamilton, had specifically requested Henry's presence. The War Office had just taken over the responsibility for correspondents from the Admiralty. The Director of Special Intelligence briefed Henry, Herbert Russell (Reuters) and Sydney Moseley (Central News and Exchange Telegraph). Russell and Moseley were initially wary of Henry, believing that he wished the campaign to be covered only by veterans like himself. Soon, however, Russell was 'hanging on to every word of Nevinson's'. Moseley was more cautious, seeing him as something of an intellectual snob but he conceded that he was 'a remarkably tough old egg. Hard as nails!'[2] In the event the younger men fell ill and returned home. Henry stayed on.

Departing on 4 July, Henry wrote in his diary that 'a new & final adventure starts'. Well aware of the risks, he told his old friend, the literary banker Edward Clodd, that 'a very stern dream begins for me again'.[3] On the way the correspondents passed the Aegean island of Skyros where Rupert Brooke had been buried in April. After attacks of dysentery, heat stroke and an insect bite on the lip, the poet had died of blood poisoning. In 1910, standing in for Massingham, the *Nation*'s editor, for a fortnight, Henry had accepted a poem by this young house-master at Rugby School. He later recalled Brooke, 'An astonishing apparition in any newspaper office', dressed in a blue shirt with a blue tie, with eyes 'really like the sky . . . the whole effect was almost ludi-crously beautiful'.[4] Brooke wanted to be Henry's 'servant' in the First Balkan War. In 1915 he was bound for the Dardanelles. His death was a reminder that climate killed as effectively as did the enemy.

Henry reached the mountainous island of Imbros (Gökçeada) on 12 July. Here Hamilton had his headquarters. Henry's book would cover the whole Dardanelles campaign. But he was present only for the latter part of the action, from mid-July until the beginning of October and for a few weeks in December, less than half of the period he examined.

The Dardanelles Straits link the Aegean Sea and the Sea of Marmara, a narrow passage of thirty miles or so and the main shipping route to the ports of southern Russia. This strategically significant waterway separates Europe from Asia. The slender peninsula on the European side of the straits known as Gallipoli (Gelibolu), after the town of the same name, was part of the Ottoman Empire, now in alliance with Germany. The story of the disastrous campaign to defeat the Turks[5] and relieve the pressure facing Russia in the Caucasus has been told many times. February 1915 had seen an ineffective British–French naval bombardment on the fortresses guarding the southern entrance to the straits, followed by an advance in mid-March with an armada of battleships. Turkish retaliation was much more effective than anticipated. On 18 March, the Turks won a significant naval victory. Allied plans now shifted to landing troops on the European side of the peninsula. An ambitious amphibious assault took place: the (in)famous landings of 25 April. There was a lack of intelligence about the Turkish situation – throughout, the discipline and spirit of the Turkish army were underestimated – and a shortage of troops and supplies.

Information about the extremely inhospitable and alien terrain was also crucially inadequate. The five divisions[6] of the Mediterranean Expeditionary Force were in an extremely hazardous position. There were severe natural deterrents. Coastal cliffs, raked like theatre seats, covered much of the seaward side of the peninsula. The 29th Division aimed for five narrow beaches at the southern tip at Cape Helles with the offshore fleet covering them. The Royal Naval Division and the French hoped to divert Turkish reinforcements by focusing on Bulair and on the Asiatic shore respectively. But the Turkish land army, having to face enemy army *and* navy together, had been busy digging trenches above all the threatened beaches. At Cape Helles, the British were exposed to Turkish artillery. At two of the beaches, only yards from the shore, Turkish rifle and machine guns caused devastation: 'never before in human history had troops assaulted a beach defended by the modern, quick-firing weapons of war'.[7] The sea turned crimson.

Australian and New Zealand troops touched ground about a mile north of their selected beach only to face climbing a succession of formidable ridges at what became known as Anzac (named after the Australian and New Zealand Army Corps). There was thick scrub and steep ravines. The Turkish counterattack and loss of life by Dominion troops created one of the most enduring tragic memories of the war. The deaths and defeat of men from six Australian states so far from home aided the making of a modern Australian nation, and Gallipoli became elided with Australia in popular memory.[8]

By early May the Anzacs alone had lost nearly 10,000 men and the British were only three miles beyond Cape Helles. This disastrous situation prompted the resignation of Lord Fisher, First Sea Lord, forced Churchill from the Admiralty and played a significant part in the creation of the coalition government. Yet when Henry arrived in July, the allies still had only a toe-hold on the peninsula, were deadlocked in static trench warfare and faced scorching heat and a water shortage. Nevertheless, as usual, his timing was propitious. For in the same month came the much-needed reinforcement of troops: 13th (Western) Division, 11th (Northern) and the 10th (Irish). Plans were being made for a new offensive.

Henry found some familiar faces. They included William Maxwell, formerly a correspondent at Ladysmith and the First Balkan War but now a censor. Ashmead-Bartlett was representing Fleet Street. He would emerge from his tent in a flowing robe of yellow silk shot with crimson and call for breakfast 'as though the Carlton were still his corporeal home'.[9] It proved to be pride before a fall. Yet Henry was not averse to luxury. The Australian correspondent C. E. W. Bean recorded one 'jolly good dinner' at camp where 'Nevinson insisted on my drinking some champagne & so did Bartlett.'[10] Henry also met the novelist Compton Mackenzie, his 'mind & eyes going full gallop'. He was with intelligence. They understood each other. Mackenzie's bedtime reading was a page or two of Homer or Thucydides. Whereas Ashmead-Bartlett showed 'contemptuous petulance' at having to sign a declaration accepting military regulations, Mackenzie noted that Henry displayed 'a courtliness of gesture that seemed to express his sense of the slight embarrassment I might be feeling at having to proffer such a superfluous document'.[11]

Pitching his tent at the new press camp in an olive grove inland from GHQ at Kephalos Bay, Henry rapidly secured a private interview with Hamilton. He then sailed across to Cape Helles at the tip of the peninsula. With him were the correspondents Malcolm Ross (a New Zealand mountaineer) and Bean, who was renowned for going to parts others never bothered to reach. They disembarked at the sandy bay code-named W Beach. The sacrifice of Lancashire Fusiliers there on 25 April had immortalized it as 'Lancashire Landing'. They witnessed the burying of some Scottish soldiers killed by Turks the previous night. The troops' objective remained the hill of Achi Baba, so near yet so far away, the ideal defensive position for the Turks. Wandering round the labyrinthine disused or reserve trenches, Henry and his companions were exposed to some desultory shelling but gun- and rifle-fire were persistent in the main trenches in the Helles sector. Henry dispatched a 600-word cable and a long letter for the paper. To his relief, the censor left it more or less intact. He and Bean also visited Anzac. The Antipodean soldier's physique, humour and lack of deference impressed Henry. Water was carefully rationed and an Australian soldier, asked by the British commander General Birdwood whether he was having a good clean-up, answered in the affirmative, adding 'and I only wish I was a bloody canary'.[12]

Henry was with the Anzacs on the night of 22–23 July. Spies had warned of a special attack in honour of the Young Turks' Constitution Day. That night not one Anzac went sick. In moonlight up on Walker's Ridge Henry lay on a 'nice flat parapet' behind some sandbags. Casual fire was followed at 2 a.m. by intense machine-gun and rifle-fire. From a gap in the parapet he glimpsed 'sharp tongues of flame flashing all along the edges, like a belt of jewels'.[13] But it ceased after fifteen minutes. There were virtually no casualties and Henry climbed back down the cliff to his seaside cavern. Back at Imbros a fortnight after leaving in England all that was 'dear to me except adventure', he wrote 'there is no place in the world I would rather be than in this dirty tent'.[14]

Critics of this campaign vary in apportioning blame, but whether singling out Hamilton for praise or derision, or attacking government prevarication, they have been equally passionate in attack. And despite claiming that, unlike the 'poetic vision' of his friend John Masefield, he was 'simply recording the events as they occurred',[15] Henry was just as wedded to a partial reading as his contemporaries and successors.

His conception of the campaign was linked to his love of Greek history and legends. For Henry, the Dardanelles spelt the ancient Hellespont. From the cliff above Cape Helles he could look across to the windy Trojan plain. With Byronic musing, he conjured up ancient scenes. Near the fortified promontory of Kum Kale, briefly occupied in April by the French, was a white, sandy shore where, for ten long years, the fleet of the invading Greeks had rested, that famous force of over a thousand. Influenced by tales of Achilles and Hector, Henry relished living vicariously *and* enjoyed telling readers that the straits were the site of Trojan war. Homer and heroes occupied his thoughts alongside the modern army.

Henry's story was laced with tragedy, ancient and modern. His book is dedicated to 'Those Who Fell On The Gallipoli Peninsula'. But two quotations follow from Thucydides (Pericles' funeral speech) and Aeschylus' *Agamemnon*: 'Beside the ruins of Troy they lie buried, these men so beautiful; there they have their burial-place, hidden in an enemy's land.' Churchill, the first British minister to focus on Gallipoli, had initially conceived of a Greek army seizing the peninsula so that a British fleet could reach the Sea of Marmara.[16]

The doomed sacrificial hero in Henry's tragic tale was Sir Ian Hamilton. He fulfilled Henry's personal criteria for bravery and admiration but was eventually recalled from the Dardanelles. He never again had a senior appointment.[17] At first sight he might seem an unlikely subject for Henry's admiration. Part of the ruling class with a military background and maternal links to the Anglo-Irish gentry, he appears neither radical nor underprivileged. Yet Henry saw him as a scapegoat for the failings of the British government. There were also many traits in his personality and career that appealed to him. They had first met in South Africa where both disliked Sir Redvers Buller. Hamilton had built up a reputation as a soldier and leader. A respected strategist and reformer, his ideas on rifle training transformed the Indian army. He even wrote against conscription. He and his father were in the Gordon Highlanders, so he could be cast as the Highland Warrior. He was also a published poet who had declared that 'I'd rather write one really sweet and famous sonnet than be QMG in India or even Commander-in-Chief himself.'[18] The man of action and words became effectively combined. And, unlike many of his rank, he cultivated good relations with the press.

In October 1915, ten days after Hamilton was recalled home, Henry spoke in London on the Dardanelles, raising £721 for the United Suffragists. He praised the brave suffragist Lieutenant Cather whom he had found commanding the wreck of the grounded collier *The River Clyde*.[19] He also paid tribute to Hamilton's personal courage, even claiming that he did not feel fear as other men.[20] He was 'a model of what we mean by the perfect knight'.[21] Such romanticization helped combat the attacks on his command but also reflected personal admiration for Hamilton's bravery, lack of ostentation and regard for others. Hamilton's fall from grace provided a new twist to Henry's now familiar quest for causes and championing the underdog. Here was a fallen hero who needed rescuing. Henry's task was all the more compelling because he had been on the spot as the final part of Gallipoli's tragedy unfolded.

This tale, suitably censored, was told in the *Manchester Guardian* from 30 July. The first few articles (in accordance with War Office advice) concentrated on the human side. Henry recounted his day with the 42nd (E. Lancs.) Division at Cape Helles. Here, at the front of the firing line, just forty yards from Turkish sandbags, was 'a wilderness of mounds and pits and trenches'. There were heaped-up stores and rows of horses, tarpaulin dressing-stations, carts and wagons continually on the move and 'Indian muleteers continually striving to inculcate human reason into mules'.[22] A cloud of dust pervaded everything and flies multiplied. Trenches had Lancashire names: a long communication trench captured in June was called the Wigan Road. Henry told of former miners, weavers and spinners almost naked in the blazing midday sun, picking lice from their clothes and cooking on little wood fires as shells flew over their heads. As he was unable to discuss tactics and strategy and discouraged from revealing technical information, this tale of the Lancashire lads was what was wanted.

Nearly a month later came Henry's eyewitness accounts of the Suvla

Bay landing in early August (sent via Alexandria).[23] With the advantage of hindsight he later put forward the original argument that the fatal first landing in April might have been better made by a combined force at Suvla Bay (four miles north of Anzac) and on Ocean Beach, just north of Anzac Cove.[24] He also claimed that Hamilton told him on 19 July (before his corps commanders were informed) of his 'great design' to break the stalemate by a new amphibious assault. The central Sari Bair range of mountains would be attacked from the Anzac bridgehead. Birdwood's troops would occupy the summits. Suvla and Anzac forces would descend to the straits at Maidos (Eceabat) and the part of the Dardanelles known as The Narrows would be open to the fleet. This would be supported by forces at Helles and by a surprise landing at Suvla Bay. That was the plan. It was not the reality.

On the evening of 6 August Henry left Imbros. Thousands of troops from 'Kitchener's Army' had arrived at Mitylene (Lesbos), Mudros, Helles, Anzac and Imbros during July. They embarked on various vessels. Henry travelled in a liner, the *Minneapolis*, reaching Suvla in darkness early the next morning. About 250,000 men had to be landed. Cruisers with landing parties had already begun their combined attacks. By nightfall they held the complete semi-circle of the bay. Henry's initial assessment was optimistic: it seemed an excellent result for one day, especially since they had new troops. But these reinforcements were not fully trained and faced both difficulties in landing and a topographical nightmare. The intense heat and flies meant that men succumbed to dysentery. Inadequate planning, leadership and logistics spelt fresh disaster, the troops failing to take the heights surrounding Suvla Bay even though they were held by relatively few Turkish soldiers. On 8 August troops reached but then abandoned Scimitar Hill, a small but crucial position on the Suvla Plain. Turkish snipers, artillery and scrub fires prevented its recovery. Churchill's ultimate goal of Constantinople seemed further away than ever. Henry later admitted that this day 'might well be called Black Sunday'.[25]

Censorship forbade disclosure of casualty figures and Hamilton's official cables had to be received before the press could have their say. *Guardian* readers therefore heard from their Special Correspondent about the 'Brilliant Charge of the Irishmen at Suvla Bay' when Irish infantrymen took the razorback ridge that formed the northern tip of Suvla Bay. 'Australians' Reckless Courage' at Anzac was announced but readers were not told the true situation. In four days the allies had lost over 12,000 men (the Turkish losses were even greater). All Turkish troops in the northern sector were now under the command of Mustapha Kemal. Three months earlier he had become a folk hero. After the war he would become known to the world as Atatürk, Turkey's great leader and modernizer. The August landings diverted the Turks from the Caucasian, Egyptian and Mesopotamian fronts but little else could be claimed of advantage to the allies. It was soon evident that the idea of converging attacks from Helles, Anzac and Suvla had failed. Suvla Bay had become the allies' third static enclave on the peninsula and at great human cost.

Henry later summarized his perspectives on 'this black chaos of slaughter'.[26] Mistakes over landing places, heat and extreme thirst (the water supply broke down) compounded the difficulties of tackling an entrenched enemy with naval guns. Divisions of the New Army and Territorials lacked experience and, despite undoubted bravery, as Henry went up and down the firing lines he felt 'their confidence shaking'. Hamilton's appeal for reinforcements on 16 August was refused.

There was one final attempt to win back Scimitar Hill. On 21 August Hamilton deployed what was left of the 29th Division. The assault failed and 'So ended the last determined attempt to secure victory in the Dardanelles.'[27] There were 6,500 casualties and one of them was Henry. Suffering from his old fever he had forced himself to go aboard a trawler bound for the north point of Suvla Bay. By mid-afternoon he was about half a mile from Scimitar Hill, on the firing ledge at Chocolate Hill, so named because of the burned scrub. Naval guns in the bay began pounding Scimitar Hill to little effect. The Turks responded by concentrating on Chocolate Hill. The men in the front trenches prepared to advance and fixed bayonets.

Suddenly Henry felt a blow like a trip-hammer on his skull and with no fear or pain:

> I fell like a slaughtered ox, but was up again next second. I heard a machine-gun officer say, 'Are you hit?' I put my hand to my head and looked at it. Blood dripped from all the fingers. 'I suppose I am', I said. I saw my brown shirt running with blood. I felt the warmth of the blood like hot water against my skin. I wondered that a man could have so much blood in him.[28]

He was told later that he kept repeating 'I'm not going away. I must see the battle!' He had a bandage in his pocket and the officer tied it round his head. He was taken to a dugout where an RAMC orderly mopped clots of 'pink jelly' off his shirt. Henry had feared they might be lumps of brain, but his pith helmet had taken the force of the shell and saved his skull. When the blood ceased to drip he returned to the trench.

Within an hour he was back in his old position, fearful but not in pain. That came later after walking four miles back to Suvla Point where surgeons examined the wound. Henry later joked how a shell struck his skull but rebounded, 'finding it impervious to all but reason'. Richard had recently painted one of his most famous pictures, *Bursting Shell*. Its use of darkness/black and light/colour dramatically evokes the precise moment of an explosion but within an urban setting. Henry claimed that his blow left only a groove suitably shaped like a scimitar: 'It makes an excuse for increasing baldness, and if I am taken prisoner by the Turks

I can point to it as an outward and visible sign of the Crescent and the Prophet's faith.' But many years later he admitted to E. M. Forster that his hand had shaken ever since that Suvla shell.[29]

Nevertheless, this battle wound helped validate Henry's military links, suggesting less of the ageing surrogate and more of the 'real' soldier. It also enhanced the legend of the fearless war correspondent. Bean acknowledged that Henry was 'very game' but noted privately that 'A good deal has been made out of Nevinson's wound.' Bean even briefly toyed with the idea of mentioning his own leg wound to help promote his literary work![30] Interestingly, he was under the impression that Henry had *fought* for the Greeks in 1897. He saw him as 'a writer of British reputation and quite as big a man in his own line as Sir Ian Hamilton is in his'.

The ethical as well as the physical role of the correspondent was now tested. After returning to Anzac and a cliff dugout, Henry visited Mitylene. The excuse was vague talk of a possible landing at Adramyti Bay opposite the island but Henry welcomed briefly escaping the terrible toll of deaths and recriminations, especially since he felt his 'blood boiling with rheumatism'. His real interest, though, was to see the home of the poet Sappho. Accompanied by other correspondents, including Ashmead-Bartlett, Henry relaxed and explored. He wrote an article but it was later cut to pieces and all mention of the navy censored. The chief of intelligence at GHQ told Bean that he would like to send every word 'that men like Nevinson and yourself write' but was hampered by regulations.[31] The press officer, Major Delme Radcliffe, however, suggested that Henry had been inventing material. But a much bigger issue now overshadowed this.

Hamilton's staff informed Ashmead-Bartlett that he must return home for attempting to send an uncensored letter highly critical of the campaign. According to Henry, he had long 'set himself to crab the whole expedition' and persistently predicted failure. In London in June he had told Henry that he was about to make his views known to the Foreign Office. Now the opportunity came to discredit Hamilton and publicize his opinions, free from censorship. In early September a keen young Australian journalist called Keith Murdoch had appeared at Anzac. He was bound for work in London but wanted to spend a few days gaining an impression of the Australian soldiers. He signed the war correspondents' agreement to communicate solely by the official sanctioned route, submitting to the censor military information of a confidential nature. But he arranged with Ashmead-Bartlett to convey his dispatch to the Prime Minister, Asquith, in London.

Sir Ian was, however, informed of this by somebody at Imbros. Murdoch got as far as Marseilles where he was arrested and had to hand over the letter. Ashmead-Bartlett meanwhile had his accreditation withdrawn and was sent home in disgrace. When the two men reached

London they made their views clear. Murdoch went to the Australian High Commission where he penned an 8,000-word letter to Andrew Fisher, Australia's Prime Minister, sensationalizing the account and urging Hamilton's recall. The novelist and former actress Elizabeth Robins, loyal friend to the Hamiltons and Henry, called it a 'farrago of falsehood, misrepresentation and calumny'.[32] Asquith read it and, without consulting Hamilton, had it printed and circulated to the Imperial Defence Committee and Dardanelles Committee. Meanwhile Ashmead-Bartlett spelt out the situation in the press.

Within weeks Hamilton was relieved of his command. Murdoch later became Sir Keith Murdoch and father of the media tycoon Rupert Murdoch. Several modern accounts have named Henry as the person who alerted Hamilton to the smuggled dispatch.[33] Phillip Knightley was given Henry's name by Bean's former batman and assistant, A. W. Bazley.[34] Bazley may have named Henry because he was often critical of Ashmead-Bartlett, had Hamilton's ear and was even suggested by the latter as a successor to the disgraced journalist (something Henry immediately refused). But Henry was not the informer. In 1917 Henry stated in a letter to Hamilton that he did not hear about the letter until after it had been discovered: 'If I had known of it, I should have urged him, since he felt like that about the situation, to resign and go home.'[35] Henry did, though, tell Hamilton that, early in August, Ashmead-Bartlett had bet Lester Lawrence (Reuters) five pounds that Hamilton would soon be recalled.[36] The historian Nicholas Hiley exonerates Henry from blame but suggests that Malcolm Ross might have been responsible.[37] Henry's diary for 19 February 1917 solves the mystery. He had been reading Hamilton's diary. When Henry talked to Hamilton the following day in private at his Hyde Park Gardens home, Hamilton revealed that the correspondent who informed on Ashmead-Bartlett was 'the navy's official photographer'.

At the beginning of October, after three months away, Henry travelled home via Malta. A fortnight later Hamilton was recalled. He told Henry that it was because of his response to a cipher asking for an estimation of probable losses on evacuation. Hamilton had suggested that the toll would be between half and three-quarters of the men. Kitchener told him that he could be proud to be recalled rather than sacrifice lives and reputation through withdrawal.

Two months later Henry returned to witness the withdrawal recommended by General Sir Charles Monro.[38] He spent a fortnight literally going over old ground and watching the evacuation shape up. Although Murdoch had claimed that officers and men held the General Staff and Hamilton in contempt and that sedition was 'talked round every tin of bully beef', Henry felt that 'all the spirit' had gone out of the campaign with Hamilton's departure.[39] The physical climate had also changed. At the end of November men froze to death in sudden snow blizzards. But from Anzac and Suvla alone over 83,000 men, horses, mules, carts, guns and supplies had to be removed and embarked. Various ruses were adopted to dupe the Turks. On the final days all ranks were ordered to show themselves on the skyline and walk where they could be observed. Henry's account of this feat could not be published in full until the following spring.

On 9 January the evacuation of Helles ended and so too, after eight and a half months, did the Dardanelles expedition, 'equal in splendour of conception, heroism, and tragedy'.[40] 'Nothing has become it better than the leaving', wrote Henry.[41] Yet despite the enormous toll of the campaign for both sides – nearly a million men had fought with over 450,000 casualties – and Hamilton's gloomy prognosis, the evacuation of 83,000 allied soldiers was virtually free of casualties.

Henry had left on Christmas Day. But, as with Angola, involvement did not end there. There were articles, lectures and, at Sir Ian's suggestion, a book. Henry was initially hesitant, fearing that it would occupy too much time and that Masefield's book *Gallipoli* (which prompted 'a rather bitter envy') had already 'taken the cream off'.[42] Anxious to resurrect his reputation, Hamilton assured Henry that there was now much more evidence available and that he could supply 'heaps of stuff'. When John Murray and Heinemann turned down the book proposal, Lady Jean Hamilton suggested financing its publication. Henry was shocked: 'I absolutely refused as paralyzing me & bringing entire discredit on the evidence.' Nisbet then offered Henry a contract. The first report of the Dardanelles Commission had just appeared.

The controversy surrounding the doomed campaign had prompted an investigation involving 168 witnesses. It began in August and sat for over a year. In November Hamilton suggested that they should hear from Henry as the most weighty of the correspondents. But Cabinet Office records[43] show that, although appreciated as a correspondent of 'sterling integrity', whose conduct and discretion in the field were 'in every way admirable', he was viewed in official circles as somewhat less reliable at home. Indeed, his comments and indiscretion in lectures on Gallipoli were thought to infringe war correspondents' regulations. Nevertheless, he was one of the few remaining correspondents of the 'old school' and judged too shrewd and seasoned in military matters to 'allow his political and private views to obtrude in despatches from the scene of operation'. These reports on Gallipoli correspondents reveal just how much class mattered. Henry was, unlike some, accepted as a gentleman.

Henry eventually gave evidence on 9 March 1917 for an hour and twenty minutes. He was asked to read out his diary account of the Suvla landing and questioned about the condition of the troops, the effect of naval gunfire on land defences and the lack of water. He suggested carelessness but stressed that he was no expert. Throughout he refused to criticize the higher command or repeat gossip or criticism about

Hamilton.[44] He unequivocally attributed the campaign's failure to the sending of 'green & half-trained troops, both officers & men ignorant of real war'. The chairman, Sir William Pickford, asked about Hamilton's alleged order to shoot laggards. Murdoch had mentioned that Henry had referred to this being written in an officer's diary. Hamilton had suggested to Henry a few days earlier that he might give evidence on this sensitive issue. Henry appears – probably genuinely but possibly expediently – to have had no recall of either such an exchange with Murdoch or of reading such words. He wrote in his diary on 5 March after meeting Sir Ian: 'I have no such memory.' The diary in question had been kept at Gallipoli by Captain Gould and Henry had agreed to convey it home to his close friend, the journalist, poet and suffragist Gerald Gould. Henry told the commission and wrote in his own diary: 'I cd [*sic*] not say it wasn't there but I don't now remember it.' His diary simply mentions reading Cyril Gould's 'excellent & terrible diary' in London in October 1915, some weeks after he met Murdoch.

Hamilton hoped for a favourable, rapid and public report. In the event it was somewhat bland, due, it has been argued,[45] to his open and secret orchestration as well as imperial relations and the wider background of the war. Much to Hamilton's annoyance, the final report only appeared in late 1919. But, all things considered, he did not fare badly and the government did not escape responsibility.[46] Henry was also anxious about the delay, fearing the War Office might reject his book. It did go ahead, slightly censored. But the delayed final report could not be included.

Henry had been wise to hesitate about whether to write this book. It occupied much of 1917 and the first half of 1918 and prevented him visiting revolutionary Russia. Going over the proofs in July 1918, he feared that it would be neither popular nor successful 'but perhaps may do Sir Ian some service, & it is true history'. Significantly, the frontispiece is a photograph of Hamilton, who saw the book as important in exonerating his name, especially after the War Office proved so reluctant to publicize all the findings of the Dardanelles Commission. At every stage he supplied Henry with information, loaning his diaries, showing him cables and reading draft chapters. There were frequent letters with detailed suggestions – one ran to thirteen pages of foolscap – telephone calls and meetings.[47] Churchill talked to Henry for an hour on the causes of the early failure in the spring of 1915. He conversed in his 'pleasant schoolboy manner' but Henry noted that, although he spoke fluently and used the right words, he 'snorts in his throat or nose like a bulldog'.

Hamilton used every opportunity to promote this 'luminous' publication.[48] He was especially impressed by Henry's description of the assault on the ridge of Sari Bair on 9 August. Although disaster struck, allegedly due to British naval shells falling short, this had been preceded by a moment of glory. Henry compared the soldiers to Xenophon's men.

Hamilton predicted that this passage would 'find an abiding place in the records of English literature'.[49] It did not. But the volume – over 400 pages long and costing eighteen shillings – sold several thousand copies in the first few months after its November 1918 publication, was reprinted twice and had, like most of Henry's books, an American edition. Masefield called it 'the best & most thoughtful history that has appeared about any part of this war'.[50] Lord Haldane praised it, and it has been well received by historians.[51]

Modern appreciation of terrain as 'a magnificent munition of war' stresses the role played by geological conditions in helping shape the outcome. Peter Doyle, an expert in the geological conditions of Gallipoli, has commented upon Henry's prescience. Henry expressed 'an almost complete understanding of the difficulties of the terrain faced by men and commanders alike'. He was the only contemporary writer to ask why Suvla Bay had not been the landing place. Doyle suggests that 'It is still tempting to follow the line of Nevinson's thinking' and ask what might have been achieved by a united force concentrated on one location.[52] But, not surprisingly given Henry's career from 1897 onwards and his position and mind-set as a British journalist attached to the allied campaign, he was reticent about Turkish ability and strength. Here he was in tune with the British government, military and press in failing to recognize from the outset that, as David French puts it, this was 'an operation against a first-class military power and not a backward oriental despotism'.[53] It has taken many decades for British and Australian historians to focus on Ottoman victory alongside British and Anzac defeat.

Henry's conclusion highlighted errors: seeking to force a passage first by naval means alone, fatal delays and an insufficient army for land operations. He was convinced that failure was attributable to the authorities at home.[54] The government saw the campaign simply as a sideshow. Henry remained consistent in apportioning blame and consequently exculpating Hamilton. He referred later to the 'Hesitating uncertainty' of Kitchener and stressed that 'the chief causes of the disaster were never near the peninsula at all'.[55] In September 1916 his review of Masefield's book helped shape this history as a romantic, tragic epic:

> The story stands isolated & complete, as one of the supreme Episodes in our national history ... Certainly a failure but no dishonour from the leader down to the Indian muleteer only the sorrowful glory of great deeds thwarted by fortune, or by far-off authorities deaf to the surrounding appeals.[56]

And 'the leader' remained a lifelong friend. In 1932 another small flare-up over Gallipoli saw Henry defend Hamilton once more in the press. Hamilton called this 'a long drink of champagne' and referred to 'our mutual campaign'.[57] 'Campaign' might mean the time they spent parrying attacks at home rather than in Gallipoli but, whatever it signified, it suggested a sustained, shared history.

Between Henry's two spells at Gallipoli came a visit to Salonika (Thessaloniki) for the provincial press syndicate. In October 1915 Bulgaria had become Germany's ally and committed to war against Serbia. Salonika had been taken from the Ottomans by the Greek army in October 1912. The Serbs now urged allied intervention so that the Bulgarians could be defeated in the south before the Germans and Austrians attacked in the north. When Bulgaria mobilized troops, the Greek Prime Minister Venizelos told the British and French governments that Greece would join the war on their side if they sent 150,000 troops to Salonika. His monarch, however, had different ideas. King Constantine was the Kaiser's brother-in-law and wanted Greece to remain neutral. Venizelos was dismissed. Salonika now became a huge allied base. Henry interviewed the new Prime Minister Skouloudis and talked to a bitter Venizelos. It was a far cry from Crete in 1897.

Salonika's streets were full of Greek troops and British and French soldiers. Many had come from Gallipoli. Neutrality meant that Germans and Austrians walked free and 'pursued espionage unchecked' though Zeppelins dropped occasional bombs.[58] Henry enjoyed this cosmopolitan city, named after Alexander the Great's sister, with its Roman walls, Turkish influence and large population of Sephardic Jews. Yet there were frustrations. Correspondents could only send copy under Greek censorship rules and it took a few days getting clearance from the War Office. During his initial three weeks in the city, Monastir was taken by the Bulgarians and they and German forces came closer. At Christmas Henry returned to Salonika for two months.[59] Some of his letters and telegrams failed to reach home. He felt as though he was marking time. Residing in a city hotel, frequenting coffee houses and trying, with difficulty, to prise information from army chiefs was a world away from Gallipoli. Some mistook him for a soldier. When the entomologist Captain Malcolm Burr invited him to dine, the troops gave the dignified, uniformed man the Present Arms.[60] He was not always comfortable with fellow correspondents. There was 'bad trouble' with Ferguson of Reuters who, over dinner, told a 'dirty story about suffragettes'.[61]

Henry departed in early March, visiting Egypt on his way home. He saw Edith Durham at Suez. At Ismailia (Al Ismāilīyah) he discovered his former Gallipoli colleagues in the correspondents' camp and travelled with them to Cairo. Hit by sciatica and terrible rheumatic pains, he had to be hoisted into a steamer 'like a sack of chilled meat'.[62] He feared that he was ending his career 'in pain & disappointment'.

War had also taken its toll on his family. Richard had been discharged with a pension from the RAMC on ill-health grounds. Philippa's daughter Margaret delighted Henry for years to come but his second grandchild, Toby, born in 1916, had meningitis sans phrase and would spend most of his life in a mental asylum. His state was attributed to a 'Zeppelin shock before birth'. He was partially paralysed and, Henry admitted, 'looks wretchedly imbecile'. When he was two Henry wrote that 'No sorrow or disaster has ever made me so wretched.' He featured little in Henry's diary over the following years yet this absence cannot simply be equated with lack of feeling.

For over three weeks in 1917 Henry was seriously ill himself with blood poisoning. He later recollected his nights in a nursing home, longing for the shot of morphine through which he 'slid into paradise'. He recuperated with the Pethick Lawrences at their Surrey home. The previous year he had taken his officer's coat to be dyed, seeing this as a symbolic ending of his ties with war. He had written: 'Have, I suppose, definitely left the life of wandering adventure behind. It lasted 19 years.' But the 'I suppose' still left room for a challenge. And that came in 1918 with a return to front-line journalism when Philip Gibbs, who had been reporting from the Western Front since the start of the war and commanded the *Daily Chronicle*'s largest readership, needed a rest. The paper turned once more to their veteran correspondent. Starting on 30 July with 'Averting Danger from Amiens', daily signed columns by Henry appeared on its front page until 27 August.[63]

Yet again he appeared on the scene at a vital moment. Henry may have missed being at the Somme in 1916 but he was present at what proved to be the turning point of the war. Not surprisingly, Gibbs was said to be aggrieved. At Château Rollancourt, about twenty miles south of St Omer, Henry found 'Dear old Russell' (Herbert Russell), Percival Phillips and the Christ Church men Beach-Thomas and Perry Robinson. Robinson, writing for *The Times* and *Daily News and Leader* was also a Salopian. Henry was now sixty-one, a little rheumatic but otherwise fit for his age.

The military had come to appreciate correspondents. At the end of 1915 Sir Douglas Haig had replaced Sir John French as Commander-in-Chief of the British and Empire forces. Never were they so 'helped, shielded and petted before', wrote C. E. Montague.[64] Henry described them 'Chirping together like little birds in a nest' in a French château with their own rooms, three meals daily and servants. How unlike the correspondent 'seeking food and shelter for himself, his horse and his man, or wandering far and wide in search of a censor and a telegraph office'.[65] They divided up areas between themselves and, accompanied by a press officer or censor (a wounded officer),[66] were driven to the front in a Vauxhall car. Lunchtime saw them back at the château pooling findings and writing composite dispatches. By tea time the press officers had read their material (2,000 words maximum) and whisked it away by motorcycle. The Newspaper Proprietors Association ran the operation.

11 War correspondents and press officers at Rollancourt, 1918. Henry is sitting on the right.

Henry remarked that 'the strain of a war correspondent's life was relaxed till it almost ceased'.[67]

He visited various points on the front between the Ypres Salient and the ridge dividing the Ancre and Somme rivers. Generals now explained their intentions, and on 7 August they were summoned to General Rawlinson's headquarters and informed by Generals Montgomery and Vivian about Haig's plans for the Fourth Army to push the German army back across the Somme battlefields. At 2 a.m. the following morning, Henry, Beach-Thomas and the press officer Montague set off for the high ridge east of Amiens. It was the beginning of the Battle of Amiens, soon dubbed 'the black day' by the Germans.

The rout began with an eerie, impenetrable mist. Montague, formerly a theatre critic, wrote how 'the stage was set, the play of plays was about to begin on the broad stage below; only, between our eyes and the boards, there hung a white curtain'.[68] By 4 a.m. they could hear the immense roar of guns. They walked along the top of the ridge towards Bray where they glimpsed tanks looming through the mist. Whole companies of disarmed German prisoners were marching in fours towards them. Only when the mist suddenly lifted did the column of British guns, wagons and troops become visible marching east over ground just vacated by the Germans. But Henry had been obliged to rush back to compose a 1,200-word telegram. A few days later, between Amiens and Roye, he was sprinkled with fragments from a bursting shell. There was heavy fire from both field guns and aeroplanes and 'something struck me on the head just as I was drawing a rough plan of the road in front'.[69] He watched a cavalry charge on the road to Roye. The Germans retaliated with machine-gun and rifle-fire from the woods and the cavalry 'melted away'. To Henry's annoyance this unfortunate episode was cut out of his dispatch. A week later he found the rotting corpses of men and horses.

The correspondents moved to a grander château at Vauchelles near Abbeville. One day Henry accompanied the King and his entourage to the front. It was over four years since the Great War had started. But most of the old Somme battlefield had now been retaken and Henry's dispatches started with increasingly positive statements tracking the steady advance. On the evening of 24 August he began with 'Some say that last night and this morning were the turning points of the present campaign, and perhaps of the whole war.' That morning he and Montague had seen Thiepval, infamous since 1 July 1916, the first day of the Battle of the Somme. They were watching British soldiers emerge from Mesnil wood overlooking the Ancre when small groups of Germans appeared. Together with a New Zealander who had a blank revolver they got them to surrender and marched seven of them back across the river to the authorities in Mesnil:

> One was a good Socialist all were dead sick of the war, all intelligent and quite good-tempered. One told me regretfully that his mother had a nice little house near Frankfurt-on-Oder, and always kept a good bed with clean sheets ready waiting for him, but here he had been for months coated in mud, sleeping in filth among rats, and covered with lice. It was the simple lament of millions on both sides.[70]

By the end of the month the allies had advanced to the outworks of the Hindenburg Line. Henry departed on 26 August but earlier that day met, under fire, a Middlesex regiment in a shallow trench. It was, he wrote in his diary, 'my last taste of battle'.

Back home after 'this charming & energetic episode', adjectives most would not have deployed for such a month, Henry experienced his customary culture shock. Margaret was away but Richard and Kathleen were installed at Downside Crescent: 'all things in chaos & grievance & obstruction as usual. How different from life at the real centre!' In 1917, thanks largely to pressure exerted indirectly by Henry and directly by his old friend Masterman (in charge of propaganda), Richard had become a war artist. He was joining a distinguished group that included Muirhead Bone, Stanley Spencer and Paul Nash. The Nevinsons had been fearful that legal changes concerning military service would mean that, despite ill health, Richard would not be exempted from active service. Now as an official (unpaid) war artist he returned to France but to sketch. The Leicester Galleries held a second Exhibition of Pictures of

War in March 1918. At the opening, Lord Beaverbrook, Minister of Information, called Richard 'an instance of inherited genius in a different art'. The Friends' Ambulance Unit awarded the Mons Star to father and son.

Both men found wartime restrictions and censorship irksome but articulated this in different ways. Whereas Henry cultivated the role of the rebel committed to exposing the establishment, Richard, as Walsh has argued, portrayed himself as 'the victim of the establishment in pursuit of truth'. Richard's most public brush with censorship came with the showing of his painting *Paths of Glory* at this 1918 exhibition. This graphic depiction of dead men borrowed its title from Gray's 'Elegy Written in a Country Churchyard': 'The paths of glory lead but to the grave.' Censorship restrictions did not permit such portrayals and, after months of wrangling over the issue and a ban on showing it, Richard included it in the exhibition but with the word 'censored' (in blue chalk on brown paper) glued on the painting across the men's bodies. Immense attention was ensured. Richard's battles with military authorities, critics and artists kept Henry anxious about his son's 'haunted mind'.

The end of the war found Henry in Belgium. The small group of correspondents had been augmented and requested that he return. He crossed the Channel on 7 November, telling *Daily News* readers of the sense of anticipation and joy pervading northern France.[71] His stay at the new headquarters at Lille was brief. A few days after arriving he heard, at the military post in the small town of Orchies, that the Armistice had finally been signed and would begin at 11 a.m. He was determined to reach Mons in time. With him were his favourite press officer Montague and the young journalist (later novelist) Cecil Roberts.

Setting off at dawn on 11 November, they drove rapidly across the Belgian frontier, passing places of earlier conflict now teeming with returning refugees. The clock was beginning to strike the hour as they drove into the Grand-Place. Gathered there were civilians and soldiers (a brigade of the 3rd Canadian Division and Irish troops, a squadron of the 5th Lancers), assembled by the lovely fifteenth-century town hall. The terms of the Armistice were read out, national anthems sung and 'Tipperary' chimed out from the old belfry. Amidst flags, singing, loud cheers and laughter, women waved handkerchiefs and aeroplanes dropped brilliant white stars on the crowd. 'I have seldom seen such joy' wrote Henry of the place where the Great War had begun back in August 1914.[72]

CHAPTER NINE
A Corresponding Cause
Ireland

There is a land too dear for a lover's words
Lying beyond the sunset like a dream
(from H. W. Nevinson, 'A Vigil')

It was at dawn in August 1897, Henry's *annus mirabilis*, that he first saw the Irish mountains rising from the sea. Many years later he wrote of that summer in Bray as the happiest time of his life. To an incurable romantic, the beauty and tragedy of Ireland and its history proved irresistible. Kingstown (Dun Laoghaire), where he set foot on Irish soil, was always 'the gateway of magic for me'.[1] After a lifetime of travel, Ireland remained 'by far the most beautiful country I have known'.[2] Henry was prone to superlatives but Ireland was dear to him. It formed part of his wider agenda for the self-determination of small nations. He wrote for the English press about scenes and campaigns there that tested his loyalties and sense of justice. He deplored his country's treatment in the decades leading to the 1880s: 'It is a history no Englishman can read without the deepest shame.'[3] But, unknown to most, Henry's commitment had a personal as well as a political dimension. Ireland was inextricably linked to Henry's intense love affair with Nannie Dryhurst. He had been with her on that first memorable visit.

Thanks to Nannie, he had been drawn into the burgeoning Irish cultural nationalism of 1890s London. And as a literary journalist he promoted Anglo-Irish poetry. In several fine essays, Henry paid tribute to Jonathan Swift, in his opinion one of the 'shrewdest and most clear-eyed writers of our literature'. Familiar with passionate indignation, sensitivity and wrath at the oppression of others, Henry defended Swift against those who ridiculed his alleged misanthropy. In 'Where Cruel Rage' Henry stressed that it was 'an intensely personal sympathy with suffering, that tore his heart and kindled that furnace of indignation against the stupid, the hateful and the cruel'.[4]

As a correspondent Henry met controversial political and artistic figures in Ireland. He first encountered the Dublin intelligentsia of the

Contemporary Club in 1899 (including Yeats's mentor, the Fenian John O'Leary, and Maud Gonne).[5] The following year he covered a special convention of the United Irish League at the Rotunda, chaired by the leader of the Irish Parliamentary Party, John Redmond.[6] He argued that a great change had occurred since Parnell's death in 1891: 'Never since the English began their blundering over the country' had the Irish been so conscious of their nationality. If the land question were settled, Ireland would become less of a financial burden and a step could be taken towards recognizing the country's identity: 'Will our Ministers have the wisdom and courage to catch such an opportunity as it hurries by?'[7]

Henry cultivated the image of himself as a rebel. Yet his causes were borrowed ones. They were deeply felt but tended not to be indigenous. The fact that suffrage was denied to English women perhaps helps explain why it was so important to him. Yet even here, as a man with a vote, he was still on the privileged side. He wanted to identify with the underdog. In several novels, for example in *The Day Before* by his colleague Tomlinson, Henry appears as an Irishman.[8] But although he could act as a voice of conscience in the British press, thereby fulfilling a vital role, he could not fully empathize with those whose voices he helped to publicize. And 'rebel' had a particular meaning in Ireland, something which he, a rebel without his own cause, could only partly comprehend. Nannie frequently criticized his limited understanding of the Irish situation as an Englishman. In 1893 his diary tells of the danger of Ireland 'falling away into a self-centred little state like Belgium – completely cut off from us in sentiment & history'.[9] He soon thought differently but there was always a chasm between Henry and Nannie. He saw her in Dublin in 1918. She was friendly but there remained the problem of 'my cursed nationality which she never lets me forget, always planting the poisoned darts in my heart'.

Celtic pride in identity surrounded Henry, even in Hampstead: Nannie's nationalism, Eleanore Podmore's involvement in Scottish folklore and Margaret's espousal of Welshness. Yet Henry's identification with Ireland does not signify straightforward antipathy towards England – far from it. His love of country ran deep. In many respects his views on Ireland were predicated on envy. Henry dearly wished that English people could articulate an attachment to their country the way the Irish did for theirs. He wrote that 'Nationality is essential for the completeness of the individual's life . . . one's being breathes nationality.'[10] An interest in the Nevinson family's Westmorland ancestry was part of this. Although he felt that the weight of the past weighed almost too heavily on the present in Ireland, the English, he believed, were too suspicious of passion to appreciate their past. Often ashamed of his country's modern imperial role, his first signed piece in the *Nation* argued that the most heroic figures of the nineteenth century – including Parnell, Mazzini and Kossuth – had 'vindicated the rights of free nationality rather than extending empires'.[11] Henry's sense of Englishness drew upon ideas about a world that appeared to have been lost: hence his interest in the rights of the 'freeborn Englishman' expressed through radical heroes such as the seventeenth-century John Hampden, the subject of his essay 'The Gadfly of Freedom'.[12]

Looking back to the principles of Gladstonian Home Rule, Henry and radical Liberal journalists such as Hobhouse and Hammond attacked, time and again, the Anglo-Irish Union.[13] As Hammond's biographer notes, Ireland touched a raw nerve and 'Home Rule was a staple conviction'.[14] These journalists sought to inform readers and influence government policy through Liberal newspapers such as the *Manchester Guardian* and Massingham's paper, pointedly entitled the *Nation*. Their international perspectives helped locate Anglo-Irish relations in a broad context. However, their critiques of colonialism and arguments for self-rule tended to underestimate the threat posed by Ulster Unionism.

The Third Home Rule Bill was introduced in April 1912. Shortly before this Henry went to Belfast for the *Daily News* to hear Churchill outline the government's scheme. Henry dined with correspondents, visited the Catholic community of west Belfast concentrated around the Falls Road and saw the Protestant Shankill Road. He attended a meeting of Orangemen and, after Churchill's speech, heard the Contemporary Club's analysis of it.

In March 1905, determined to resist their inclusion in a self-governing Ireland, the Ulster Unionist Council had been formed, centred on Belfast. From 1910 Sir Edward Carson led the Unionist Party. Dublin-born, he saw himself as Irish but was passionately committed to maintaining the union. For Carson, the Crown signified essential imperial unity. The Parliament Act of 1911 abolished the Lords' veto over legislation. The Lords could no longer delay for more than two years a bill passed by the House of Commons in three parliamentary sessions. The prospect of a Home Rule Bill becoming law was now a reality. Carson's party issued the Craigavon Declaration threatening to establish a separate Ulster government in Belfast should Home Rule succeed. By the end of the nineteenth century Protestants accounted for about 57 per cent of the province of Ulster even though they formed only a quarter of Ireland's entire population. Four out of the nine counties in the province had Protestant majorities and in two other counties the Protestants and Catholics were almost evenly divided. Ulster Unionists saw Britain as essential for prosperity. They and southern Unionists equated Home Rule with a Catholic takeover and feared that extremists would dominate an Irish parliament on a slippery slope to an independent Ireland.

Henry returned to Ulster in the autumn of 1912, writing for the *Manchester Guardian* (for two guineas daily) on the signing of the Ulster Solemn League and Covenant.[15] Although critical of the ten-day 'roadshow', it was his idea to cover it. He joked about his qualifications:

'brought up a violent Orangeman, I became a peaceful Nationalist before Gladstone; but have many Ulster friends and so could describe events with my habitual moderation and judicial balance'.[16] A quarter of a million men and as many women pledged to resist Home Rule by all means. Henry observed Carson read the draft of the Covenant at Craigavon with all the Unionist MPs present. Known to be partisan, Henry was not allowed inside, was refused a copy of the document and was not included in the press lunch at Portadown. The journalists followed Carson and his entourage as the Covenant was taken round the province. Henry sent his paper several thousand words nightly. On 28 September the Covenant was placed in Belfast's City Hall where Carson knelt to sign what Henry called 'that melodramatic and sinister document'.[17]

With habitual *im*moderation, Henry had already made clear his antipathy towards Carson. In February on the front page of the *Daily News* he had argued that old Ulster Unionist hatreds were being stoked by such men. They represented 'the last struggle of a dominant minority to retain the ascendancy of generations'.[18] From Belfast in late September he reported that he knew many prepared, despite intimidation, to refuse to sign the Covenant.[19] An article disparagingly entitled 'Carson, Smith & Co.' suggested that, if only the government would hold on to Home Rule and follow true Liberalism and democracy, then 'we should hear no more of Ulster fighting and being right'.[20] Henry does not seem to have appreciated that, for many, retaining the Union mattered as much as challenging it did for his friends. His claim that he could understand the dominant character of Protestant Ulster, 'for many of us were brought up to a similar aspect of God and the world', speaks for itself.

The autumn of 1912 also saw a fatal rupture in the WSPU and Henry's final quarrel with Nannie. Disagreement over Ulster precipitated the parting. Nannie had told Henry to leave the subject alone because he could not understand it. She was a member of the Inghinidhe na hEireann (Daughters of Erin) started in 1900 by Maud Gonne and other women to give Ireland its first nationalist feminist organization.[21] Along with Countess Markievicz, Nannie helped found its paper *Bean na hEireann* (Women of Ireland) and sat on its committee. It only survived for just over two years but it was the first women's journal in Ireland, its slogan 'Freedom for Our Nation and the complete removal of all disabilities to our sex' declaring its priority. Henry was more inclined to the views of the Irish Women's Franchise League, whose secretary was Hanna Sheehy Skeffington, who supplied Evelyn with items for *Votes for Women*.

In the autumn of 1913 Henry reported on the Dublin Lock Out. As a consequence of the transport strike organized by James Larkin's Irish Transport and General Workers' Union, employers locked out 250,000 workers who refused to give an undertaking not to join a union. Nationalism and socialism were fused through James Connolly's Irish Citizen Army. Against a background of sporadic arming and drilling of volunteer soldiers, the Ulster Volunteer Force had been formed. Within months, republicans and moderate nationalists in the south founded their own defence force, the Irish Volunteers. After war broke out, the majority (now called the National Volunteers) split from the significant anti-war minority who were not prepared to join the British army. From the start the Irish Republican Brotherhood had infiltrated the Volunteers and plans were soon made for an armed rising. The Home Rule Act had been passed in September 1914 but was suspended during wartime. Henry retrospectively dubbed this a fatal decision, though at the time people believed war might be over quite quickly.

On the morning of Easter Monday, 24 April 1916, a detachment of Irish Volunteers and members of the Irish Citizen Army famously marched into Dublin's centre. Without a single shot fired they took control of the General Post Office. From its steps Patrick Pearse proclaimed the Irish Republic as a sovereign independent state claiming the allegiance of every Irishman and Irishwoman. But within a week the rebel forces surrendered unconditionally. The Easter Rising was largely confined to Dublin. The British had gained prior knowledge of German involvement in insurrectionary plans and, although caught unawares, the insurgents (probably between 1,000 and 1,500) were put down by about 2,500 British troops, many of whom were Irish. They shelled the Post Office, there was street fighting, about 450 lives (rebels and civilians) were lost, several thousand were injured and property was destroyed. The picture is, however, easily muddied and not only by political bias. Press censorship also helped shape how the rising was portrayed at the time and consequently interpreted later.[22] Fifteen executions followed.

Henry, still recovering from Gallipoli, had not been in Ireland. This partly explains his focus on the leaders' personalities rather than their politics. He was also keen to stress their humanity. Henry argued that they were not part of a homogeneous movement. He also stressed that they had been his friends and that he had the credentials to pronounce opinions (whatever Nannie might think) based on a closer acquaintance with the key protagonists than most English journalists had. He had worked in both north and south. In March 1914 in Belfast and Newry he had sought (in vain) information about the Curragh Mutiny. Officers had threatened to mutiny if ordered to go into action to coerce Ulster to accept Home Rule.[23] In the same month in Dublin he had investigated paramilitary organizations and sought the views of figures such as Æ (George Russell), whom he admired as president of the Gaelic League, poet and practical farmer. He had been delighted to see a donkey and cart advertising a St Patrick's Day talk on women and war by 'Mr. Henry Woodd Nevinson, the famous war correspondent'.

His comments on Easter 1916 were, though, careful to condemn the brutal treatment of the rebels rather than condone their action. His language suggested that the choice of an armed rising was a deluded one. He wrote in his diary on 28 April about the 'terrible news' from Ireland: 'James Connolly reported killed & I fear many others of my finest friends. They could not keep out of such an enterprise, however insane. The horror of it hung on me all the beautiful day'. In print he suggested what a difference the executions made. But for this creation of martyrs 'the Irish people as a whole would have taken the rising as a gallant but crazy affair, a possible danger to Home Rule but nothing more'.[24] The executions were an offence against reasonable treatment in time of war. In the *Atlantic Monthly* he discussed the leaders in turn, each name followed by the stark word 'executed'.[25] He met Yeats and 'talked the whole time of the Irish Sinn Féin rising'. Irish news dominated his diary.

Henry had known Pearse slightly, having met this 'clever & devoted man' in 1912 at St Enda's School where he was headmaster. He moved from advocating Home Rule to belief in 'blood sacrifice'. Henry portrayed him as 'the finest idealist and most poetic dreamer among them' and was proud that Pearse had praised his *Essays in Rebellion*.[26] He was more sympathetic, though, to the views of Connolly, shot at dawn in Kilmainham Gaol. Prior to the Easter Rising, Henry believed that working-class consciousness rather than nationalism would dominate Irish politics. He had argued that issues such as female sweated labour were what mattered for Belfast people.[27] At a meeting (chaired by Connolly) he had declared that labour was 'the coming Irish question, surpassing all talk of machinery of government'.

Henry later wrote the Preface to Desmond Ryan's biography of Connolly, arguing that he had a greater breadth and depth of vision than many of his comrades: 'He knew the crimes of English government but he was not perpetually mumbling and grumbling over them.'[28] Here was a man who was at home with Ulster and Dublin workers whilst years outside Ireland had shaped a 'world-wide revolutionist'. He was never doctrinaire. Henry thus distanced him not only from Pearse but also from the strand of civil war republicanism associated with men like Erskine Childers. In 1916 Henry described himself as 'a very concrete and personal person'.[29] Connolly, he felt, was in the same mould and a doomed martyr: 'In any free country he would have guided the people. In Ireland he could but die in a struggle which he knew to be hopeless.'[30]

So troubled was Nannie when she heard of the first execution (of the young poet and dramatist MacDonagh) that she allowed Henry into her home for the first time for years. It was Francis Sheehy Skeffington's execution by a firing party of seven that most affected Henry. His widow sent him a 'terrible' letter, explaining that, although unarmed and a non-combatant, he had been dragged from the street into Portobello barracks, given no legal representation and summarily executed. She was never officially notified of his arrest, trial or burial, permitted to see him or remove his body. One English officer in Dublin, Sir Francis Fletcher Vane (who had organized Cadets with Henry in the 1890s), refused to collude in the cover-up and so was dismissed. Henry wondered 'When will indignation cease to tear & paralyse me?'

In 1912 Henry had described Francis Sheehy Skeffington, with his bushy ginger beard and tweed knickerbockers, as 'rather cranky'. Now he portrayed him as 'the most violent pacifist I have known', no fomenter of armed rebellion.[31] His wife was the activist. She had brought food to the insurgents and conveyed messages. 'Skeffy's' implacable opposition to militarism and avowed pacifism stopped him assisting them and he tried to halt the looting. Henry discussed his case with MPs and in the press questioned the military authorities' right to seize and exterminate him without even a confirmation of the sentence by the commander-in-chief.[32] The officer responsible, Bowen-Coulthurst, was court-martialled and found guilty but insane. Retired on full pay he spent eighteen months in Broadmoor and then 'in a remarkable recovery of sanity . . . sailed off to a new life in Canada'.[33]

Not so fortunate was Sir Roger Casement. Henry first met him in 1905, a 'large, blue-eyed, very handsome, & soft-voiced' Irishman who 'Talked well but never listened'.[34] Casement had served in the British consular service in Africa and South America. His report on the Congo was the first to expose fully the treatment of natives in its rubber trade. This and his commissioned investigation into rubber collection in the Amazon earned him a knighthood. In 1911 Casement sent Henry his draft report on what became known as the Putamayo Atrocities. Henry dubbed it 'one of the most awful documents ever written'.[35] Casement suggested how Henry might write about it: mankind was only beginning to realize that slavery 'did not perish on the plains of Gettysburg . . . a viler slavery – more atrocious by far – rules today vast areas of South and Central America'.[36] Henry duly obliged. His *Nation* article declared that 'we think the atrocious system died on the plains of Gettysburg. It is not true. The problem of slavery is still before us.'[37]

Resigning his post because of ill health, Casement continued a life of danger. With Ulster loyalists increasingly vocal and militaristic, he helped arm the opposition, raising money in America. After war broke out he tried (unsuccessfully) to recruit Irish prisoners of war in Germany into a pro-independence Irish Brigade. Correcting proofs for his article on Casement and Sinn Féin, Henry added a note that Casement 'seems to have intended an "alliance" for Ireland's safe neutrality during the war, with independence as a check to England's sea-power afterwards'.[38] Casement determined to go to Ireland in time for the projected rising. His motive has long been debated. What is indisputable is that he landed near Tralee on 21 April 1916, was arrested and, later that year, tried, found guilty of high treason and executed in England.

Since Henry had serious reservations about the wisdom of the rising, why, then, was he 'occupied perpetually day & night' for Casement for three months?[39] Casement had been the first to see that Henry's account of Angolan slavery was not only true but also understated. Indeed, their anti-slavery crusades were viewed similarly by many. Both men encouraged the romantic rebel image. Conscious of Nannie's jibe that 'you English never know when to leave us alone',[40] England's demonization of Casement also helped validate Henry's involvement. He objected to Sir F. E. Smith appointing himself as prosecutor, as he was 'the most prominent Englishman in the Ulster movement which advocated armed resistance to Home Rule'.[41] Believing in old liberal values and fair play, Henry viewed the besmirching of Casement's reputation as questioning the very meaning of British justice.

Henry had heard 'the horrible story of Casement's intriguing with Berlin' and a rumour that he was 'under arrest for sodomy' back in November 1914. After Casement was captured, Henry chose to depict his traducers as the uncivilized ones. Once more, Henry and Margaret's antipathy towards each other was sharpened by articulating opposing opinions: 'At lunch M. said she & all her friends hoped Casement wd [sic] be hanged, drawn & quartered – that noble personality, my dear friend. And such are the bestial people I have to live among.' Professor John Hartman Morgan, on Casement's legal team, told Henry in early June that a member of the government, either Herbert Samuel or Smith, had got newspaper editors together and read them bits from Casement's diary 'to show that he practised unnatural vice & to prejudice them against him. In consequence we can't bring evidence of his character & services.' These 'Black Diaries' detailed Casement's sexual encounters with male friends and procurement of 'native boys' from Madeira to the Amazon. They conveniently skewed opinion. Here was a sex scandal where media attention might rival that of another distinguished and then disgraced Irishman, Oscar Wilde.

There has been much speculation about whether British intelligence fabricated the contents of the diaries, making their origin as murky as their content. Even modern editors of the infamous diaries hold divergent views. In 1999 the Irish government ordered an investigation into their origin. Forensic examination showed them to be genuine.[42] Henry's diary is illuminating. On 19 July, just after the Court of Appeal heard the case, Henry spoke to fellow humanitarian John Harris. Harris had initially thought the diaries were Casement's translation from writings kept by 'some Putamayo scoundrel'. But after reading them he told Henry that he 'couldn't doubt' that they were genuine. Henry saw this as 'All very horrible & perversion of physical state: that Intermediate sex gone mad'. Yet the accusations were unproven and, as he wrote in his own diary, 'the vice is irrelevant to the charge'. The government had made shameful use of the document. Had Casement seduced 'a score of girls' and thrown them on the street, 'no one wld [*sic*] have said a word'.

Neither the *Daily News* nor the *Manchester Guardian* would touch Henry's letter about this. But he lashed out wherever possible against the smear campaign. It was a 'whispering scandal, spreading suspicions, sowing hints' as in the Dreyfus Case, fabricated against a man on trial for his life. Justice decreed that there be 'no prejudice against the accused by charges outside the immediate charge' and:

> It is for the honour of the English name that I have spoken, and with the object of maintaining unsullied our reputation for justice throughout the world – a reputation grievously exposed to danger by political animus and further machinations. For we may as well abandon all thought of justice if we allow the Cabinet or the Home Office or Scotland Yard to override us without a word.[43]

Henry provoked opposition from some unexpected quarters. His old ally R. B. Cunninghame Graham made a 'vile & poisonous attack' on his letter in the *Nation* so was 'cut' by Henry for twelve years. Casement, though, was 'very much touched' by it and asked Henry to visit him. He was now in Brixton Gaol, and six days before the trial began Henry saw him for three-quarters of an hour. He looked 'much aged, wrinkled, careworn, his hands at first working nervously'.[44] Casement argued that the Germans longed for peace but feared national destruction. He wondered whether it would be best to say nothing in court but Henry advised against this, stressing the powerful effect of speeches from the dock by Irish patriots. He told Henry that no Englishman except 'Wilfred Blunt[45] and me cd [*sic*] understand the Irish question & he didn't count me as an Englishman'.

At the trial Henry sat with the nationalist historian Alice Stopford Green, Casement's cousins and Mrs Duffy, the solicitor's wife. Casement smiled and bowed to Henry who stood up, bowing back.[46] He thought Casement looked the noblest and happiest man there. Henry was disappointed by the defence's focus on the aim of opposing the Ulster Volunteers after the war 'instead of boldly proclaiming the right of a subject nation to strike back'. Massingham had already told Henry that this fine quixotic attitude would not save him but Henry would have liked the principle asserted. He called Casement's statement 'that superb vindication of nationalist patriotism – I suppose one of the greatest speeches ever made from the dock to judges for whom the abhorrent little "black caps" were waiting'. Casement asserted his right to be tried in Ireland before an Irish court and jury. Self-government was 'a thing born in us at birth; a thing no more to be doled out to us or withheld from us by another people than the right of life itself'.[47] Ireland was being treated like a convicted criminal and, 'If it be treason to fight against such an unnatural fact as this, then I am proud to be a rebel and shall cling to my rebellion with the last drop of my blood.' This, Henry felt, should have formed the sole defence. The death sentence was passed.

The next day Gavan Duffy (Casement's solicitor) told Henry the 'whole truth' about Casement's expedition, that he initially went to Germany 'to arrange that Ireland if invaded sh. [*sic*] not be treated as Belgium but as a friendly country'. Hearing misleading information from America about a probable Sinn Féin rising and knowing that Germany would give no real support, he went to Ireland to stop it. He carried arms in case the Sinn Féiners were intent on rising, in which case he 'would have felt obliged to join in'. Naval and military intelligence had interrogated Casement about the intended rising but did nothing as 'they wished things to come to a head so sent no warning to Ireland'.

Henry's diary account was written on 30 July 1916 after talking to Casement's solicitor. Yet only in 1998 with the release of previously withheld papers was Casement's account formally confirmed from government sources. These papers show that a desperate Casement was aware that the rising would fail after Germany reneged on its promise to send troops to help the rebels. Nevertheless, he determined to proceed with the 'wholly futile scheme' lest he be 'branded by his friends in Ireland and America as a coward and traitor to their cause'.[48] Casement admitted to British intelligence that he knew 'that you were bound to catch me'. He asserted, 'I have done nothing dishonourable, as you will one day learn.'

Henry had to be careful what he said in print. Duffy advised him not to say much about Casement's objective. But in his memoirs in 1928, Henry quoted from Casement's Munich and Berlin letters expressing his despair at the hopeless situation.[49] Henry also mentioned that Casement had told him in Brixton that he had gone to Ireland 'to tell his friends not to attempt the Rising for it was useless to expect any adequate help from the Germans'. And he reproduced a letter from Pentonville Gaol to his sister: 'It is a cruel thing to die with all men misunderstanding – misapprehending – and to be silent for ever.'

Immediately after the trial Casement's supporters swung into action. George Bernard Shaw orchestrated much of this. He sought Henry's advice 'because there is nobody else accessible whose judgment I think as good as my own'.[50] Henry wrote formal letters 'to people of well known distinction' urging them to sign one of three petitions.[51] He attended the Court of Criminal Appeal on 17 July knowing that there was no hope. He was right. The hearing lasted just half an hour.

Incalculable damage was done by the insinuations about Casement's private life. Henry claimed that they constituted 'a more loathsome crime than the worst that could possibly be unearthed in the career of the criminal himself'.[52] But appeals for reprieve also met a mixed response for other reasons. After receiving Henry's requests for a signature and letter to Asquith, Wilfred Scawen Blunt argued that pleading for a reprieve would do Casement a disservice.[53] The government wanted penal servitude since they knew that martyrdom would boost the Irish cause. Gertrude Bannister, Casement's cousin, admitted that he was 'absolutely unshaken in his refusal to ask clemency, & in his desire to die for his country'.[54]

Henry persisted with letters to the press, Asquith and the Home Office. He lobbied MPs. Redmond turned away as soon as Henry mentioned the name Casement, uttering 'Please don't.' Despite a last-minute appeal to the King, Casement went to the scaffold on the morning of 3 August 1916. Henry attended a night vigil at Mrs Green's home. Out of this experience came his most powerful poem. 'A Vigil' never mentions Casement by name but its sub-title is 'August 2 to 3, 1916'. Casement, like Henry, had been entranced by Ireland's natural beauty and had been a poet. Henry imagines the final thoughts and actions of the condemned man in his whitewashed cell. As 'the light of death is breaking', he conjures up a scene far away where 'This very dawn steals down a mountain side':

> Now on the shore the slow-descending light
> Touches the whitening ripples as they break
> In bubbles against the sand with the flowing tide,
> And rouses wild birds up in whitening flocks
> Of crying terns and Solan geese that go
> Through the clear air of this same morning hour
> Swooping and plunging.

From such lyricism we are plunged rudely back to reality and anger:

> The life's example, calling to us still
> To stand untamed, unconquered, and defy
> Legalised murderers, spewing poisonous breath,
> Successful ghouls of purchased infamy,
> Life's prostitutes, suckers of noble blood,
> And freedom's hypocrites whose zeal is spent
> In praising distant freedom;
> . . .
> And all the Might, Dominion, Majesty,
> Thrones, Principalities, and Kingly Powers
> Rejoicing now he is dead.[55]

The next day, 'torn with rage', Henry sought solace in Oxford with Evelyn.

In October he attended Gertrude Bannister's wedding. They 'talked secretly amid general noise' and she 'kissed me once ag. [*sic*]'. Here was yet another attractive, intelligent younger woman committed to a cause who appealed to the apparently incorrigible Henry.[56] This fair haired, blue-eyed schoolmistress dubbed him 'Knight Errant'. Henry claimed that she loved him, 'age & all: really loves me. It is best to end such impossible things.' After she decided to marry Sidney Parry – 'a sharp sword to me' – Henry told her 'how deeply I envied him'. With a breathtaking disregard for the fact that he had himself been married for over thirty years, since before Gertrude was born, he wrote 'Yet I do not wish to marry anyone: for that kills love, being too daily an affection & intermixed with common affairs.'

In fact the Parrys became lifelong friends. Henry would sometimes stay with them on the Antrim coast. In May 1918 he escorted Gertrude across the water en route to a lunch in his honour at Dublin's Shelbourne Hotel. Guests included the former Attorney General James O'Connor and James MacNeill, later Governor-General of the Irish Free State. Henry met Nannie nearby in Terenure, and talked to Mrs Green, who received him 'imperiously like Queen Elizabeth greeting Drake after a failure'. Sinn Féin had not recognized the convention set up by Lloyd George in Dublin the previous year to frame a constitution for a United Ireland, and Henry the journalist was keen to canvass opinions.

Although founded by Arthur Griffith as a militant, non-violent nationalist organization some years before the Easter Rising, Sinn Féin (Ourselves Alone) gained strength in its wake. It was not a Sinn Féin rising but came to be seen as such. In October 1917 Éamon de Valera became its President and then headed the Irish Volunteers. Sinn Féin's opposition to a proposal to introduce conscription in Ireland boosted its popularity. Henry saw conscription as 'The Proposed Murder of a Nation'.[57] Growing friendliness would be replaced by 'sullen resentment on our side' and 'an envenomed hatred' on the Irish side. He warned, 'In Ireland the greatest admiration is reserved for the most defiant.'

Conscription was not introduced there but Henry believed that the crisis 'laid the tombstone on Home Rule', Irish politics entering a new phase.[58] In the bitter election of December 1918 Sinn Féin won almost all of the seventy-five seats outside Ulster. The Irish Parliamentary Party returned just six MPs, the Unionists twenty-six. But the Sinn Féin MPs refused to take their seats in the House of Commons. On 21 January, constituting themselves the Dáil Éireann (Parliament of the Irish Republic), they issued a Declaration of Independence. De Valera became the provisional government's president.

In this month, attempting to get explosives from a quarry in Co. Tipperary, the Irish Republican Army (IRA), as the Volunteers were now called, killed two policemen. This began the Irish War of Independence, also known as the Anglo-Irish War or Tan War, with guerrilla attacks on the police and British troops by IRA irregulars organized by Michael Collins. The IRA saw itself as the legal army of the Republic proclaimed at Easter 1916.

Returning to Ireland in March, Henry remarked on the growth of a 'grim & hostile spirit', believing that 'one thing only was certain: all was made ready for the shedding of Irish blood'.[59] That summer he commented on raids, imprisonment and men and women 'like hares chivvied upon the mountains and from cover to cover'.[60] Evelyn was with him for part of the time. It was the relative calm before the storm. The Dáil was declared illegal in the autumn. Sinn Féin, the IRA and all nationalist bodies except the Gaelic League were proscribed. As the IRA campaign became more widespread, martial law was imposed, along with curfews, night raids and more arrests. Many left the Royal Irish Constabulary in fear. Now former soldiers were recruited, nicknamed Black-and-Tans because of the colour of their uniforms. In Limerick a local pack of hounds sported this name. Even more detested were the ex-officers, the Auxiliaries, who arrived in March 1920. An infamous campaign of reprisals followed. Henry called the 'Auxis' 'ex-gentlemen' but amended this since 'none of them could ever have been a gentleman'.[61] There was a gulf between the British government's and the IRA's depictions of nationalist fighters: a small murder gang was not easily reconciled with an Irish national army legitimately defending its republic.

Henry now publicly identified himself with Sinn Féin. He sat on the platform in February 1920 at their large meeting at London's Albert Hall. In the spring he lectured in the United States and Canada.[62] In Montreal he spoke 'from the Sinn Féin side' to a private gathering of Irish people who listened in 'sympathetic silence'. At the University Club in Philadelphia the audience 'gasped as at a confession of murder & adultery when I championed Sinn Féin'. In New York he and Yeats participated in an 'Open Table' on the poets of the Irish Rebellion. And at the Waldorf Astoria Henry met de Valera. His diary reads as though he, rather than de Valera, were the expert on Irish politics: a 'tall, thin, fine featured, very intelligent, very nice looking' man who 'Holds exactly my view: thinks Ulster wld [*sic*] settle itself if England would leave it alone'. He told Henry that he saw the Dominion movement as a hindrance. Dominion Home Rule (the policy for Ireland favoured by some moderate nationalists) implied the wide powers of self-government possessed by Dominions like Canada and Australia. But before legislation was passed, Ireland saw a dramatic intensification of violence.

In August Terence MacSwiney, Lord Mayor of Cork, was arrested and brought to London, charged with possessing a Royal Irish Constabulary secret cipher and seditious documents. Jailed for two years and denied the status of a political prisoner, he went on hunger strike in Brixton Gaol. Henry, Evelyn and the Professor of English at Cork University addressed a crowd at Brixton from a coal cart. A resolution was passed demanding MacSwiney's release. Henry knew nothing would be done, 'But we have shown some decent rage & Ireland will hear of it.' He penned a middle on martyrdom, admitting that it was not very good, 'reflection being mingled with rage'. In October, after a seventy-four-day fast, MacSwiney died. Henry joined Sir Horace Plunkett (founder of the Irish Dominion League, he chaired the Irish Convention), Hammond, Tawney, Bernard Shaw and others in the Peace with Ireland Committee. But he was disappointed that no constructive practical schemes were suggested and that 'My beloved [Nannie] was there but purposely did not see me.' Chaired by the Tory Lord Henry Cavendish-Bentinck, it sought to halt reprisals and get 'undisciplined forces' withdrawn. Henry and Evelyn were on a list of its principal speakers. He was identified as one of those 'who did most for us'.[63] For five months Henry faithfully attended most of its weekly meetings at the House of Commons and then switched to the Irish Self-Determination League of Great Britain. By 1921 it had about 300 branches, organized meetings and distributed literature. Henry and Evelyn joined its poster parade in Whitehall.

Henry's autobiography implies that he made a personal pilgrimage to Ireland for MacSwiney's funeral, following the coffin all the way to Cork City Hall.[64] In fact he attended after a last-minute request from the *Daily Herald* for three 500-word articles. In his diary he admitted being 'uncertain' about going. He marched with university graduates in the funeral cortège. The IRA lined the route to the cathedral. Arthur Griffith spoke at the cemetery. Revolvers were fired into the air. Under the cedars was left 'one whose name will never be forgotten in Irish history', declared Henry, 'a symbol of glorious sacrifice' who 'in our English history will be remembered with bitter shame, and indignant humiliation'.[65]

Earlier that month Henry had spent five days in Dublin. Discovering that he was sharing the boat train with Black-and-Tans he moved to a first-class compartment. He stayed with his friend Diarmid Coffey. Returning from the nearby University Club, he found Coffey's street guarded by regular soldiers in iron hats with fixed bayonets. An armoured car stood outside the gate. The house was being raided for the second time in two days. About twenty men searched it and dug up the garden, taking away a small bundle of papers. The next day Henry visited villages where houses had been burned. He found 'Up the Republic' the most common response. He called on Erskine Childers. The author of the famous spy story *The Riddle of the Sands*, he had been born into the Anglo-Irish ascendancy. But, encouraged by his American wife Molly, he was fast becoming one of the most uncompromising of all republicans and would be executed by the Irish Free State. Henry noticed how he had completely ceased to smile. Violet Bonham Carter, who visited Ireland in 1921, thought similarly: 'He cannot smile. He has a set – pale – bitter face – a mind with no "give" in it at any point.'[66]

Amid rumours of atrocities on both sides, the *Herald* sent Henry back to Ireland in mid-November. He headed south west in a motor car driven by Dr Neil Watson. James MacNeill accompanied them for part of the journey. Aware that he might be searched, Henry replaced his usual hardback diary with a small soft notebook that could be hidden more easily. It was a precarious journey. Hugh Martin of the *Daily News*, known for criticizing British policy in Ireland, had already been threatened by the Black-and-Tans. Driving through glorious country-side they saw the ruins of police barracks and creameries. Henry sent 700 words from Tralee, a centre of Black-and-Tan activities. At night he heard doors smashed in raids. His stories made the paper's front page. His account of the death of a sixteen-year-old daughter of a butter-maker in Dingle Creamery, rumoured to be the result of a shooting competi-tion between Black-and-Tans, was raised in Parliament.[67] In several places police demanded permits and, as they drove up to the mouth of the Shannon, they saw groups of men attacking villages. At Limerick they called on Lord Mayor O'Callaghan, who was soon afterwards shot in his home. They saw the bodies of four youths pierced with bullet holes in Killaloe. There was a brief respite at Coole Park, home of the playwright and poet Lady Gregory. Then, after the kind of mountain journey Henry loved, came tales of British officers murdered in their beds in Dublin on 21 November and rumours of 270 slaughtered: all the 'good of my journey & peace policy gone at once'. Lester of the *Freeman's Journal* (collaborating with the *Herald*) sent a telegram requesting Henry's help in Dublin.

The IRA had shot dead fourteen plain-clothes policemen and intelli-gence officers in their Dublin homes or hotels that morning. Retaliation came swiftly. In the afternoon the Black-and-Tans opened fire on the unarmed crowd at an Irish football match between Dublin and Tipperary at Croke Park, Dublin, killing at least eleven (seventeen in Henry's account) and wounding about sixty. The day became known as Bloody Sunday. Henry saw the funeral procession for nine of the British men. His travelling companion Watson had his home raided but all that was removed was Henry's book of poems *Lines of Life* (which included 'A Vigil'). He kept sending copy home but complained that 'most of my stuff is cut down'.

Lloyd George suggested a truce but on the night of 29 November Henry heard the Sinn Féin Bank being blown up in Dublin. The offices of the *Freeman's Journal* were set alight. Henry travelled to Belfast with fellow journalist James Good to investigate the distress and relief meas-ures, but was called south by the *Herald* to report on a delegation of Labour MPs visiting Cork. Here Black-and-Tan officers brandishing revolvers searched Henry and A. P. Wadsworth (*Manchester Guardian*). The following day, O'Brien, a distraught sweetshop owner, appeared at the Imperial Hotel, complaining that 'ruffians' had wrecked his shop and terrified his family. A Black-and-Tan officer put a revolver to O'Brien's head and dragged him into the hotel. Henry intervened, protesting that the officer had come up from behind so O'Brien could not have been making a personal comment. He was released. That afternoon, in his ruined shop, O'Brien and his family welcomed Henry, claiming that he had saved his life. Later that day Henry saw Auxiliaries lash passers-by with whips in retaliation for the killing of an armed party of Auxiliaries in the mountains nine days earlier. Soon after Henry left Cork the city centre was burned. Auxiliaries wore burned corks on their hats. Martial law was proclaimed there and in neighbouring counties.

Henry was reminded of scenes he had witnessed in South Africa, Macedonia and Russia. In 'The Desecration', for which Nannie actually thanked him, he argued that in such a climate of constant fear there could be no hope for peace until, as a first step, the Auxiliaries and Black-and-Tans were withdrawn. Such arms as deemed necessary should be limited to Irish police 'who have some feeling for their countrymen' and to regular troops 'who have some respect for their officers and the honor [*sic*] of our English name'.[68]

Secretly warned in Dublin that 'the Auxiliaries were breathing out slaughters against me' he left Ireland on 10 December.[69] Reflecting on five weeks as the *Herald*'s correspondent, Henry deplored the attempts to

> break a noble people's spirit, the insults to the weak and unarmed, the contumely and scorn, the grotesque brutality to prisoners and captives, the mothers hiding their children in bogs and mountains, the children growing up in an atmosphere of sleepless terror.

He did not believe that the present government could last long. 'But how long will it be before the memory of its abominations fades from the Irish heart?'[70] In the New Year the British government sanctioned reprisals. Over 750 IRA members and civilians died in the seven months before a truce was agreed.

In January 1921 Henry and Evelyn, now in the Labour Party, participated in its campaign for peace in Ireland.[71] About 500 protest meetings were held nationwide with audiences of between 500 and 5,000. Henry addressed Newnham women and Trinity men in Cambridge and packed audiences at venues such as Ladywell Baths, south east London. He shared a platform with Evelyn in Bedford. The finale was a vast gathering at the Albert Hall. For Henry, militant suffrage remained the litmus test for successful English protest meetings so he detected 'a want of something the WSPU used to get'. A couple of weeks later came the Ladysmith Dinner. Henry enjoyed these evenings and worked on his speech. But on learning that General Sir Nevil Macready (who commanded the British forces in Ireland) might attend, he explained that he could not 'endure feasting & gaiety while boys are being executed for fighting for freedom in Ireland'. Six rebels had just been executed. Dining alone at the 1917 Club instead, he went on to by-election meetings in Woolwich.[72]

Just before Christmas, Lloyd George's coalition government had passed the Government of Ireland Act. Partition was implemented in May: separate parliaments for northern and southern Ireland, each with an elected House of Commons and Senate with governments responsible to the parliaments and elections by proportional representation. The State of Northern Ireland would consist of six counties with no jurisdiction over foreign policy. The supremacy of the United Kingdom Parliament remained intact. Both parts of Ireland were to be represented at Westminster. Henry covered the May elections for the *Herald*, using another special notebook. Leaving his Dublin hotel he narrowly missed being hit by two bombs thrown at a passing military car. He found people 'much hardened'. At election meetings in the north he heard the rattle of the Orange drum and speeches full of Old Testament fervour until 'I am worn out with listening.' The election was 'running hot' here 'as between angels of light and devils of darkness, each party claiming to stand on the side of the angels'.[73] Unionists won the majority of seats. One prominent Partitionist (Unionist) told Henry that the new act was so bad that it could actually lead to the union of the whole country. In the south, Sinn Féin won 124 out of the 128 seats unopposed and then boycotted Parliament. On 25 May, the day Henry left the country he called 'my adopted mother', Sinn Féiners in Dublin burned down the Custom House. Editors in England were wary. When G. P. Gooch agreed to Henry writing an article for the *Contemporary Review*, he stressed that it must be descriptive and 'not definitely Sinn Féin'.

In June, George V visited Belfast to open Parliament. He urged conciliation. Secret talks had been taking place since April, and 11 July saw a truce. Less than two weeks later Henry greeted de Valera and delegates at Euston station en route to preliminary peace discussions with Lloyd George and Sir James Craig, head of the Unionist government. Henry jumped on to the running board of de Valera's car, snatching a few words with him. In mid-August Henry heard the proposed terms in Dublin. Dominion status signified much more than Home Rule and allowed full control of home affairs but it also spelt allegiance to the Crown, membership of the British Empire and recognition of Northern Ireland. On 16 August, Henry attended yet another seminal and symbolic national gathering: the first meeting of the new Dáil in the Rotunda of the Mansion House. Evelyn and Nannie were also present. Members took an oath to defend the Irish Republic. In his diary Henry described de Valera's speech as 'very threatening & warlike'.

The Dáil categorically rejected the terms. A despondent Henry recognized the power of de Valera's speech. It allowed no retreat from defending their position and 'What Irishman, what Irishwoman could resist such an appeal?'[74] Henry had suggested to the Speaker (MacNeill) a compromise, terminable twenty-year treaty. Now he was bitterly disappointed that the doctrinaires had triumphed. 'All our efforts at practical arrangement end,' says Henry's diary. 'I came away much depressed & apprehensive of ghastly war.' To his surprise, he learned in America on 6 December that the Treaty between Great Britain and what was now called the Irish Free State had been signed.[75] He hoped that 'at last the immemorial shame which made true patriots loathe the very name of Englishman was about to be wiped out'.[76]

What followed was therefore 'all the more terrible'.[77] De Valera could not accept the oath of loyalty to the King, resigned as President and was succeeded by Griffith. The Dáil accepted it by a narrow majority. In January Michael Collins headed the new provisional government. Power was handed over. After visiting his sister Marian in North Wales, Henry went to Ireland for St Patrick's Day. He rejoiced to see the Irish flag flying over 'that symbol of ancient subjection', Dublin Castle, but not only were there increasing campaigns against Catholics in Northern Ireland but also the likelihood of internal bloody conflict – 'the worst kind of murder' – in the south.[78] Using the familial analogy he reserved for Ireland, he feared 'for the brutal murder of born brothers'. Families were divided internally, the atmosphere exacerbated by delays in the withdrawal of British troops. Henry and Nannie's views did not coincide.[79] He listened to Countess Markievicz and the 'inelastic' Childers. He thought he understood why they felt as they did but regretted their sentiments, leaving in 'deep sadness'. He told a colleague: 'Been in Wales (for a sick sister) and in Ireland (for a sick country). In spite of my exultant hopes, the "Women-and-Childers" gang are bringing your country into great danger.'[80]

A June election endorsed Collins's government but the country drifted towards civil war, anti-Treaty IRA members seeing themselves as the lawful army of the Republic. On 22 June the Ulster Unionist Field Marshal Sir Henry Wilson was murdered in London. Six days later the Free State government had shelled the Four Courts, occupied since April by a rebel republican unit. Henry went to Ireland the following day. Big guns were firing every ten minutes. At lunch time he heard a loud explosion and the classical buildings of the Four Courts were engulfed in flames. The next day (reduced to 'a few hours afterwards' in his memoirs) Henry clambered over smouldering ruins. Walking round the city armed with a revolver, he found 'All the streets and squares were lively with death'.[81] At the corner of St Stephens Green he and the *Daily Chronicle* correspondent saw a bomb thrown at a lorry full of soldiers. It exploded in the middle of the street and 'Bullets hissed all round us'. In August, Griffith died and Collins was killed, 'the worst possible blow to Ireland' in Henry's opinion. Both sides engaged in direct confrontation and guerrilla tactics. In December the Irish Free State adopted a formal constitution and the government of Northern Ireland promptly opted out of its jurisdiction. Henry had written in July that people had become so accustomed to 'fighting, bloodshed and murder, that they find it hard to imagine life without them'. But he did believe that there was a deep longing for peace.[82]

Committed to civil liberties and minority rights, Henry later upheld the rights of nationalists in the north. But after the civil war ended officially in May 1923, he did not write much more about the Free State.[83] It was no longer at the centre of news. Much of the indignation articulated during Henry's long career had anyway been directed at claims for freedom rather than its operation. His involvement in Irish affairs was largely against British governments behaving badly rather than investigating why certain issues were important for republicans. He did not appreciate the significance of Irish being spoken at the opening of the Dáil in August 1921 (had he still been involved with Nannie he might have evinced more sympathy). He failed to recognize how important symbols might be for national identity. He expressed impatience with the Irish concern over 'that tiresome oath of allegiance', adding 'as though that mattered'! Such sentiments suggest that, although bravely championing causes, he ultimately failed to grasp the complexities of Irish nationalism.

Yet he knew when he was not wanted. Nannie helped him to understand that 'Nothing could be more difficult or dangerous than for an Englishman to speak to the Irish about Ireland.'[84] When the imprisoned nationalist poet Joseph Campbell described Henry as a 'well-meaning English Liberal' who could not understand the anti-Treaty perspective, he replied that he was neither a Liberal nor, 'if possible, an armchair writer'. He added a fair question: 'But would the Republicans during the late trouble have admitted me to their lines or their counsels? You know they would not.'

Over the years Henry and a handful of journalists helped sustain publicity on Anglo-Irish affairs. His outspoken views and blunt words alienated Unionists, some of the British public and historians.[85] There was no sitting on the fence. As with India and women's suffrage, Henry was more involved than most correspondents. Branded the rebel journalist par excellence, he displayed 'decent rage'. He did, however, believe that the Irish Parliamentary Party deserved more credit than it received. In November 1917 after talking to a Sinn Féiner he noted privately that 'I was angered as usual at their contemptuous ingratitude to men like Dillon who have suffered & done so much all these 40 years for Ireland.'

Summarizing the events of 1921, Henry wrote: 'It has been mainly an Irish year for me.' Even though covering Irish affairs was part of his professional work, his sustained commitment was remarkable for someone not of Irish descent. 'Nevinson was of great importance in the relations of nationalist Ireland and the new Liberals', writes a modern historian.[86] Massingham complained that Henry would rush off to Ireland when he might have been at home composing middles. Yet although he wrote books about most conflicts he covered, unlike Hugh

Martin and Hammond who produced both newspaper articles and books on Ireland Henry did not turn his Irish experience into a volume. He may have felt that by 1923 it was too late to embark on the kind of hefty tome needed for a serious study.[87]

From reviews of Irish culture and defending Roger Casement to articles and talks on its recurring conflicts over many years, Henry wrote from the heart. And although he sometimes generalized and simplified issues, this passion and publicity counted. He was appreciated where he felt it mattered. In 1932 the *Cork Examiner* suggested that 'probably of all English journalists' Henry had 'given the most effective aid to Ireland in the past'.[88]

CHAPTER TEN

Old and New Worlds

On Christmas Day 1918 Henry was on his own in Cologne. A 'lonely but expensive lunch' encouraged self-pity and guilt as he sat amidst the splendour of the Dom Hotel in a country reeling from food shortages. Fellow correspondents Gibbs, Robinson and Phillips had returned home but, wishing to 'Get at the truth about the social state of things here', Henry stayed on. He wrote to Gertrude Parry, telling her how he had hoped to 'retire into a peaceful and contemplative life in preparation for my latter end! Now I see nothing but a series of boiling points, new every morning like the love.'[1] That exclamation mark hints at the absurdity of Henry Nevinson ever courting a peaceful existence.[2] 'Boiling points' had characterized his life up until now. There was to be no simmering into old age.

For another decade Henry would cover assignments abroad. He was in a highly privileged position, witnessing and commenting upon the shaping of the post-war world order yet informed by experiences that reached back into the nineteenth century. Unlike the foreign correspondent resident in one country, he moved around, observing how nations handled peace, economic problems and nationalist claims. He had made the transition from war correspondent to special correspondent and, being freelance, had the freedom of not being tied to one newspaper. However, in the 1920s he wrote regularly for the *Manchester Guardian* (£25 weekly for most foreign assignments) and the *Baltimore Sun*.[3]

At the end of 1917, depressed at the way war was dragging on, Henry had written in his diary: 'I think it is the end of an age – the European age.'[4] He now observed the new in the Middle East as eastern immigrants poured into Palestine. The 1920s also enabled him to see at first hand the growth of a twentieth-century superpower, the United States. He had never been to the New World but made three visits to America in these years, all closely associated with the workings of the presidency. For Richard Nevinson too, the United States beckoned.[5] Paintings of Manhattan skyscrapers replaced missiles. Yet both men were quintessentially defined in the public imagination by past work and, for the ageing Henry rooted in the classical tradition, modernity had its price.

After the joyful Armistice scene at Mons in 1918, Henry travelled round Belgium. One of the first uniformed Englishmen to reach Ghent, he felt like 'him who brought the citizens good news'.[6] He witnessed thousands of returning refugees and saw acts of revenge. On 1 December, Henry, Roberts and Beach-Thomas drove into Germany. Three days earlier the Kaiser had abdicated. The journalists were just ahead of the 4th Dragoon Guards and a regiment of Lancers advancing as vanguard to the 1st Cavalry Division. Within a few days they had reached Cologne. At the Dom Hotel, overlooking Cologne's majestic cathedral, waiters fresh out of army uniforms served them. Just before Christmas, General Haig gathered the correspondents together at the entrance to the Kaiser Bridge over the Rhine. Presenting them with tiny Union Jacks on sticks – 'like good children at a school-treat' – he praised their work and then stated that the ensuing peace must not be a peace of vengeance.[7]

Keen to gauge the level of deprivation and with the advantage of understanding German, Henry listened to socialist speakers, to advocates of a Rhineland Republic and to mayors, including Konrad Adenauer, later first Chancellor of the Federal Republic of Germany. One mayor told him they were too exhausted to hate their conquerors. Henry felt he was witnessing the disintegration of a nation and, as in India pre-war, speculated on the degree to which 'unquestioning submission to authority' accounted for the ruin.[8] The early stages of a British blockade on food supplies and jobs and the influenza pandemic exacerbated the situation. At the children's hospital in Lindenburg he saw many children dying of starvation. Mothers had no milk, the French had requisitioned large numbers of cows and there was no rubber for milk bottle teats. Henry's appeal in the *Manchester Guardian* resulted in a million teats being sent to Germany.

Henry sounded a warning: 'We have a choice before us. It is easily in our power to reduce Central Europe to a desert of ruin inhabited by skeletons, such as Germany was at the end of The Thirty Years' War.' Yet world peace would not be ensured by 'the destruction of a great and laborious people, or by implanting among them the poisonous seed of revenge'.[9] This was intended as an antidote to the Northcliffe press. Journalists like Ward Price of the *Daily Mail* suggested that Germany was prosperous and unharmed. The artist Rothenstein, also based at the Dom (where he sketched Henry), later recalled a telegram from an English newspaper magnate stating that 'no news testifying to the plight of the Germans, likely to arouse sympathy in England, must be telegraphed home'.[10] Henry still disdained correspondents who 'hardly stirred out of the best hotel except to walk down the fashionable street'. He became the first to 'break through the conspiracy of silence in the press'.[11]

After two months Henry returned home. He had turned down a request from Dent to write a history of the war. Now he addressed meetings against the blockade, working with Quakers in the Fight the Famine Council. He joined the council of the Save the Children's Fund that grew out of this. But tragically there was a baby closer to home that could not be saved. Kathleen Nevinson had given birth to Anthony Christopher Wynne. Yet by the time Richard returned from a triumphant New York tour, the son he had never seen had died. Henry's diary recorded the birth on 20 May 1919 yet did not mention him again until early June when he was dying. Then, rather curiously, he wrote 'I was strangely unhappy.' Henry could be hard on himself as well as others when it came to expressing family emotions. The baby was buried with Henry's father in Hampstead churchyard. Henry, who set such store by his family name, chose not to dwell on this in his diary. Instead he immersed himself in relief work for starving German children, all the while deploring the peace terms and 'our acquiescence in the crime of Versailles'.[12]

The treaty had stipulated that Germany pay the allies compensation for war damage. France chaired the Reparations Commission. Germany's offer of free labour and materials to restore the devastated regions of northern France was rejected. In April 1921 liability was fixed at a rate exceeding Germany's capacity to repay. When the country defaulted on payments early in 1923, French and Belgian troops occupied the Ruhr to force the Weimar Republic either to pay its debts or suffer dire economic consequences from the loss of its industrial centre. To disarmed Germans this represented a violation of the peace treaty. Passive resistance in the Ruhr, encouraged by the Weimar Republic, effectively halted most production. The United States and Britain disapproved of the Franco-Belgian action. The Americans withdrew their troops from the Rhine in protest. After consideration Britain retained its presence. Despite Henry's implacable opposition to the French action, he believed that this was the correct decision.

At the end of January 1923, Henry and Evelyn spent over a fortnight reporting on conditions in Germany: Henry for the *Guardian* and Evelyn for the *Daily Herald*. Neither his memoirs nor diary indicate that they were together though Evelyn's autobiography mentions him as a colleague. However, Evelyn now kept travel diaries and from her opening entry for this trip she mentions travelling with 'GD', an abbreviation of Grand Duke, Henry's nickname.[13] Their diaries show them following identical itineraries. They stayed, investigated and socialized together, both deeply troubled by what they saw. Henry's brief was to write on conditions in cities outside the Ruhr. Of Berlin he wrote: 'I do not know where in the world's history one could find a parallel to so overwhelming an overthrow, so complete a reversal of fortune, and in so short a time.'[14]

In Berlin and in Leipzig they witnessed a ruined middle class and the total collapse of the currency. The relationship of wages to food prices dominated as the value of the German mark plummeted. It took a worker a day and a half to buy a pound of margarine. Then came news of the blockade of the Ruhr. The textile centre of Chemnitz revealed 'Human misery about at its lowest'. Fellow correspondent Morgan Philips Price, who had witnessed the Russian Revolution, wrote that the condition of Germany 'literally beggars description'. Unlike Russia there seemed 'scarcely a ray of light on the horizon'.[15] The one bright spot for Henry was returning to Jena after nearly forty years. He was delighted to hold a seminar at his old university.

Jena must have stirred youthful memories and heightened the contrast between German cultural and intellectual traditions and the current lack of prospects for the intelligentsia, especially in the occupied territory. With his propensity for defending the underdog, he gave the Germans his sympathy and the French were cast as desiring revenge and commercial prosperity. Schools in the Ruhr were commandeered for barracks. Countless teachers lost their jobs and nearly 130,000 children an education. With the Ruhr and Rhineland encircled by French outposts and a customs barrier between occupied and unoccupied Germany, Henry condemned French plans to weaken Germany still further through Separatism. This advocated turning its territories on the Rhine, the Palatinate and Saarland into client states dependent on France. How, Henry asked, could England and America look calmly on while a nation was destroyed?[16]

Yet that nation had recently been the enemy, and British readers who had fought or suffered losses were not very likely to reason thus. There were objections to Henry's depiction of French politicians rejoicing at the spectacle of Germans dying of hunger and disease.[17] His irony, which puzzled some at the best of times, became excoriating in depicting the French premier, Raymond Poincaré. He should be the happiest man on earth: 'he ruins his enemy and enriches his people. Was ever happiness like unto his happiness?'[18]

In late September, with infant mortality soaring and a steep fall in the birth rate, the German government formally ended nine months of passive resistance. A month later Henry returned to Germany for the *Guardian*. Scott was concerned that hunger and hunger riots might develop 'in a rather serious way . . . anything might happen'. Henry, just turned sixty-seven and once more victim to the ill health induced by past assignments, agreed to go only as a 'stop-gap'. Refusing to accept age as a factor, he explained that malaria and rheumatism had put paid to being a correspondent, 'who has to run about for telegraphic news, though I think I could still do "descriptives"'.[19]

In the event he stayed a month, providing impressions of the Rhineland and Ruhr. Somewhat disingenuously, he wrote in his autobiography of 'a new and welcome figure' joining old colleagues in Cologne: Evelyn Sharp![20] Henry and Evelyn went by car to Aachen (where the Belgians had stationed soldiers with machine guns). At

Duren, the Rhineland Republic seemed to be in 'full swing'. Henry stressed that only 1 per cent of the Ruhr population allied itself with the Separatist Movement and that the French encouraged these 'scallywag youths and gaolbirds'.[21] With headings such as 'The Revolver Republic', he reflected the views of those on the Left who feared that France would destroy the Weimar Republic.[22] At Trier, the Separatists' green, white and red flag flew. Attempts to remove it saw the cavalry charging the crowd.

Henry wrote that he was 'sick of horrors and misery. So is all the world. Still they continue, and I cannot let them go without protest.' But even protest could be difficult. Modern communications did not necessarily aid correspondents. He wrote 600 words after meetings in Koblenz with Matthes the Separatist leader and with Lord Kilmarnock at the headquarters of the Rhineland Commission. But he then had a wretched thirty minutes shouting his message on the telephone to Antwerp. His telegram to Scott (text messaging from the early twentieth century!) raises questions about the effectiveness of air mails and telegraphs: 'THE DIFFICULTY IS TT ONE HS TO COME TO COLOGNE TO WRITE OR TELEGRAPH AND TT TKES NRLY ALL ONE DAY.'[23]

Neither was travel easy. Henry and Evelyn's train journey to the Ruhr took a circuitous route. But they were used to such challenges and it was Henry's disdain for French treatment of the Germans rather than inconvenience that prompted an incident at Dusseldorf station. They sat in the waiting room with crowds of German passengers. A French officer entered and peremptorily ordered bags to be opened for inspection. Henry was commanded to 'Ouvrez.' As Evelyn recalled, 'It was a great moment. The correspondent of a hundred wars just looked at the intruder, then turned away his head as from an insect that had buzzed in his ear. The officer was at first speechless, then repeated in an awful tone "Ouvrez, ouvrez".' Believing that the kind Englishman (who spoke excellent German) did not understand French, the passengers translated for him, begging him to comply. He simply carried on smoking. The Germans now explained that this rebel was English. 'The effect was magical' and Evelyn, always kind-hearted and aware that the French were themselves fed anti-German propaganda and had anyway faced atrocities on their land and people, began to feel sorry for the officer.[24]

Henry described the Ruhr as 'one of those unhappy districts where man has made a desolation & called it wealth'.[25] Starving people populated one of the world's richest coalfields. Most mines were closed and factories and railways were running slowly, if at all, operated by foreigners. The mark, 'unstable as water, was running down from nothing to nothing'.[26] Henry and Evelyn visited the vast Krupp works where 62,000 workers had been discharged. Pleading for intervention, his impassioned articles told of the desperation of trades union leaders.

At the request of the British a new enquiry into reparation potential-
ities was set up under an American general. The Dawes Plan became
operational in the autumn of 1924. It involved a two-year moratorium
on payments, return of the Ruhr to Germany and a foreign loan in return
for a German undertaking to resume payment in increasing annuities.
The next five years were better. But Henry had witnessed the economic
situation at its nadir. In November 1923 he was, for once, relieved to go
home.

He also travelled further afield in these years. His first visit to the
United States was a lecture tour, organized by an agent in Boston. Billed
as the 'Dean of English War correspondents', he offered twenty-five
lectures.[27] During the Atlantic voyage a mother hushed her child by
murmuring 'Look at pretty grandfather' when he passed by. On 16 April
1920, sailing past the 'painfully straight' arm of the Statue of Liberty,
'pretty grandfather' had his first, unforgettable vision of New York. He
called it a 'magic city of dreams', marvelling at Manhattan's skyscrapers.
The Woolworth Building towered above all others. He stayed, for less
than two dollars a night, at the National Arts Club off Gramercy Park in

12 Henry Nevinson – a studio portrait.

Lower Manhattan. A brownstone with a spectacular glass dome, it was both exclusive and inclusive: women had, since its opening in 1898, been admitted as full, equal members.

Although Henry offered talks about his varied experiences across the globe, the only topic Americans seemed to want was English literary figures. He addressed over a dozen clubs and fraternities, mainly in the north eastern states. The hospitality was impressive but the passivity of audiences disappointed him. Cornell was his favourite university. Enchanted by its campus above Ithaca, complete with ravine and lilacs in full bloom, 'a sweeter place for youth could not be imagined'. The freedom of its female students (about one-sixth of the student population) fascinated him.

In June, Henry covered the Republican Convention in Chicago for the *Manchester Guardian*. This began a campaign to select the presidential candidate that continued until November. After two terms of Democrats and with the ailing President Wilson standing down, the Republicans were spoiling for a fight. Three candidates emerged at the end of the first day of balloting. But a seasoned newspaperman warned Henry that none of them would succeed. The next day he saw their votes 'melt away like the Assyrians at the breath of the Lord'.[28] On the tenth ballot the conservative Senator Warren G. Harding of Ohio triumphed. The previous night a cabal of party leaders in a smoke-filled room had agreed that Harding was their man. Having secured the nomination, Harding won the presidential election with a seven million majority. Henry so loathed the pretence, private politicking and open razzmatazz of the Convention that he joked it 'almost made a monarchist of me'.[29] It was close to 100 degrees Fahrenheit in the vast Coliseum. The public spectacle was accompanied by the deafening noise of cheerleaders. Henry wondered what it cost both lungs and purses, especially since he could see no real difference between Republicans and Democrats.

He did, however, witness another historic event. Women (on the brink of gaining the right to vote in presidential elections) had never addressed the Republican Convention. Now Henry heard Mrs Robinson (Theodore Roosevelt's sister) speak. He judged her speech militarist and reactionary but preferable to the men's. He stayed at Hull House, the famous settlement house founded by Jane Addams in the 1880s. Somewhat patronizingly, he saw British women's suffrage as more militant and, by implication, more significant than its American counterpart. Henry defended 'the old militancy in the old way, & with the old passion. They didn't like it. They are alarmed or afraid even of standing still with flags to picket.' Watching the National Woman's Party outside the Convention, he remarked, 'They call it militancy but it is peace.' This ignored historical differences between suffrage in the two countries as well as within America, the effect of current repressive policing and earlier actions such as Woman's Party members chaining themselves to the White House. Nevertheless, Henry enjoyed having his photograph taken with the party's founder, Alice Paul, who had been active in English suffragette circles and force-fed in prison.

Henry noticed 'a peculiar absence of indignation' in American life.[30] He attributed this to the size of the country: it was too vast for concentrated rage, lacking one symbolic rallying point at which protesters could gather relatively easily. He deplored the continual threat to personal liberty, reserving his most scathing comments for under-cover informants, the 'filthiest form of tyranny'.[31] Those fearing Bolshevism conveniently confused radicalism with terrorism. Against a background of violence and bombings as well as strikes by organized labour, dissenters from 'pure Americanism' were vulnerable. Henry attended workers' meetings in New York City on May Day. Its entire police force of 11,000 had been mobilized because of unsubstantiated claims that the day would trigger a communist uprising. Returning to the States in the autumn of 1921,[32] Henry petitioned Congress at the request of the American Civil Liberties Union, urging amnesty for the socialist leader Eugene V. Debs and other political prisoners. Although the 1917 Espionage Act had been suspended, nearly 150 sentenced under it were still imprisoned. The petition was read in the Senate on 12 December and twenty-three people including Debs were released a fortnight later. His rapturous greeting of Henry was captured on film.

Henry remained in the United States for over four months, covering the Disarmament Conference in Washington for the *Guardian* (duplicated in the *Baltimore Sun* and *New York World*). The naval armaments race between Great Britain, the United States and Japan threatened peace. There was also American unease about the Anglo-Japanese alliance in the Pacific. Nine European and Asiatic powers were invited. At its first plenary session, Secretary of State Charles Hughes delivered a revolutionary statement. He proposed real disarmament: that the major powers freeze their naval strength. Henry noted that the speech shook the delegates like an explosion. Plans were outlined for a ten-year break from constructing capital ships with specific details of the destruction of national battleships. The Americans would scrap the most. Henry's colleague Colonel Repington remarked how it 'took us off our feet. We seemed spellbound.' In thirty-five minutes Hughes had sunk more ships 'than all the admirals of the world have destroyed in a cycle of centuries. More, he appeared to me to condemn by anticipation all the armaments of the globe.'[33] In the long term the conference did little to resolve underlying tensions between the United States and Japan and was unable to tackle fundamentally the problem of naval armaments.[34] But it was perceived as a diplomatic triumph for the United States.

Conference meetings were private but the press attended plenary sessions. President Harding, 'a master of platitude',[35] met them at the White House at least once a week. Hughes held meetings most days,

Henry and his colleagues standing in a semi-circle, firing questions. The British press also had twice-daily sessions with Lord Riddell of the National Proprietors' Association and attended grand dinners with Arthur Balfour and other delegates at the British Embassy. Henry discovered that journalists commanded respect and received assistance in America. As Repington put it, with Harding and Hughes constantly briefing them it was as though the King and Lord Curzon held weekly press meetings at which journalists could ask what they wished![36]

This was the first conference with radio as well as extensive newspaper coverage. Given the time difference, Henry had to compose and get his copy (usually about 900 words daily) to the telegraph clerks by about 3 p.m. for it to reach Manchester. The weighty plenary sessions left him with a tight margin and the pressure manifested itself in skin problems. The British press included Maurice Low, Wickham Steed and H. G. Wells. Henry greatly admired Wells's intellect. Both men opposed France's claims. Wells's anti-French comments resulted in him moving from the *Daily Mail* to the *Daily Express*. Henry's diary denounced speeches by the French premier Briand, especially his bellicose attacks on Germany. But the chief bone of contention with France concerned the French rejection of a British proposal to scrap submarines. At one press briefing with Hughes, Henry asked whether England might now build anti-submarine vessels and light cruisers against France. The next day an American newspaper denounced 'Liberal or Manchester' journalists who spread 'poisonous propaganda' against France.

Over the New Year, Henry received a delegation from Chità, capital of the Siberian Eastern Republic, which for the previous three years had been occupied by Japanese troops. The delegation gave him documents demonstrating that, before the conference, France and Japan had 'caucused', agreeing to work together during meetings. This inflammatory material even showed earlier evidence of France agreeing to attack the Bolsheviks from eastern Siberia, enabling Japan to dominate Siberia. Henry persuaded the delegation, which had approached him first, to delay showing the material to other journalists by one day since his paper had no Sunday edition and he wanted a 'scoop'. His diary shows that he thought the documents genuine, at least in part. He confidently told his paper that 'I can have little doubt that the documents are authentic.'[37] He and the British delegates understood that, genuine or forged, the documents could blow the conference 'sky high like a kite' and cause the French to walk out.

Henry got his 'exclusive'. But, despite press speculation about whether any substance lay behind the claims, the incident blew over quickly. Both the French and Japanese dismissed the documents as forgeries. As Henry knew, allegations about Japanese atrocities were embarrassing for a conference involved in delicate negotiations between Japan and other major powers. Moreover, the Chità delegation was not an official one. Nevertheless, one result of the conference was Japan's withdrawal of troops from Siberia.

Henry recognized other tangible gains. Naval competition had been checked, costs cut and, he hoped, the horrors of submarine warfare reduced. Important agreement had been made with Japan. At last, difficult questions were being discussed internationally. Above all, good will had been stimulated between Britain and the United States. Against this background, during his voyage home in February 1922 he composed one of his most successful works. 'Farewell to America' appeared in the *Baltimore Sun* and the *Nation* and was reprinted on both sides of the Atlantic into the 1950s. Allan Nevins's compilation of twenty-eight of the 'ablest' travel writers on America since the Washington era ends with it.[38] It even enjoyed that double-edged mark of popularity: pirated editions.

Short – a middle par excellence – it is Henry's commentary on American confidence, consumerism and modernity compared to Britain's traditions. It opens with a sentence that carries, for the modern reader, a chilling post-9/11 significance: 'In mist and driving snow the towers of New York fade from view.' Then Henry bids:

> Good-bye to central heating and radiators, fit symbols of the hearts they warm! Good-bye to frequent and well-appointed bathrooms, the glory of America's art! . . . I am going home. I am going to . . . a land of open fires and chilly rooms and frozen water-pipes, of washing-stands and slop pails, and one bath per household at the most . . . Good-bye to the copious meals – the early grape-fruit, the 'cereals' . . . I am going to the land of joints and roots and solid pudding; the land of ham-and-eggs and violent tea . . . Good-bye to the long stream of motors – 'limousines' or 'flivvers'! Good-bye to the signal lights upon Fifth Avenue, gold, crimson and green . . . I am going to the land of the policeman's finger, where the horse and the bicycle still drag out a lingering life . . . Good-bye to the land of a new language in growth, of split infinitives and cross-bred words . . . where strangers say 'glad to meet you, sir,' and really seem glad . . . I am going to a land of ancient speech . . . where we never say we are glad to meet a stranger, and seldom are . . .

Its rhythm and repetition – six of its seven paragraphs end with 'Good-bye, America! I am going home' – lull the reader and soften both its implicit criticism of America and its exaggerated claims for British customs:

> Good-bye to the land where Liberals are thought dangerous, and Radicals show red! . . . I am going to a land of politics violently divergent; a land where even Coalitions cannot coalesce . . . a land fierce for personal freedom, and indignant with rage for justice . . .

He ends with 'Good-bye, Americans! I am going to a country very much like yours. I am going to your spiritual home.'[39]

Henry's final visit to the United States came in 1929 when he accompanied Ramsay MacDonald on the first visit from a British Prime Minister to an American President. Henry had known MacDonald since the 1880s. Post-war, Henry saw the Labour Party as Britain's best hope politically though was never a party man and declined invitations to stand as Labour candidate for Hampstead and for the Universities. He covered the 1922 election for the *Baltimore Sun*, sending daily cables of just under 1,000 words and describing the victor, the Conservative Bonar Law, as 'a worthy, puzzled Colonial gentleman, rich but honest'. Early in 1924 when MacDonald formed the first Labour government and old friends like Noel Buxton became Cabinet ministers, Henry found himself invited to receptions at 10 Downing Street. But in October, for the third time in three years and dogged by red scares, the country went to the polls again. MacDonald asked Henry to accompany him on his pre-election tour from Newcastle upon Tyne down to his Aberavon (Aberafan) constituency.[40] It took an hour to travel the last mile through Port Talbot. 'Never', wrote Henry, 'have I been in such crowds, never heard such cheering, and such singing, never felt so wild a passion of enthusiasm around me.' But there was a Tory landslide.

In 1929 Henry reported once more from America on naval disarmament. Hoover and MacDonald's historic meeting was the preamble to a naval conference held in London the following year but announced during this visit. The *Guardian* required 'something substantial every day' with politics as 'the chief thing' and 'a good deal of attention' to the ' "human scene" '.[41] Henry sent Cunard wireless messages from the ship. Landing on Manhattan's southern tip, MacDonald was granted the Freedom of the City and greeted with a ticker-tape parade. At Penn Station, Henry, who had learned to use a typewriter at the end of the war, hurriedly typed 800 words kneeling on a wooden bench before joining the train to Washington. Here he received preferential treatment. After a meeting at the State Department he was the sole correspondent selected to walk with MacDonald. The two leaders then retreated to Hoover's Blue Ridge Mountain retreat. Henry was unimpressed by their briefing by White House officials. 'Fifty grown men' were told that the two men had 'walked downstream this morning, had sat on a log & seen a fish'!

On 11 October, Henry's seventy-third birthday, MacDonald delivered three important speeches in New York. The final speech to the Council of Foreign Relations was on disarmament. It reached the largest audience of MacDonald's career, being broadcast in the United States and relayed to Britain on short-wave radio. Henry represented the tour as a triumph for the Prime Minister. He suggested that he might have paid more attention to the Progressives but wrote effusively of the day of the three speeches: 'I suppose no single statesman has ever accomplished more for the benefit of mankind in so short a time.'[42]

In New Jersey MacDonald met a deputation of Zionists. Over the last decade American Jews had sent five million pounds to Palestine under the British mandate and he thanked them for their efforts. By this time Henry had made his own visit to Palestine and lectured about this at Boston and Yale. In 1926 the Zionist Organization had asked him to publicize in Britain the developments in Palestine. Zionism was still a young movement, its first congress held in Basle in 1897. Its Viennese founder, Theodor Herzl, had been a journalist in Paris influenced by the anti-Semitism surrounding the Dreyfus Case. A letter of November 1917 from the British Foreign Secretary, Sir Arthur Balfour, to the prominent British Jew Lord Rothschild contained what became known as the Balfour Declaration. This boosted Zionism. In words that have since been much debated, Balfour declared that the government viewed with favour a 'National Home' for the Jewish people.

In mid-1916 the secret Sykes–Picot Agreement had provided a tripartite arrangement between Russia, Britain and France for partitioning the Ottoman Empire. Palestine, the most contested area, was to be separated from Syria and placed under international administration until settled in the peace conference. A month after the Balfour Declaration, Jerusalem fell, ending nearly 1,300 years of Islamic rule in Palestine. General Allenby's entry into the city began British rule. A civilian government headed by Sir Herbert Samuel as High Commissioner existed from July 1920 to create the preconditions for establishing a Jewish National Home and to safeguard the rights of the Arabs, the overwhelming majority. Apprehension and anger about the implications of the Balfour Declaration resulted in serious anti-Jewish riots in 1920–1. Not until 1922 did the Council of the League of Nations approve a British Mandate for Palestine and Transjordania (Jordan).

A Zionist Commission had been in place since early 1918. The Zionist Organization now paid Henry's expenses for six weeks in September 1926. The *Guardian* agreed to take eight articles for ten pounds apiece. A week in Turkey introduced Henry to Atatürk's modernized Istanbul. He had last seen Constantinople, 'one of those cities, like Rome, before whose history the mind stands stupefied', in 1907.[43] Now he noted women with short hair in place of the veil, wearing European clothes, frequenting cafés and smoking. He acknowledged the part played in this change by the novelist and feminist Halidé Edib Adivar, whom he had met several times in England. Then he went south to Palestine.

Henry's descriptions suggest almost a homecoming. Knowledge of the Old Testament and places such as the Sea of Galilee and Nazareth had been 'driven into my soul as a child'.[44] This established his own links with Palestine's past and present, suggesting how much more powerful emotions must be for the Jew at last touching the soil of the promised land. Henry claimed that he had grown up knowing more about tales of what was called the Holy Land than about his own country, in a curious appropriation of History that was remote in several senses. The Bible was regarded as 'so essentially British that, though we were accustomed to despise and hate the Jews, we identified with the Jewish race as belonging to the "Chosen People" '.[45] Yet, although he critiqued his upbringing, Henry was deeply influenced by it and profoundly stirred on entering the Holy City through the Damascus Gate: 'Even to an Englishman, the first sight of Jerusalem is one of life's greatest events.'[46] He stayed at the modest Austrian Hospice where his room faced the Via Dolorosa and the supposed site of Calvary. He wandered around the ancient city and marvelled.

But his task was to report on the new. Over 17,000 Jewish immigrants settled annually in Palestine. Henry began in Tel Aviv, the symbolic modern city by the sea, 'brilliant, white and clean', where everybody seemed to be under thirty and 'so indifferent to starchy tradition'.[47] Although unemployment was now a serious problem for this burgeoning centre that had rapidly overtaken ancient, adjacent Jaffa, Henry saw it as a city of hope. He talked to labour leaders including Ben-Gurion, the future Prime Minister of Israel. He visited old Jewish colonies. And he saw modern Zionist settlements, both individualistic ('Moshav Ovdim'), such as Balfouria where each family worked for its own profit, and communal ('Kvutzah') communities, like Beth Alpha at the foot of the mountains of Gilboa, where he spent a night. For Henry, Beth Alpha was a fascinating experiment and challenge to the stifling nature of family life that hinted at Plato's Republic. He watched the land being worked and marshes drained around Haifa. But he could not cope with the mosquitoes and heat and collapsed. He spent a week in hospital in Jerusalem.

Henry had long shared some literary and suffrage interests with the Zionist Israel Zangwill, founder of the Jewish Territorial Organization. He had also written about Jewish persecution in Odessa, was renowned as a champion of causes and known to be not only a powerful and influential writer but also a seasoned investigator, good at teasing out information far from home. Moreover he had a record of advocating rights for small nations and so appealed to the section of British Jewry that focused on nationality rather than religion. But, on his own admission, he knew little about either section. When he had lived amongst poor immigrants in London's East End his personal writings had contained stereotypes and flippant comments about Jews. Yet, once interested in a public cause or movement, Henry was proficient at defending its precepts. Seeing Zionism in practice impressed him. He told of a heroic project: inspired young immigrants devoting their lives to working for the common good on land 'sanctified to them by history and by an exile so long lamented'.[48] Henry might comment that 'The Zionist was to the Arab what the motor car was to the camel' and add 'As an old-fashioned Englishman, my tastes and sympathies are naturally on the side of the camel.'[49] But, as with Futurism, he believed that Zionism held out promise, looking forward 'instead of waiting for ever over the dead ruins of the past'.[50]

However, at the end of an article on his brief visit to Amman, Henry added a postscript at the request of Dr Hans Kohn, a correspondent who had been a guide in Palestine. Explaining that 'rather violent Zionists' were advocating occupation of the strategically important Transjordania, it argued against such colonization. Dr Eder, who headed the Zionist Commission, took Henry to task for these comments. This episode encapsulated his problems. Zionists had funded his investigations yet, despite being influenced by what he had seen in Palestine, Henry was not committed to the movement in the way that he had tended to support causes in the past. He was writing about a highly charged, sensitive and evolving situation and some of his statements were accorded more significance by Zionists than he had intended. Henry's brief meant a necessary focus on the positive work of the settlers. He also argued that Palestinian Arabs were now freed from Turkish conscription and 'without really much complaint to make against Jew or Briton'.[51] He did add that 'one can understand their apprehensions' but failed to address their perspectives and so invited their criticism too. Neither was he patient with the views of the Anglican clergy he encountered in Palestine. And his acceptance of the Balfour Declaration and praise for the efficiency of the British Mandates annoyed others.

In 1927 Henry lectured on his travels at the Parliamentary Club, noticing that he disappointed the Jews who had expected a talk on Zionism. The following month he addressed the left-wing Union of Democratic Control. He pronounced it a 'gloomy failure'. The chairman had clearly hoped for an exposé of abuses by the administration of the Mandates. At a Chatham House (Royal Institute of International Affairs) debate in 1930 on Palestine opened by Arnold Toynbee, Henry spoke briefly at the end. He suggested that the controversial Balfour Declaration's description of Arabs as 'the non-Jewish communities' was some sort of reparation for centuries of Jewish misery and persecution. The pro-Arab Freda White deliberately turned her back on him afterwards.

Henry's journey to the Middle East ended in Iraq. He visited the French Mandates of the Lebanon and Syria and travelled across the Syrian Desert with the Nairn overland mail convoy. Reminded of the slow caravans carrying the commerce of Nineveh and Babylon, he passed the ancient site of Palmyra. After a night in a crowded dormitory at Rutbah, the desert rapidly turned into liquid slush. The rains had begun earlier than usual. To avoid Druze attacks, the convoy had taken a more northerly route than usual but now faced new perils. A journey to Baghdad that should have taken two to three days became treacherous, the cars weighed down by mailbags. For four long days Henry and the drivers toiled with spades, digging the cars out of the mud and laying down stones. The mail was abandoned.

After another delay outside Felujah where a torrent of rain had made the track to its bridge impassable, they finally reached Baghdad. Encrusted from head to toe in hardened mud, Henry resembled a Rodin statue. This once 'great and famous city' was also engulfed in mud, its side streets under water and its inhabitants suffering. Henry was, though, constantly reminded of former times, conjuring up images of ancient Ur and the Tower of Babel. He visited the excavated mud bricks foundations of Babylon, savouring the cradle of civilization by 'the candlelight of imagination'.[52] Two days later he returned across the desert and was home in time for Christmas. The old adventurer knew how to make the most of a story. Well aware that Ruskin had once mobilized Oxford undergraduates to build a road in flooded Ferry Hinksey, Henry ended his triple-decker autobiography carefully. The mail company drivers had told their boss in Baghdad that, whatever happened, he must keep 'Old Bill as a digger on the Staff!' Henry called this 'the finest compliment ever paid me in the course of a long and variegated life'.[53] His labours were never in vain.

This final volume, published in 1928, was entitled *Last Changes, Last Chances*. But these years also saw the ageing correspondent regretting some lost chances. In 1925 an American syndicate asked Henry (he now had a telephone) to accompany Amundsen and Ellsworth in attempting to fly across the North Pole. He declined, citing age and the need to complete his memoirs. Forced to abandon their flight, the explorers were presumed dead. Henry had regretted his precipitate refusal. He now mused on what might have been: 'The distinction, the flattery, the change, the fine form of death & burial!' He was even sorrier when three weeks later, after digging themselves out of ice, the men emerged to tell the tale.

The *Guardian* then dangled the offer of an assignment in China. Again Henry refused only to suffer pangs of self-contempt when Arthur Ransome went instead. But the Grand Duke was fast becoming 'an almost legendary figure'[54] in his own land. Henry's reputation rested on former exploits but throughout the inter-war years he enhanced it, fulminating against injustice in meetings, newspapers and books. His punishing routine would have daunted many younger men. But it was like food and water to him. He joked that he had founded a League of Age with the motto 'The Older the Bolder'.

Many inter-war activities echoed nineteenth-century interests. Henry was a founder member of the Ruskin Society, attending its annual dinner up to 1940. One of the few happy occasions shared by Henry and Margaret had been in 1888 when they met Ruskin at an inn close to Mont Blanc. Another early influence had been Goethe and, to celebrate the centenary of his death in 1932, Henry wrote *Goethe: Man and Poet*. Marketed as a readable introduction, its style was somewhat out-dated and it failed to do justice to both subject and author. Loyal to old friends too, Henry remained close to John Masefield, who wrote a poem about America welcoming 'Nevi'.[55] Henry published 'An Appreciation' of Masefield the year after he became Poet Laureate and was an annual judge at the Oxford Recitations established by the Masefields to uncover talented verse speakers.[56]

In 1920 Unwin published Henry's poems. Masefield complimented him but was much more effusive about his prose. He wrote the Preface to *Fire of Life* (1935), the abridged version of Henry's memoirs, proclaiming that 'No better autobiography has been written in English in the last hundred years.'[57] It sold 8,000 copies in the first few months of publication. Many of Henry's books enjoyed only modest sales but these years saw some new editions and foreign translations. He also published four substantial books of essays. His most famous volumes on the themes of freedom and rebellion had appeared pre-war. Now he tried new approaches. *In The Dark Backward* invoked the past through the present, in imaginative essays stimulated by the power of place. *Films of Time* conjured up the past through fantasy, drawing on his new passion for the cinema. His concept of rolling back the film reel of the past enabled him to replace temporal constraints with visual power, imagining, for example, that he was *present* in ancient Olympia. And he earned much-appreciated guineas from the medium said to be ruining the book trade: radio. He did at least eight BBC broadcasts.[58] During a dinner at the Anglo-Palestinian Club at the Savoy he nipped out for a fifteen-minute broadcast on Albania between the grapefruit and the chicken.

Another novelty for Henry was folk dancing. Evelyn's eldest brother Cecil Sharp founded the English Folk Dance Society (EFDS). Henry gradually came to appreciate Sharp and his work and sat on the executive committee of the EFDS.[59] Evelyn was an accomplished dancer. So Henry, aged seventy, learned folk dancing. He joined England's leading folk dancers at a Toronto festival (playing the Hobbyhorse in the old Horn Dance of Abbotts Bromley); then they danced their way over the Rockies. He had an ear for music and fine posture, appreciated rhythm and had been a graceful skater. To his delight his granddaughter Margaret became a talented dancer and they attended summer schools together. But sciatica gradually forced a shift to the sidelines.

Both Henry and Evelyn found that work opportunities were diminishing. Evelyn was a professional reader as well as a novelist but publishers now hinted that her judgement and fiction were dated. Massingham, whom Henry called 'The Greatest Editor of the Age',[60] died in 1924; then Brailsford ceased to edit the *New Leader*, ending a regular source of income and platform for Henry's opinions. Domestic life had not improved. Richard's volatile and aggressive behaviour added 'terror to every Sunday'. Henry feared he had lost the artistic inspiration provided by war: the 'sunshine' had been taken out of him. Margaret doted on Richard but he treated her badly and periodically threatened suicide.

Philippa's presence exacerbated family tension. Henry was upset by what he (and his nephew John) saw as rudeness and greediness. Yet Philippa's son was in an asylum, there were financial problems (Henry lent money and paid his granddaughter's school fees) and Philippa's behaviour was probably affected by thyroid problems. She had never really been able to please Henry. Perhaps she was too like Margaret, whom she resembled physically. Even in the last months of his life Henry would call her 'inconsiderate & annoying'. In revealing language he wrote of this musical daughter: 'to think what trouble we spent on her & how well she promised'. Sadly, Henry wrote in 1928, 'Children are a quiverful of arrows that pierce the parents' hearts.' In the same month EB died and, six months later, Marian.

Margaret's health was rapidly deteriorating. She had angina and was depressed. When EB's widow, Ellen, visited Downside Crescent, she noted not only that Henry and his wife ate separately (apart from the dreaded family Sunday lunches) but that the seventy-year-old Margaret wanted to go into a nursing home 'and have done with it'.[61] Now that Henry was no longer away so much and Margaret was unable to travel, tensions mounted. John L. Nevinson called their home 'a cheerless

13 C. R. W. Nevinson's portrait of his father, *Daily Graphic*, 14 March 1924.

uninhabited house'. By 1932 Margaret was in severe physical and mental distress. She tried to drown herself in the bath and needed constant care. The experienced magistrate now terrified herself that she was about to be arrested for an imagined crime. She believed there was a plot to poison herself and Richard. He wanted her institutionalized but Henry resisted this, not least because she still had periods of lucidity. He told his old friend Elizabeth Robins:

> At present I am in great tribulation, for Mrs. Nevinson's mind is rapidly failing, and I am perplexed what is best for her. To send her to a mental home among strangers seems to me cruel, but all are urging it, partly in hopes of reducing the great expense. I am so much opposed to it that I should far rather go on spending my small savings in the hope that she may end quietly here.[62]

Returning home from Cambridge on 4 June 1932, he found Margaret unconscious. She died four days later from kidney failure.[63] After her death Henry wrote that he had given her 'an unhappy life, but for Richard', adding 'and with her I was unhappy too. But it was impossible to part.' He conceded his early 'wrong to M. under my passionate love for my dear lady [Nannie]'. Less than a fortnight after Margaret's death Henry discussed the future with Evelyn. When Evelyn had gone to Switzerland on holiday in 1926, Henry had written that 'It was like parting with life, so close are we.'

On 18 January 1933 at Hampstead Register Office, Evelyn aged sixty-three married Henry, now in his seventy-seventh year. It was almost half a century since his first marriage. MacDonald, fond of both of them, offered to be best man. They were flattered but declined. It would have caused difficulties with some guests (he headed a national government and had been expelled from the Labour Party) and would have turned a private occasion into a public event. They invited just a handful of friends. They had booked the previous day but then Henry was asked to speak at a protest meeting against the imprisonment of the union leader Tom Mann. So the veteran radicals postponed events by one day. This was not a conventional wedding and they were not a conventional couple: the bride wore black.

Evelyn moved into 4 Downside Crescent and the following month about 150 friends gathered at Gertrude Parry's London home for a celebratory reception. Then, in late June, came 'my apotheosis' as about 450 (including Albanian, Bulgarian and Greek ministers) honoured Henry's achievements at a luncheon at the Criterion. It was fifty years since the publication of his first book. Hamilton called Henry his 'good angel'. Masefield compared him to Boswell. Lansbury praised his service to working people, and tribute was paid to his suffrage work, his support of Irish, Jewish and Indian peoples and general commitment to freedom. The presentation of £360 was especially welcome given the economic

climate and the loss of Henry's annual £200 for *Baltimore Sun* articles and
Evelyn's *Guardian* income. Their joint income of £400 was fast diminishing whilst health bills soared.[64] Henry became diabetic and had a
hernia. He spent his wedding anniversary in hospital. He then got peri-
tonitis. But in 1937 he told an old friend, Charles Grinling, that 'Like
the white eagle I am fettered but still alert and savage.'[65]

At the end of the war Henry had turned down a CBE on principle. Yet
there were signs that he was more prepared than before to accept the
status quo. For example, he supported the Simon Report on India. Based
on a commission composed of British MPs, some influential Indian politicians boycotted it. When he addressed an Independent Labour Party
meeting on the beneficial changes in Britain of the last seventy years, he
was accused of being bourgeois and ignorant of the workpeople and of
glorifying the past. So he criticized those who merely repeated 'the
familiar Socialist suspicions & doctrines'. In a very honest statement he
admitted that:

> owing to our inequality of life and food and education there yawns
> a disastrous gulf between the worker and the gentleman. Strive as I
> may to be one of them, I have always felt that gulf, and the workers
> have felt it too.[66]

But he still wrote and spoke about causes. They ranged from the
League for the Prevention of Cruel Sports – an article on foxhunting was
called 'Our Sportive Butchers' – to the Scottsboro campaign to save
'Negro boys' charged with raping white women in Alabama and sentenced to death.[67] He exposed in the *Guardian* (at Scott's request) the
peremptory dismissal of the Hon. Violet Douglas-Pennant, first Com-
mandant of the Women's Royal Air Force, who, it was eventually
revealed, was accused of lesbianism.[68] He and friends such as Hammond,
Hobson and Gilbert and Mary Murray endorsed *The Next Five Years:
An Essay in Political Agreement*, with its programme of social, economic
and international policy, and he urged radical constitutional change in
Yugoslavia. It was Henry who chaired the Foyles Literary Luncheon in
1933 when Emma Goldman spoke on 'An Anarchist Looks at Life'
with votes of thanks from Paul Robeson and Rebecca West.[69] Henry
liked to see himself as central to what he called 'The Stage Army of the
Good'.

In 1936 he was eighty but events in Europe were pitching him back
into the thick of protest: 'I boil with rage day and night about Spain.'[70]
He used his pen to explore the meanings of British freedom and stress
that obedience was 'the easiest & most comfortable of the vices'. With
accounts of Jewish victims in Nazi Germany, 'How', he asked, 'can we
refrain from rage?'[71] He insisted on 'our national duty to strike agst [*sic*]
cruelty & injustice wherever it appeared'. A few days after his birthday
he went on a deputation to Hampstead Town Hall to try to prevent a

fascist meeting on his own doorstep. Permission was not rescinded though it was never again granted. Henry had a dinner engagement in the City that night and gave a twenty-five-minute impromptu speech denouncing the British Union of Fascists. Such was his reputation for interrupting meetings that, although he was not present at the Hampstead meeting, the journalist Ivor Brown later described him as being there and scarcely able to contain his disgust![72]

In 1936 Henry also replaced E. M. Forster as the new President of the National Council for Civil Liberties (NCCL), the watchdog to uphold and promote civil liberties founded two years earlier.[73] Honours were now heaped upon Henry. He was made a Fellow of the Royal Society of Literature and, six months later, a Vice-President. He joined the council of the Society of Authors, becoming 'both a brother and a leader' to the society.[74] Christ Church made him an Honorary Student and he received two Honorary Doctorates. Trinity College, Dublin, bastion of Britishness and Protestantism, awarded him a D.Litt., the University of Liverpool an LLD. Professor Lyon Blease, erstwhile suffrage supporter, delivered

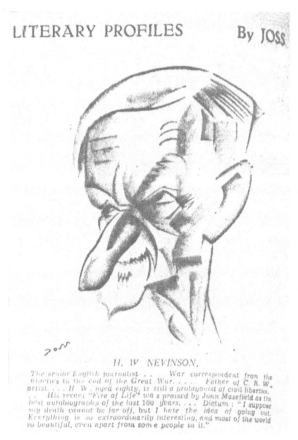

LITERARY PROFILES   By JOSS

H. W. NEVINSON,

The senior English journalist . . War correspondent from the nineties to the end of the Great War. . . . Father of C. R. W. artist. . . . H. W. aged eighty, is still a protagonist of civil liberties. . . . His recent "Fire of Life" was praised by John Masefield as the best autobiography of the last 100 years. . . . Dictum : "I suppose my death cannot be far off, but I hate the idea of going out. Everything is so extraordinarily interesting, and most of the world so beautiful, even apart from some people in it."

14 Literary Profile by Joss in the *Star*: H. W. Nevinson, 'The senior English journalist', 27 May 1936.

LITERARY PROFILES   By JOSS

EVELYN SHARP

Novelist, writer of children's stories. . . . Formerly suffragette, twice imprisoned. . . . Entered literature by way of the "Yellow Book" but denies that the "naughty nineties" were particularly naughty . . . Recently married, as his second wife, H. W. Nevinson, friend and fellow humanitarian of 30 years' standing.

15 Literary Profile by Joss in the *Star*: Evelyn Sharp, 29 May 1936.

the eulogy at the Liverpool awards ceremony in May 1936, describing Henry as:

> a journalist and a man of letters; a sensitive critic and a master of English prose. A romantic artist in the safe custody of a scholar . . . the most trustworthy as well as the most brilliant special correspondent of his generation . . . the natural enemy of the official, the pedant and the herd, and all his life he has contended with them for liberty, justice and toleration . . . He is the Bayard of English journalism, whose pen has fought more than one lost battle, but never in a mean cause, or without honour.[75]

Evelyn too enjoyed some success with her libretto for 'The Poisoned Kiss', a 'Romantic Extravaganza' by their good friend Ralph Vaughan Williams.

The following year Henry became the fourth president of English PEN (Poets, Essayists and Novelists) following Wells, Galsworthy and Priestley. As part of this 'League of Nations for writers'[76] he sought to further the freedom of the written word internationally. In 1938 at a PEN dinner with the Czech ambassador, he stressed the duty of helping 'a small democratic country to defend itself against the lies, abuses, and threats heaped on us by a bully'.[77] He was keen to fly to the PEN congress in Prague in June but Evelyn had minor heart problems so they went by train. Five days of talks, dinners and sightseeing were followed by a tour of the country. Just a few months later, on 30 September, the Munich Agreement was signed between the British and French Prime Ministers, Chamberlain and Daladier, and Hitler and Mussolini. Sudetenland, the German-speaking mountainous area of north Czechoslovakia was, without Czech consultation, handed to Germany. Henry promptly changed Chamberlain's infamous words 'Peace in our Time' to 'Peace with Dishonour'.[78] Yet, when he said as much at the PEN dinner four days later, a member protested that he was being political. So Henry resigned his presidency. The next day Hitler crossed into the Sudetenland. Six months later, a bitterly disappointed Henry recorded that, despite the vows at Munich, 'our beloved Czechoslovakia ceased to exist'. Hitler had occupied the rest of the country.

Interspersed with meetings were concerts and holidays, from the Black Forest to the Forest of Dean. But Henry was not skilled at relaxing and preferred combining work and leisure. He and Evelyn accompanied the Royal Naval Division of the 8th Corps on a free Cook's cruise to the Dardanelles. Henry showed lantern slides on Gallipoli and Athens and helped guide several hundred ex-soldiers round the sites. An Anglo-Hellenic cruise on board the *Cairo City* in 1937 was his farewell to Greece. He lectured to 200 cruisers but caught a chill on Crete and then fell down the side of an amphitheatre at Delos.

On his eighty-second birthday he reported 'Throat, cough bad, walking almost gone, memory fading, mind slow, but otherwise well & quite sane'. Two weeks earlier he had written, 'For the first time I realised that war is inevitable.' Depressed by 'the diffusion of the totalitarian spirit', the outbreak of war saw a further decline in their finances. Hit by taxation and with the shortage of paper restricting their newspaper work, Evelyn lost her regular *News Chronicle* slot. War became the first item in Henry's daily diary, charting his mounting 'rage at the treatment of Hitler's victims'. But Henry and Evelyn also faced personal danger. For in 1940 they were bombed out of their home.

By June the Nevinsons had their own sheltered room at home to save descending 400 steps to join crowds at Belsize Park tube. Day and night sirens wailed, taking their toll on Evelyn's nerves. Early on 8 September three large bombs fell nearby. One took the latch off the front door, smashed windows and damaged two ceilings. Bombing and gun-fire intensified. In one week Henry recorded thirty air raid warnings. Lives were lost in neighbouring streets. By 21 September their suitcases were packed ready for flight. An oil bomb struck Richard's studio. A new diary began with the words 'At home in a beleaguered city, exposed to bomb fire day and night'. Day and night merged: 'We miss the sunshine

16 The elderly Henry Nevinson.

for many windows are boarded up and we live like things forbid.' The day before Henry's eighty-fourth birthday, a bomb burst about twenty yards away. Then on 13 October came a 'Day of terror' as the man who had gone in search of war saw it come home to him. At 7.30 p.m. came a rushing, hissing noise followed by a huge explosion in the garden beyond. Their back windows were blown out and, as Henry sat composing a letter to his old colleague Beach-Thomas, the base of a 250-pound bomb struck their roof above the well of the staircase. Ten minutes later a bomb burst on the other side of Haverstock Hill bringing down three houses. Henry, Evelyn and their help, Marguerite Scott, all cowered in the kitchen amidst thick dust, ash, glass splinters and acrid smoke.

Friends had long urged them to leave. Now, with holes in the roof and no gas or water, the house was not habitable. Henry saw this as 'the end of my existence as I had hoped to live it'. On 19 October, Henry and

Evelyn joined folk-dancing friends Douglas and Helen Kennedy near Harpenden.[79] On 2 November they moved to the Cotswolds. Henry spent the rest of his life in Chipping Campden. His old Hampstead friend, the writer and socialist Joseph Clayton, now lived there. At the height of its prosperity in the fifteenth century as a centre for the collection and export of wool, Campden then become a quiet market town. Not yet a magnet for tourists, it was a haven from the bombs.

It was an artistic community. In 1902 C. R. Ashbee (whom Henry met at Toynbee Hall) had moved his Guild of Handicraft there, bringing craftspeople to the town and stimulating its own School of Arts and Crafts. Like Hampstead, it was popular with the intelligentsia. Friends included the Oxford professor J. W. Mackail, married to Sir Edward Burne-Jones's daughter, and Felix Crosse and Tatiana Crosse, Tchaikovsky's niece. There were weekly talks at the Cotswold Hotel. They participated in debates at the town hall.

Yet Henry was unhappy away from London: 'That was the centre of the living earth.'[80] He had spent a lifetime seeking action. His letters were now headed 'In Exile'. He knew that to call himself a prisoner of war was an impertinence, that on a clear day from nearby Dovers Hill thirteen counties were visible and that he was among welcoming people who all ' "fell for him" '.[81] But he was old, with failing health, away from the home he had lived in for decades, and he missed his books. He now lacked roots and wings.

They took rooms (£6 weekly) in Stamford House, one of Campden's imposing but cold stone houses. Their landlady (a former headmistress) had an excellent library. It helped Henry to complete his last book, a biography of Thomas Hardy.[82] But she found the catering too much so they moved to the sixteenth-century Kings Arms Hotel. The poet Ursula Wood (later Vaughan Williams) recalled her father, an army general, supplying butter.[83] American and Canadian friends sent money and food. It was six months before Richard and Kathleen visited. Henry regretted 'the entire absence of Richard' above all else. May was also enlivened by a brief visit to 'blessed London' for a PEN lunch. But news of the loss of Crete plunged Henry into depression. This was exacerbated by the final move on 11 June 1941 to three unfurnished rooms in the Victorian wing of St James's vicarage.

One consolation was that the former railway worker George Ridley MP had compiled an anthology of some of Henry's poems and essays. Henry wrote the Preface and did the proofs and index, his writing now barely decipherable. But lack of staff at Penguin Books (the printing trade had recently been de-reserved) meant that his 'sixpenny immortality' appeared too late for him to see it.[84]

The elderly artist Joseph Southall, of the Birmingham School, sketched Henry (head and shoulders) in mid-September. The two-day sitting produced, in Henry's opinion, a good pencil sketch but made him appear too young and inexperienced, 'wanting wrinkled lines'. Perhaps the artist was being kind to the ailing Henry, who that day for the first time was put into a bath chair. He suffered from neuritis, had lost a lot of weight through diabetes and was too feeble to walk much. But the portrait also represented the Nevinson of popular imagination. It was how people wanted to see him.[85]

Henry received so many telegrams on his eighty-fifth birthday that the post office ran out of gold envelopes. He still spent his better days writing poetry and short articles. A fragment of his final poem, composed in October, survives. The nostalgia and regret of recent verse had disappeared. Now 'Peace like a sun lies on the Midland wold.'[86] Henry began sending farewell letters to his closest friends. His last diary entry, more than half a century after he had started recording his life, was on 20 October 1941. He noted that the Russian government was 550 miles from Moscow but that the city still held out. Evelyn had stumbled on the stairs while carrying supper: 'Poor ES terribly stiff & pained'. And Henry too had fallen and cut his legs. He was now too feeble even to carry on writing.

Several times over the next few weeks Henry seemed to be slipping away, only to rally. Richard and Kathleen visited and granddaughter Margaret. But by 8 November he was barely conscious. Evelyn was always by his side. The next day she deliberately misquoted a word (which he used to tease her about) from *The Ancient Mariner*, saying 'Sleep. It is a *blessed* thing.' Henry opened his eyes and corrected her with the word 'gentle'. It was his last word. Henry Nevinson had done his raging. He went into a coma from which he never awoke. There was a flaming red sunset and that night 'A great hurricane rose.'[87] It was wartime but it was also Armistice Sunday.

Afterword

Even in death Henry Nevinson defied convention and expectations. The man who made his living through communication stipulated that no words be spoken at his funeral. There was, though, music at Golders Green crematorium: folk-tunes and the slow movement from Beethoven's 7th Symphony. And many words were spent praising his life and work at his Memorial Meeting at Caxton Hall on 11 December 1941.[1] Organized by PEN and the NCCL, it was a gathering of the great and the good. How did they choose to remember Henry and how might we, a hundred and fifty years after his birth, sum up his achievements?

At Caxton Hall, individuals from the Anti-Slavery Society rubbed shoulders with the Rationalist Press Association. The Royal Society of Literature came together with the Suffragette Fellowship, the Poetry Society, Labour Party, the Society of Authors and the National Liberal Club. Messages were received from many quarters including Czechoslovakia, the USSR, Greece, the Abbey Wood branch of the National Guild of Co-operators, the Electrical Trades Union and the English Folk Dance and Song Society. The meeting opened with a piano recital by Edith Vogel as a tribute from wartime refugees. Noel Brailsford spoke about Henry the journalist and read one of his poems. Professor Gilbert Murray recalled him as a Man of Letters. General Sir Ian Hamilton focused on the War Correspondent and Emmeline Pethick Lawrence paid tribute to Henry's championship of women's rights. He was praised as the friend of Ireland by Professor Farrington and of Africa by Lapido Solanke, who also sang an African funeral dirge. Vera Brittain, who had suggested the event, read from his prose.

E. M. Forster, who presided at Caxton Hall, once asked whether Henry sought 'Literature or Life?'[2] In a sense he pursued both. But although drawn to the notion of the man of learning, he recognized that he was never going to be one of the giants of literature. After a meeting with Yeats he admitted feeling 'rather overwhelmed as often by a fine mind. Am too much of a journalist now.'[3] He opted for a life of action. In that he was reporting rather than actually fighting, it seemed, for him at least, a vicarious sort of action (hence his great pride in that Gallipoli wound). But Henry came much closer to conflicts and dangers than many of his fellow correspondents and his was a singularly well-informed pen. His literary companions envied his ability to eschew the sedentary life. Military men, war correspondents and social reformers praised his eloquence and admired the way classical, literary and historical knowledge inflected his writing. His versatility was applauded though he viewed it as a shortcoming. So, his significance lay partly in the way he inspired others during his lifetime. Then, in his moment of posthumous glory at Caxton Hall in the midst of world war, the Victorian rebel and principled champion of liberty was celebrated as a hero in a world that seemed to be slipping away.

This biography has stressed the attraction of the role of war correspondent for Henry Nevinson. He was a wonderful advertisement for the capabilities of the older man, and his almost breathless pursuit of the latest danger, combined with the journalist's instinct for a good story, gave him a significant role in alerting and rousing readers. He provided, through vivid images, breaking news from across the globe whilst his experience and radicalism suggested angles that other correspondents might miss. Ultimately it was these skills and a distinctive, well-honed style essentially informed by his classical training, rather than in-depth analysis, that won him admirers. By the same token, the catholicity of his concerns, admirably demonstrated at Caxton Hall, ensured that he reached further and wider than many of his contemporaries.

And as a writer and fighter for social justice, Henry did make a difference, not least because his words inspired others. What he saw in Angola was translated into sustained campaigning. From conflicts at home and across the early-twentieth-century world he brought vivid reportage. In numerous newspapers, journals and books – providing a rich source for the historian – and on the platform, he hazarded opinions that were not always aired in the British press. His solutions to troubles, however, sometimes confirmed, as in the case of India, the degree to which he was ultimately a product of his privileged English upbringing. But his commitment and compassion also helped to inform readers about devastation in places less familiar to British readers, such as Georgia and Macedonia. In 1970 the novelist Storm Jameson asked 'Are there left men such as Henry Nevinson was? Passionate quixotes who feel injustice anywhere in the world as a nail driven into their own flesh?'[4] Perhaps today's society could do with more such figures to provoke reflection on the substantive issues that underlie major world events.

APPENDIX I

Books and Pamphlets by Henry W. Nevinson

First place of publication is London unless otherwise mentioned. Square brackets denote abbreviations used in Notes.

Single-authored books

A Sketch of Herder and His Times, 1884 [*SHT*]
Life of Friedrich Schiller, 1889; New York, 1889; Honolulu, HI, 2001
Neighbours of Ours: Scenes of East End Life, Bristol, 1895 (published as *Slum Stories of London* in New York)
In the Valley of Tophet: Scenes of Black Country Life, 1896; New York, 1896
Scenes in the Thirty Days' War between Greece and Turkey, 1897, 1898 [*STDW*]
Ladysmith: The Diary of a Siege, 1900; New York, 1900 [*L*]
The Plea of Pan, 1901, 1914; New York, 1901 [*PP*]
Between the Acts, 1904; New York, 1904 [*BA*]
Books and Personalities, 1905; New York, 1905 [*BP*]
The Dawn in Russia or Scenes in the Russian Revolution of 1905–6, London and New York, 1906 [*DIR*] (reprinted as *Russia Observed*, New York, 1971)
A Modern Slavery, London and New York, 1906, 1963; New York, 1968 [*AMS*]
The New Spirit in India: Scenes during the Unrest 1907–8, London and New York, 1908 [*NSI*]
Essays in Freedom, 1909 [*EF*]
Peace and War in the Balance, 1911 [*PW*]
The Growth of Freedom, 1912; New York, 1912
Essays in Rebellion, 1913, 2004 [*ER*]
The Dardanelles Campaign, 1918; New York, 1919 [*TDC*]
Lines of Life, 1920; New York, 1920 [*LL*]
Original Sinners, 1920; New York, 1921
The English, 1929
Essays in Freedom and Rebellion, 1921; New Haven, CT, 1921; Freeport, NY, 1967
Changes and Chances, 1923; New York, 1923 [*C&C*]
More Changes, More Chances, 1925; New York, 1925 [*More C*]
Last Changes, Last Chances, 1928; New York, 1929 [*Last C*]
England's Voice of Freedom: An Anthology of Liberty (compiled by and with Introduction by H. W. Nevinson), 1929; New York, 1929

Rough Islanders, 1930 (published as *The Natives of England* in New York, 1930)
Goethe: Man and Poet, 1932; New York, 1932; Freeport, NY, 1971, 1977
In the Dark Backward, 1934; New York, 1934 [*IDB*]
Fire of Life, 1935; New York, 1935 [*FL*]
Between the Wars, 1936 [*BW*]
Running Accompaniments, 1936 [*RA*]
Films of Time: Twelve Fantasies, 1939 [*FT*]
Thomas Hardy, 1941, 1972; Folcroft, PA, 1969; Norwood, PA, 1977
Henry Nevinson: The Augustan Book of Modern Poetry, ed. E. Thompson, 1926

Published posthumously:
Words and Deeds, Harmondsworth and New York, 1942 [*WD*]
Visions and Memories, arranged E. Sharp, 1944; New York, 1944 [*V&M*]
Essays, Poems and Tales of Henry W. Nevinson, ed. H. N. Brailsford, 1948 [*EPT*]

Joint publications

A. H. Hallam Murray accompanied by Henry W. Nevinson and Montgomery Carmichael, *Sketches on the Old Road through France to Florence*, 1904; New York, 1904, 1927
John Fulleylove RI and Henry Nevinson, *Pictures of Classic Greek Landscape and Architecture*, 1897

Booklets, pamphlets

'Women's Vote and Men', reprinted from the *English Review*, October 1909
'The Case of Mr. William Ball', 1912
'The Claim on Oxford', *New Tracts for the Times*, No. 2, Oxford, 1914
'Farewell to America', reprinted from the *Nation*, 4 March 1922, in various pamphlet editions, 1926; New York, two versions, 1922; Stamford, CT, 1953
John Masefield: An Appreciation, 1931
Also pamphlets based on Henry's newspaper articles, e.g. the Douglas-Pennant Case, and the Dardanelles
Song:
'An Old Warrior' (words by H. W. Nevinson, music by R. Chignell), 1923

APPENDIX 2

Books/Booklets to which Henry W. Nevinson Contributed

R. F. Burton, *First Footsteps in Africa*, 1910

G. Renwick, *Finland Today*, 1911

G. Sigerson, *Honesta Custodia*, 1913

The Sister Nivedita (M. E. Noble), *Studies from an Eastern Home*, 1913

J. H. Whitehouse (ed.), *Ruskin the Prophet, and Other Centenary Studies*, 1920

C. T. Winchester, *An Old Castle and Other Essays*, New York, 1922

D. Ryan, *James Connolly*, 1924

H. J. Massingham, *HWM: A Selection from the Writings of H. W. Massingham*, 1925

C. P. B. Osmaston, *A New Presentation of Greek Art and Thought: The Handiwork of a Hellenist*, 1928

J. Ishill (ed.), *Havelock Ellis in Appreciation*, published privately, New Jersey, 1929

K. Foss, *Black Bread and Samovars*, 1930

P. G. L. Webb, *Poems*, 1933

H. Leslie, *Where East is West: Life in Bulgaria*, 1933

M. Burr, *A Fossicker in Angola*, 1933

W. R. Inge, *The Post Victorians*, 1933

A. Barrett Brown, *Great Democrats*, 1934

BBC, *Anywhere for a News Story*, 1934

I. Steinberg, *Spiridonova: Revolutionary Terrorist*, 1935

D. R. Kahn, *Spring Up, O Well*, 1936

Friends of Europe, *Hitler the Man*, 1936

H. Ripper, *Vital Speech: A Study in Perfect Utterance*, 1938

R. Kidd, *British Liberties in Danger*, 1940

E. F. Howard (H. Leslie), *Across Barriers*, 1941

Notes

For abbreviations of book titles see Appendix 1. Unless otherwise indicated, the place of publication throughout this book is London. All references to Henry Nevinson's books (unless stated otherwise) are to the first United Kingdom edition. Throughout the text Henry Nevinson's use of place names is given. Where appropriate, modern names follow in parenthesis.

Introduction

1 Nevinson to P. Webb, 13 July 1922, Evelyn Sharp Nevinson Papers (ESNev.) MSS. Eng. Lett. c 278, The Bodleian Library, University of Oxford.
2 *Observer*, 20 October 1935.
3 He contributed to many more. See Appendix 2. In May 1904 he travelled through France for a lavishly illustrated travel book, *Sketches on the Old Road through France to Florence*. Henry wrote the Introduction and just under 100 pages of text to accompany Hallam Murray's watercolours.
4 Interview on Channel Five, 26 July 1998.
5 Advertisement from the *Sunday Sun* in H. W. Nevinson, *The New Spirit in India: Scenes during the Unrest 1907–8*, London and New York, 1908 [*NSI*].
6 He never visited China, Japan, Latin America, Australia or New Zealand.
7 E.g. A. Best *et al.* (eds), *International History of the Twentieth Century*, 2003. The first chapter on 1900–17 opens with a section called 'The End of the European Era'.
8 *Daily Herald* [*DH*], 27 August 1932.
9 Ibid., 28 December 1932.
10 See Appendices 1 and 2.
11 R. L. Purdy and M. Millgate, *The Collected Letters of Thomas Hardy*, 3, Oxford, 1982, p. 228.

12 H. W. Nevinson, Preface to C. T. Winchester, *An Old Castle and Other Essays*, New York, 1922, p. xvi.

13 New Journalism was so named by Matthew Arnold in 1887. At the turn of the century London had thirteen national morning newspapers and five evening papers. See A. Jones, *The Power of the Press: Newspapers, Power and the Public in Nineteenth Century England*, Aldershot, 1996.

14 J. Masefield, *So Long to Learn*, 1952, p. 93.

15 *Fortnightly Review*, March 1945. His fiction, poetry, literary essays and biographies are discussed in greater detail in my forthcoming study of his literary work.

16 H. W. Nevinson, *Words and Deeds* [*WD*], Harmondsworth and New York, 1942, p. 11.

17 J. Galsworthy, *The Patrician*, 1911, pp. 24, 38.

18 P. Gibbs, *The Middle of the Road*, 1922, p. 63.

19 S. Koven, *Slumming: Sexual and Social Politics in Victorian England*, Princeton, NJ, 2004, p. 261.

20 Henry Woodd Nevinson Papers (HWNP), Nevinson Journals (NevJ.) MSS. Eng. Misc. e 624/2, 22 March 1927, Bodleian Library.

21 *Christian Commonwealth*, 3 November 1915.

22 *Listener*, 8 May 1941.

23 F. Frankfurter, *Reminiscences*, 1960, p. 93.

24 File 2.43/53, July 1933, Winifred Holtby Papers, Hull Local Studies Library.

25 *News Chronicle*, 10 November 1941; A. V. John, 'Imag(in)ing H. W. Nevinson: War Correspondent, Literary Journalist and Rebel' in M. Hewitt (ed.), *Representing Victorian Lives*, 1999, pp. 140–51.

26 *New Leader*, 16 October 1925.

27 Although he kept a diary in the early 1880s, those that survive cover 1893–1941.

Chapter One

1 H. W. Nevinson, 'How I Began', 1 February 1938, BBC Written Sound Archives, Caversham. All quotes in this chapter, unless otherwise indicated, come from Henry's diaries, HWNP, MSS. Eng. Misc. e 610/1 – 610/5, 1893–8 (NevJ.), Bodleian Library.

2 A reference to the anonymous Latin tomb inscription, 'Et in Arcadia ego'. H. W. Nevinson, *Changes and Chances* [*C&C*], 1923, p. 1.

3 H. W. Nevinson, *The Natives of England*, 1930, p. 182.

4 See L. Davidoff *et al.*, *The Family Story: Blood, Contract and Intimacy 1830–1960*, 1999.

5 J. Tosh, *A Man's Place: Masculinity and the Middle-Class Home in Victorian England*, 1999.

6 *Harper's Monthly Magazine* [*HMM*], cxx/1910, pp. 230–5.

7 Henry suggests that he received most of his education at Shrewsbury but he only spent two and a half years there. For the schools see J. B. Oldham, *A History of Shrewsbury School 1552–1952*, Oxford, 1952; A. M. Carr and T. Fullman, 'Shrewsbury Library: Its History and Restoration', 1983;

Register for Shrewsbury School 1873–5, School Lists 1873–5, Shrewsbury School Archives; Nevinson to A. Waugh, 5 October 1917, Sherborne School Archives.

8 *C&C*, p. 28.

9 NevJ. e 622/5, 18 September 1922; H. W. Nevinson, *Running Accompaniments [RA]*, 1936, pp. 14–29; *Nation*, 1 June 1918.

10 A. H. Gilkes, MA, *Boys and Masters: A Story of School Life*, 1887, p. 183.

11 T. H. Quilter, *Graham Wallas and the Great Society*, 1980, p. 4; M. Vivian Hughes, *A London Family 1870–1900*, Oxford, 1991, p. 55.

12 Murray to E. Sharp, 2 March 1942, ESNev. MSS. Eng. Lett. d 278.

13 F. M. Turner, *The Greek Heritage in Victorian Britain*, New Haven, CT, 1981.

14 *Listener*, 8 August 1940, pp. 193–4.

15 This covered tuition fees, rental of two rooms, a pantry, four daily meals and services of a scout and boy.

16 H. W. Nevinson, *In the Dark Backward [IDB]*, 1934, p. 123.

17 H. W. Nevinson, *Between the Acts [BA]*, 1904, pp. 35–70; *New Leader [NL]*, 3 July 1925. In 1940 his former lecturer Reginald Macan told Henry that he had been learning his trade in the 1870s, like a dentist at the cost of his patients. 14 November 1940, ESNev. MSS. Eng. Lett. c 279.

18 H. W. Nevinson, *Visions and Memories [V&M]*, arranged E. Sharp, London and New York, 1944, p. 131. Corroborated by a contributor to the *Oxford Magazine*, 17 February 1945.

19 *C&C*, p. 35.

20 As 'B. G. N.' S. S. Goldsmith, *Elgar's Enigmas: Basil Nevinson and Charles Gorton*, Christ's College, Finchley, 2000. The eldest of the Nevinson children, Bas was a non-practising barrister. Widowed young, he suffered from depression, gambled and drank. He died aged fifty-seven. His lifestyle and Tory politics alienated him from Henry, who rather underplayed his musical talent.

21 M. G. Brock and M. C. Curthoys, *History of the University of Oxford*, VII, *Nineteenth-Century Oxford*, 2, Oxford, 2000.

22 N.d., MS. Eng. Lett. d 338, f 95, Bodleian Library.

23 *RA*, p. 17.

24 Ibid., p. 24.

25 *V&M*, p. 129. The title of Henry's poem was originally 'A Foul Blow'. It was modified on advice that it could be libellous. Correspondence between Henry and J. H. Whitehouse, Isle of Wight Record Office.

26 9 October 1923, ESNev. MSS. Eng. Lett. c 278.

27 *RA*, p. 17.

28 *V&M*, p. 122.

29 Ibid., pp. 1–2.

30 *C&C*, p. 48.

31 *RA*, p. 26.

32 H. W. Nevinson, *Between the Wars [BW]*, 1936, p. 124. He wrote long articles and a book on Goethe. See Chapter 10.

33 At 14 Cecil Street. *V&M*, p. 132.

34 H. W. Nevinson, *A Sketch of Herder and His Times [SHT]*, 1884.

35 26 April 1930, 911/3/XV; 11 June 1932, 911/3/XXa, John L. Nevinson Diaries, The Society of Antiquaries of London.

36 NevJ. e 626/3, 15 October 1935; e 627/3, 1 December 1938.
37 A. V. John, 'Margaret Wynne Nevinson: Gender and National Identity in the Early Twentieth Century' in R. R. Davies and G. H. Jenkins (eds), *From Medieval to Modern Wales: Historical Essays in Honour of Kenneth O. Morgan and Ralph A. Griffiths*, Cardiff, 2004, pp. 230–45.
38 Quoted in P. Rose, *Parallel Lives: Five Victorian Marriages*, New York, 1984, p. 26.
39 R. N. Smart, 'Literate Ladies – A Fifty Year Experiment', *Alumnus Chronicle*, University of St Andrews, 59, 1968, pp. 20–31.
40 Both recalled seeing George Eliot there with her new husband. *RA*, p. 210; M. Wynne Nevinson, *Life's Fitful Fever*, 1926, p. 66. This would have been in December 1880 when she made her first public appearance with John Cross, a few weeks before her death. K. Hughes, *George Eliot: The Last Victorian*, 1999 edn, p. 481.
41 They were married by licence. Marriage certificate 281 for 18 April 1884, The National Archives: Family Records Centre, London; Communication with the Archivist of the Stadtarchiv Jena, 15 February 2001.
42 H. W. Nevinson, *Essays in Freedom* [*EF*], 1909, p. 256.
43 Now Jennergasse 14. They also lived in what is currently the Post Office.
44 E. C. Bentley, *Those Days*, 1940, p. 25; *Nation*, 24 February 1923.
45 Bedford College for Women Council Minutes, iv, 1883–93, GB 110/1/4, pp. 70, 218, Archives, Royal Holloway, University of London.
46 *C&C*, pp. 96–7.
47 HWNP, MS. Eng. Misc. d 624; S. Koven, *Slumming: Sexual and Social Politics in Victorian London*, Princeton, NJ, 2004; Annual Reports of the Universities' Settlement in East London; Canon Barnett's Toynbee Hall Scrapbook, Tower Hamlets Local History Library and Archives; Toynbee Hall Educational Plans, Winter Term 1895, A/TOY/26/11/1A, London Metropolitan Archives (LMA).
48 In 1901 when relations between Henry and Margaret were especially strained, she told their children that she had written the book. It is in Henry's style but her contribution was probably substantial since she visited homes regularly. The title suggests familiarity and a joint venture. See E. Ross, 'Women's Neighbourhood Sharing in London before World War One', *History Workshop Journal*, 15 (1983), p. 13; Idem, *The Lady Explorer in the Slums of London*, Berkeley, CA, forthcoming.
49 In P. J. Keating (ed.), *Working-Class Stories of the 1890s*, 1971; W. V. Harris, *British Short Fiction in the Nineteenth Century: A Literary and Bibliographic Guide*, Detroit, 1979, p. 126.
50 Nevinson MS. vi, Shrewsbury School Archives; *Toynbee Record*, 3/12, 1891; H. W. Nevinson, *Peace and War in the Balance* [*PW*], 1911, pp. 60–2.
51 Tophet, in the Valley of Hinnom, was used for idolatrous worship and then became the refuse centre for Jerusalem's rubbish.
52 Quoted in D. Langley Moore, *E. Nesbit: A Biography*, 1933, p. 132.
53 In 1899 it became the London Playing Fields Society. First Annual Report of the London Playing Fields Committee, May 1891, LMA.
54 *BA*, p. 192.
55 It cost the thirty-one travellers just under £20 each. Thomas Okey, later first Professor of Italian at Cambridge, was in charge. They prepared

by studying Thucydides, Herodotus and Plutarch. A/TOY/26/11/1A, LMA.

56 *V&M*, p. 147.
57 *C&C*, p. 145.
58 E.g. *V&M*, p. 148.
59 A. F. Havighurst, *Radical Journalist: H. W. Massingham*, Cambridge, 1974, p. 56; *C&C*, pp. 175–6.
60 H. W. Nevinson, *Scenes in the Thirty Days' War between Greece and Turkey, 1897* [*STDW*], 1898, p. 158.
61 *C&C*, p. 147.
62 *STDW*, p. 16.
63 Ibid., p. 74.
64 *Daily Chronicle* [*DC*], 29 April 1897; *C&C*, p. 158.
65 *STDW*, p. 83.
66 Christian to E. Sharp, 10 November 1941, ESNev. MSS. Eng. Lett. d 280.
67 *Manchester Guardian* [*MG*], 18 November 1933.
68 *DC*, 13 May 1897.
69 *BA*, pp. 149–79.
70 *RA*, p. 35.
71 *STDW*, p. 234.
72 Ibid., p. 287.
73 *V&M*, p. 149.
74 Quoted in L. Furneaux, *News of War*, 1964, p. 154.
75 H. W. Nevinson, *Essays, Poems and Tales of Henry W. Nevinson* [*EPT*], ed. H. N. Brailsford, 1948, p. 8; F. M. Leventhal, *The Last Dissenter: H. N. Brailsford and his World*, Oxford, p. 32.
76 *DC*, 17 June 1897.
77 Ibid.; Leventhal, *The Last Dissenter*, pp. 35–6. In 1898 Great Britain, France, Italy and Russia made Crete a British protectorate. Cretan union ('enosis') with Greece was announced in 1905.
78 *DC*, 24 June 1897.
79 *DC*, 17 June 1897.
80 *STDW*, p. 258.
81 Nevinson, 'How I Began'.
82 *DC*, 13 May 1897.
83 Furneaux, *News of War*, p. 156.
84 *Daily Graphic*, 14 July 1897.
85 *DC*, 11 May 1897. See too *IDB*, pp. 58–70.
86 Quoted in Havighurst, *Radical Journalist*, p. 58.
87 H. W. Nevinson, *Lines of Life* [*LL*], 1920, p. 47.
88 War correspondents Kinnaird Rose and Ashmead-Bartlett published their books in 1897.
89 *STDW*, p. 288.
90 J. Fulleylove and H. W. Nevinson, *Pictures of Classical Greek Landscape and Architecture*, 1897, p. xiv. Fulleylove gave Richard Nevinson drawing lessons.
91 *MG*, 1 August 1901.
92 *EPT*, p. 12. In 1934 Richard produced a large oil painting entitled *Pan Triumphant*.

Chapter Two

1 *DC*, 24 August 1899.

2 *DC*, 15 October 1900, though the diary entry (3 October 1899) says 'the heart in his soul was bloody with grief'. The quotes in this chapter, unless otherwise indicated, are from NevJ. e 610/6 – 611/4, 1899–1902.

3 H. W. Nevinson, *Essays in Rebellion* [*ER*], 1913, p. 189.

4 Boers were Afrikaners of Dutch extraction. The word 'Boer' means 'farmer'.

5 J. Beaumont Hughes, draft of 'The Making of a War Correspondent: Lionel James of *The Times*', p. 1.

6 H. W. Nevinson, 'Memories of War Correspondence', 28 January 1930, BBC Written Sound Archives, Caversham.

7 P. Knightley, *The First Casualty: From the Crimea to Vietnam, The War Correspondent as Hero, Propagandist and Myth Maker*, 1975 edn, pp. 13–14.

8 T. Royle, *War Report: The War Correspondents' View of Battle from the Crimea to the Falklands*, 1989, p. 17.

9 K. O. Morgan, 'The Boer War and the Media (1899–1902)', *Twentieth Century British History*, 13/1, 2002, pp. 1–16; *Timewatch*, BBC2, 'The Boer War: The First Media War', 18 March 1997; D. Lowry, *The South African War Reappraised*, Manchester, 2000.

10 *C&C*, p. 317.

11 Beaumont Hughes, 'The Making of a War Correspondent', p. 1.

12 Nevinson, 'Memories of War Correspondence'.

13 His target was Captain Pollen.

14 In *C&C*, p. 230, he praised Majors Altham and Henderson, who became distinguished First World War generals, but the former was unpopular at Ladysmith.

15 T. Pakenham, *The Boer War*, 1979, pp. 139, 146. See too G. Foden, *Ladysmith*, 1999.

16 H. W. Nevinson, Introduction to *Anywhere for a News Story*, BBC, 1934, p. 13.

17 R. T. Stearn, 'War Correspondents and Colonial War *c*.1870–1900' in J. M. Mackenzie, *Popular Imperialism and the Military*, 1992, p. 140.

18 S. Barnett, 14 October 1900, F/BAR/225, LMA.

19 J. Beaumont Hughes, 'The Press and the Public during the Boer War', *The Historian*, 61, 1999, p. 10; Idem, draft of 'The Liberal Press and the South African War', *Social Democrats Historical Journal*, December, 2000.

20 *V&M*, p. 157.

21 *C&C*, p. 235.

22 Jacqueline Beaumont gives evidence of this from mid-December. J. Beaumont, 'The British Press during the South African War: The Sieges of Mafeking, Kimberley and Ladysmith' in M. Connelly and D. Welch (eds), *War and the Media: Reportage and Propaganda, 1900–2003*, 2005, p. 16.

23 B. Farwell, *The Great Boer War*, 1999 edn, pp. 219–34.

24 R. Sibbald, *The War Correspondents: The Boer War*, Stroud, 1993, p. 85.

25 Nevinson to J. Lea (John Lea's sister married E. B. Nevinson), 15 March 1900, MSS.RP2679(ii), British Library. Methuen and Fisher Unwin asked him for a book. Eleanor Podmore revised it. Nevinson to Fisher Unwin, 5 April 1900, Henry W. and Albert A. Berg Collection, The New York Public Library.

26 Henry was annoyed that some of his statistics, including casualty figures, were omitted.
27 J. B. Atkins's *The Relief of Ladysmith* appeared two months after the event. Steevens's posthumous, incomplete letters/diary for the *Daily Mail* appeared in February 1900. Harry Pearse's book beat Henry's by one day. Methuen's Colonial Library series also printed an edition of Henry's book in India and the colonies.
28 He later suggested that this might have influenced the issuing of jam rations in the Great War. *MG*, 22 November 1933.
29 *BA*, p. 224.
30 *V&M*, p. 161.
31 H. W. Nevinson, *Ladysmith: The Diary of a Siege* [L], 1900, p. 89.
32 Ibid., p. 178.
33 Ibid., p. 179.
34 Sibbald, *The War Correspondents*, p. 84.
35 *L*, p. 204.
36 *DC*, 13 October 1900.
37 H. W. Nevinson, *The Plea of Pan* [PP], 1901, p. 96.
38 *C&C*, p. 236; *V&M*, p. 158.
39 *BA*, p. 243.
40 *L*, p. 285.
41 Nevinson to Lea, 15 March 1900.
42 H. W. Nevinson, 'Siege of Ladysmith', 16 December 1933, BBC Written Sound Archives, Caversham.
43 *C&C*, p. 256.
44 This copy is in the Bodleian Library.
45 *C&C*, p. 257; Nevinson, 'Siege of Ladysmith'.
46 *DC*, 16 April 1900.
47 Nevinson to Lea, 15 March 1900.
48 *V&M*, p. 158.
49 Nevinson to Lea, 15 March 1900.
50 Although signed by both, Henry drafted it and then went through it with Donohoe.
51 Back home he stressed the War Office's ignorance about decent maps of the country. *East London Advertiser*, 27 November 1900.
52 *C&C*, p. 282.
53 H. W. Nevinson, *Books and Personalities* [BP], London and New York, 1905, p. 294.
54 *C&C*, pp. 295–6.
55 In a letter to Lea, 10 April, MSS. RP2679(ii), British Library, she wrote that at first she had thought it an unrighteous war but had 'more or less come to the conclusion that the Boers meant war'.
56 M. Wynne Nevinson, *Life's Fitful Fever*, 1926, p. 143.
57 C. R. W. Nevinson, *Paint and Prejudice*, 1937, pp. 4, 10–11.
58 NevJ. e 618/1, 30 August 1913.
59 *DC*, 22 February 1901.
60 *C&C*, p. 323.
61 *DC*, 1 June 1902.
62 *C&C*, p. 319.

63 B. Nasson, *The South African War 1899–1902*, 1999, p. 282; P. M. Krebs, *Gender, Race and the Writing of Empire*, Cambridge, 1999, pp. 5, 175.

64 J. Beaumont from forthcoming book on the sieges of the South African War.

65 *BA*, p. 202.

66 *C&C*, p. 339.

67 *BA*, pp. 265–82.

68 Nevinson to E. C. Bentley, n.d., Camden Local Studies and Archives Centre, London.

69 *The Times*, 30 November 1936.

70 *EF*, p. 87.

71 G. Dawson, *Soldier Heroes: British Adventure, Empire and the Imagining of Masculinities*, 1994, pp. 146–7, 235.

Chapter Three

1 E. M. Forster, *NL*, 2 October 1925. Henry dubbed them 'The Islands of Doom', *HMM*, cxii/669, p. 327.

2 The quotes in this chapter, unless otherwise indicated, are from NevJ. e 612/3 – 615/4, 1904–9.

3 J. H. Harris, *Portuguese Slavery: Britain's Dilemma*, 1913, p. 23.

4 H. W. Nevinson, *More Changes, More Chances* [*More C*], 1925, pp. 38–9.

5 Henry requested from Cadbury introductions to planters. Cadbury also provided Portuguese regulations and the firm's book on cocoa. 180/845–54, Cadbury Papers, University of Birmingham.

6 *Nation*, 3 August 1907.

7 H. W. Nevinson, *A Modern Slavery* [*AMS*], New York, 1968, pp. 5–7.

8 Ibid., p. 22.

9 *IDB*, p. 211.

10 *AMS*, p. 27.

11 Ibid., p. 49.

12 Ibid., p. 59.

13 Ibid., p. 69.

14 W. G. Clarence-Smith, *Cocoa and Chocolate 1765–1914*, 2000.

15 *EPT*, p. 11.

16 *More C*, p. 72.

17 *LL*, p. 46.

18 H. W. Nevinson, *Films of Time: Twelve Fantasies* [*FT*], 1939, p. 173.

19 *More C*, p. 81.

20 *IDB*, p. 204.

21 W. G. Clarence Smith, 'Labour Conditions in the Plantations of Sao Thomé and Principe, 1875–1914', *Slavery and Abolition*, 14/I, 1993, pp. 149–67.

22 Small numbers came from Dahomey, Gabon and even China and some short-term indentured labourers from the Cape Verde Islands.

23 Blurb composed by Henry for *RA*.

24 *HMM*, cxi/663, p. 341.

25 Ibid., cxi/664, p. 535; Nevinson to William Cadbury (who also objected to this tactic), 1 September 1905, 180/856–7, Cadbury Papers.

26 *Anti-Slavery Reporter* *[ASR]*, series 4, xxv/4, August to October 1905, pp. 91–4, November to December 1905, pp. 125–9, xxvi/1, January to February 1906, pp. 3–6.

27 *NL*, 2 October 1925.

28 Cadbury supported many of Casement's humanitarian schemes. He published his own *Labour in Portuguese West Africa* in 1910.

29 *Nation*, 17 March 1923.

30 Chapters IV, V and VII were not included in the *HMM* letters. Before learning about the book the ASS had considered approaching Henry about reprinting them as a pamphlet, 2 March 1906, ASS Committee Minutes, MSS. Brit. Emp. S20, E2/12, Bodleian Library of Commonwealth and African Studies at Rhodes House, Oxford (BLCAS).

31 Nevinson to Travers Buxton, 13 May 1906, S18, C86/36, BLCAS.

32 *NL*, 8 August 1924.

33 The book had only a third of the forty-seven photographs printed in the *HMM* articles.

34 *AMS*, p. 83.

35 T. W. Laqueur, 'Bodies, Details, and the Humanitarian Narrative' in L. Hunt (ed.), *The New Cultural History*, Berkeley, CA, 1989, pp. 176–204.

36 *AMS*, p. 179.

37 *More C*, p. 75.

38 *AMS*, p. 12.

39 *The Aborigines' Friend*, viii/5, January 1908; *Tribune*, 7 June 1906.

40 *Nation*, 2 May 1914.

41 Ibid., 20 March 1909, 12 April 1913.

42 *RA*, p. 133. Henry pointed out that nineteenth-century legislation in Berlin and Brussels bound Britain and Portugal to put down the slave trade from the Congo Basin and Central Africa.

43 Harris, *Portuguese Slavery*, p. 80.

44 *The Times*, 4, 5 June 1909.

45 Ibid., 28, 30 September 1909.

46 *ASR*, series 4, xxvii/5, November–December 1907, p. 126; Nevinson to A. Bryant, 24 March n.y., MSS. Brit.Emp. S22, G268/B, BLCAS.

47 *MG*, 14, 15 April 1908.

48 *The Aborigines' Friend*, viii/7, May 1908.

49 S. Koss, *Fleet Street Radical: A. G. Gardiner and the* Daily News, 1973, pp. 112–13.

50 On 5 October 1906 Henry told William Cadbury 'a complete change' was needed 'in the disposition of the Portuguese people', adding that, if an American gunboat held up a mail steamer 'with its usual cargo of slaves, they would be compelled to think about it', 180/858, Cadbury Papers. See too *DC*, 30 March 1906.

51 *ASR*, series 5, 1/5, October 1910.

52 *Nation*, 20 March 1909.

53 Nevinson to W. Cadbury, 9 April 1909, 180/867, Cadbury Papers.

54 H. W. Nevinson, 'The Angola Slave Trade', *Fortnightly Review*, 88, 1907, pp. 488–97.

55 I. O. Williams, *The Firm of Cadbury 1831–1931*, 1931, pp. 205–11;

Nation, 12 April 1913; Draft Notes for cross-examination of Mr Nevinson, 121, Cadbury Papers.

56 Harris, *Portuguese Slavery*, p. 81.
57 *Millgate Monthly*, xxii/1, January 1927.
58 J. Duffy, *A Question of Slavery*, Oxford, 1967, p. 187.
59 R. Mildam, 'The Anti-Imperial Archive?', Historical Geography Seminar, Institute of Historical Research, University of London, 6 March 2001.
60 Duffy, *A Question of Slavery*, p. 186.
61 Ibid., p. 187.
62 Ibid., pp. 187–8.
63 *HMM*, cxi/663, p. 350.
64 *Nation*, 6 July 1912.
65 *More C*, p. 95.
66 See his revealing Introduction to Richard F. Burton, *First Footsteps in East Africa*, 1910.
67 NevJ. e 624/2, 4 May 1927.
68 ESNev. MSS. Eng. Lett. d 280, 1941–2. Henry had become a vice-president of the ASS.
69 Duffy, *A Question of Slavery*, p. 186.
70 *AMS*, pp. ix, xix.
71 A. V. John, 'A Modern Slavery?', *History Today*, 52/6, June 2002, pp. 34–5. See too *Guardian*, 12–19 April, 5 May 2001; *Financial Times*, 20 April 2001; 'The Slave Children', BBC2, 7 October 2001; *File on 4*, BBC Radio 4, 20 October 2001.

Chapter Four

1 'Journalism is the first draft of History' emanated from Philip Graham, publisher of the *Washington Post*. John Pilger narrowed it to the best journalism. Introduction to P. Knightley, *The First Casualty: The War Correspondent as Hero and Myth Maker from the Crimea to Kosovo*, 2000 edn.
2 The quotes in this chapter, unless otherwise indicated, are from NevJ. e 613/1 – 613/4, 1905–7.
3 *More C*, pp. 101–2; F. M. Leventhal, *The Last Dissenter: H. N. Brailsford and his World*, Oxford, 1985, pp. 51–5.
4 Nevinson to Mrs Hammond, 20 November 1905, vol. 15, f 250, Hammond Papers, Bodleian Library.
5 Russia still used the Julian calendar, thirteen days behind the Western Gregorian calendar used in this account.
6 *Nation*, 10 May 1913 (unsigned). The draft ('The Satire of Rage') is in the National Library of Scotland, Acc.8693.
7 H. W. Nevinson, *The Dawn in Russia or Scenes in the Russian Revolution of 1905–6 [DIR]*, London and New York, 1906, p. 63.
8 This was the high point of political feminism. L. H. Edmondson, *Feminism in Russia 1900–1917*, 1984.
9 *DIR*, p. 33.
10 *More C*, p. 129 differs slightly from the *DC* original version of 23 December 1905. Mr Ruby, a new recruit to the paper, had altered Henry's words.

11 House of Lords Record Office, Stow Hill Papers, STH/DS/1/NE, 1–15. Henry later met him in Moscow working for the *Tribune*.

12 *DIR*, p. 58.

13 Socialist Revolutionaries assassinated him when he returned to St Petersburg.

14 *More C*, p. 107. What is generally considered to have been the first Soviet (in all but name) took place some months earlier in the textile town of Ivanovo Voznesensk in Central Russia.

15 *Nation*, 10 May 1913.

16 *More C*, p. 114.

17 Ibid., pp. 118–23; *DIR*, chapter V; *DC*, 10 February 1906 (sent by consular mail); *NL*, 31 July 1925; *EF*, pp. 267–73.

18 *EF*, p. 273.

19 *DC*, 23 December 1905. Compare this with *DIR*, pp. 121–2.

20 *DIR*, p. 163.

21 Ibid., p. 158; *MG*, 25 November 1933; *NL*, 23 December 1927.

22 *DIR*, p. 176.

23 Ibid., p. 182.

24 W. Harrison, 'The British Press and the Russian Revolution of 1905–7', *Oxford Slavonic Papers*, ns. vii, 1974, p. 79.

25 *DC*, 23 December 1906.

26 Ibid., 29 December 1906.

27 Possibly prompted by a conversation with P. N. Miliukov, historian and leader of the 10,000-strong main party of Russian liberalism, the Constitutional Democratic Party or Kadets.

28 H. W. Nevinson in K. Foss, *Black Bread and Samovars*, 1930, p. 8.

29 T. U. Raun, 'The Revolution of 1905 in the Baltic Provinces and Finland', *Slavonic Review*, 43/3, 1984, pp. 453–67.

30 *Nation*, 8 September 1917. Many were slaughtered in the countryside. Latvian peasants burned the country houses of their German landlords in 1905. Now Germans used the Russian troops to exact revenge. In reasserting the authority of the Empire, they were conveniently terrorizing the landlords' former dependants.

31 *DC*, 17, 19 February 1906; *DIR*, pp. 283–7; *More C*, pp. 157–8.

32 *DIR*, p. 284. Henry did not mention him by name in his article or book.

33 *More C*, pp. 160–2.

34 *DIR*, p. 260.

35 They arrived during the election. Elections were then protracted affairs, covered very closely by the press.

36 *DIR*, p. 77. A second edition followed six months later, reprinted in 1971 as *Russia Observed*.

37 E.g. Galsworthy in *The Reader*, 10 April 1907.

38 *DC*, 26 June 1906.

39 31 July 1909, ESNev. MSS. Eng. Lit. c 278.

40 *Westminster Gazette*, 14 May 1906; *DIR*, p. 322.

41 *More C*, pp. 167–8.

42 *DIR*, p. 337.

43 Campbell-Bannerman's famous words 'La Douma est morte. Vive la Douma' had apparently already been coined by Henry to end his leader on

the dissolution. Henry later claimed that he rejected them at proof stage as too commonplace, only to hear 'C–B' utter them in Parliament the next day at a conference attended by six Duma members. Yet Henry's diary does not mention this. *More C*, p. 170.

44 B. Hollingsworth, 'The British Memorial to the Russian Duma, 1906', *Slavonic Review*, LIII/33, 1975, pp. 540–1.

45 Henry's appeal for support was rejected by some, e.g. George Meredith.

46 W. Harrison, 'Mackenzie Wallace's view of the Russian Revolution of 1905–7', *Oxford Slavonic Papers*, ns. lv, 1971, pp. 73–82.

47 Hollingsworth, 'The British Memorial', p. 557.

48 British Embassy in St Petersburg to London, 11 October 1906, FO 181/865, The National Archives: Public Record Office, Kew (TNA: PRO).

49 Hollingsworth, 'The British Memorial', p. 551. According to Henry's diary, Pethick Lawrence was 'very vehement & cross about the change of plan, Robertson was 'quite straight & fine' and Brailsford wished to carry it through even with a rump deputation.

50 Henry's diary says that 'rather than reduce the deputation to an absurd rump I proposed to send one man privately'.

51 *Daily News [DN]*, 12 October 1906.

52 *More C*, p. 184.

53 Hollingsworth, 'The British Memorial', pp. 554–5.

54 *More C*, p. 182.

55 Ibid., p. 188.

56 *DC*, 10 December 1906.

57 He had been in the revolutionary federalist section of the First International. In London the Cherkesovs were active with Nannie Dryhurst in anarchist circles. He was later in the Georgian Menshevik government in exile.

58 See Chapter 5. Dryhurst family papers (in private hands). She gave £100 from the Relief Committee to the Georgians. Many years later a Georgian Legation was established at Sylvia Dryhurst's London home.

59 *More C*, p. 206.

60 *HMM*, CXVI/692, January 1908, pp. 256–65.

61 Ibid., CXVI/695, April 1908, pp.760–8. In the *DC*, 7 January 1907, Henry argued that nationality was the key to understanding this region, feuds between Armenians and Tartars ultimately mattering more than revolutionary movements against the Russians.

62 *HMM*, CXVI/696, May 1908, p. 935.

63 *DC*, 4 February 1907.

64 *Nation*, 20 April 1907.

65 A. J. A. Morris, 'The English Radicals' Campaign for Disarmament and the Hague Conference of 1907', *Journal of Modern History*, 43, 1971, pp. 367–93.

66 Henry's diary describes it as 'a mere waste of time'. He would have abandoned it had it not been for Nannie.

67 *Westminster Gazette*, 26 September 1907.

68 Leventhal, *The Last Dissenter*, p. 61.

69 For the deliberately euphemistic correspondence on this sensitive subject, see the Nevinson–Blunt letters in the West Sussex Record Office, County

Hall, Chichester, Blunt MSS.46. Henry wrote the Introduction to I. Steinberg, *Spiridonova: Revolutionary Terrorist*, 1935, pp. xi–xxii.

70 *More C*, p. 284.

71 *MG*, 6 June 1908.

72 *NL*, 11 November 1927.

73 *Nation*, 25 June 1910. Henry sat on the Anglo-Finnish Society committee.

74 Ibid., 1 October 1910.

75 NevJ. e 616/1, 15 September 1910. Henry also spoke at (the more conservative) Old Finn Party's dinner, stressing the importance of nationality and need to protect freedom everywhere.

76 H. W. Nevinson, Preface to G. Renwick, *Finland Today*, 1911, p. 8.

77 *Nation*, 1, 15 October 1910.

78 *More C*, p. 284.

79 Written in March. *Contemporary Review*, CXI, April 1917, pp. 409–18.

80 *Votes for Women*, April 1917.

81 'Russia Free!' Authorized Report, 1917, p. 7; NevJ. e 620/2, 31 March 1917.

82 H. W. Nevinson, *Last Changes, Last Chances* [*Last C*], 1928, p. 124.

83 M. A. Hamilton, *Remembering My Good Friends*, 1944, p. 79; NevJ. e 625/2, 23 January 1931.

84 HWNP, MS. Eng. Misc. c 497; NevJ. e 621/2, 11 January 1920, 22 July 1921, e 622/3, 14 March 1922.

85 HWNP, MS. Eng. Misc. c 497.

86 *EF*, p. xvi.

Chapter Five

1 See A. V. John, 'Men, Manners and Militancy: Literary Men and Women's Suffrage' in A. V. John and C. Eustance (eds), *The Men's Share? Masculinities, Male Support and Women's Suffrage in Britain, 1890–1920*, 1997. The quotes in this chapter, unless otherwise indicated, come from NevJ. e 610/1 – 620/2, 1893–1917.

2 E. Pankhurst to Nevinson, 4 October 1909, ESNev. MSS. Eng. Lett. c 278.

3 P. Gibbs, *The Pageant of the Years*, 1946, p. 128.

4 *ER*, p. 184.

5 G. Sigerson, *Custodia Honesta*, 1912, p. 7.

6 F. M. L. Thompson, *Hampstead: Building a Borough 1650–1964*, 1974, p. 438.

7 W. Marsden, 'Charles Booth and the Social Geography of Education in Late Nineteenth-century London' in D. Englander and R. O'Day (eds), *Retrieved Riches: Social Investigation in Britain 1840–1914*, Aldershot, 1995, pp. 253–4.

8 C. Mackenzie, *Gallipoli Memories*, 1929, p. 237.

9 *EPT*, p. 37.

10 NevJ. e 625/2, 31 October 1930.

11 Manuscript papers compiled by Mrs Dryhurst's granddaughter, Mrs Maire Gaster; family papers held by Pat Paget and Nancy Nicholls.

12 R. Schuchard, 'An Attendant Lord: H. W. Nevinson's Friendship with W. B. Yeats', *Yeats Annual*, 7, 1990, p. 90.

13 1891 census, RG12/107, f 118, p. 32.
14 In Irish publications she wrote under the pseudonym of Nic Eoghain (Daughter of Egan – her mother's maiden name).
15 *LL*, p. 15; NevJ. e 621/2, 29 September 1919.
16 Letters to Mrs Dryhurst presented by A. R. Dryhurst, MS.AM464473A, Dryhurst Papers, British Library.
17 NevJ. e 625/2, 28 October 1930.
18 John L. Nevinson Diaries, 8 April 1940, 911/3/**XXXIX**, The Society of Antiquaries of London.
19 Journals of George Sturt, 9 August 1899, in papers supplied by Pat Paget.
20 M. Olivier (ed.), *Sidney Olivier: Letters and Selected Writings*, 1948, p. 77.
21 *The Yellow Book*, xiii, April 1897, pp. 153–5.
22 Schuchard, 'An Attendant Lord', p. 95.
23 J. Masefield, *So Long to Learn*, 1952, p. 124.
24 *C&C*, p. 300.
25 S. Hinely, 'Charlotte Wilson: Anarchist, Fabian and Feminist', Ph.D., Stanford University, CA, 1987, p. 303.
26 *Freedom*, February 1892; J. Shotton, *No Master High or Low: Libertarian Education and Schooling in Britain 1890–1990*, Bristol, 1993, p. 35. The school was closed after the discovery of bombs and bomb-making equipment in the basement.
27 A. Barrett Brown (ed.), *Great Democrats*, 1934, p. 101; *C&C*, p. 129.
28 M. Wynne Nevinson, *Life's Fitful Fever*, 1926, p. 113.
29 NevJ. e 625/4, 8 June 1932.
30 M. Wynne Nevinson, *Fragments of Life*, 1922, pp. 11–23.
31 A. V. John, 'A Family at War: The Nevinson Family' in M. J. K. Walsh (ed.), *C. R. W. Nevinson: The Lives of a Modern Bohemian*, Newark, DE, forthcoming.
32 Compare the comments of modern Reuters correspondent A. Hartley, *The Zanzibar Chest*, New York, 2003, p. 299.
33 NevJ. e 625/4, 8 June 1932.
34 Ibid., 8 November 1932.
35 Wynne Nevinson, *Fragments of Life*, pp. 70, 119–20, 133, 137.
36 T. Broughton, *Men of Letters, Writing Lives, Masculinity and Literary Auto/Biography in the Late Victorian Period*, 1999.
37 *PP*, p. 182.
38 E. Sharp, *Unfinished Adventure: Selected Reminiscences from an Englishwoman's Life*, 1933. Evelyn Sharp's life is the subject of my forthcoming biography published by Day Books.
39 E. Sharp, 'Fairy Tales as They Are, as They Were and as They Should Be', 1889, p. 2.
40 S. Gwynn, *Experiences of a Literary Man*, 1926, p. 137.
41 Author's copy of *Last C*.
42 See Chapter 7.
43 *English Review*, October 1909.
44 Dryhurst Family papers.
45 *Nation*, 17 August 1912.
46 A. V. John, 'Behind the Locked Door: Evelyn Sharp, Suffragette and Rebel Journalist', *Women's History Review*, 12/1, 2003, pp. 5–13.

47 Nevinson to P. Webb, 16 January 1913, ESNev. MSS. Eng. Lett. c 278.

48 E. Sharp, *Rebel Women*, 1910, 1915, reprinted 2003.

49 Nevinson to Sharp/ESNev. MSS. Eng. Lett., December 1911, d 277.

50 F. Meynell, *My Lives*, 1971, p. 72. Meynell got the date wrong.

51 A. V. John, 'The Privilege of Power: Suffrage Women and the Issue of Men's Support' in A. Vickery (ed.), *Women, Privilege and Power: British Politics 1750 to the Present*, Stanford, CA, 2001, pp. 243–52.

52 Three million women below thirty remained voteless, as did older professional women in furnished lodgings.

53 In recognition of suffrage work, Evelyn was presented with a cheque for over £320 at a United Suffragist party. Henry was the first speaker. Elizabeth Robins, Massingham and Lady Sybil Smith organized a dinner celebrating Henry's 'many-sided public services' as war correspondent, suffragist and man of letters. He received a casket and cheque for £280. HWNP, MS. Eng. Misc. c 496 for the 187 guests.

54 *More C*, p. 339.

Chapter Six

1 12 December 1907, MSS.EUR, Morley Papers, D573/13, India Office Library and Records (IOR), The British Library. Morley became a viscount in 1908.

2 A term about knowing and caring coined by the television war correspondent Martin Bell. M. Bell, *In Harm's Way*, 1996, p. 128.

3 Intelligence Reports on the Political Situation. Proceedings B. Weekly Report of the Director of Criminal Intelligence (CIR), 19 October 1907, National Archives of India, New Delhi, Microfilm in IOR.

4 September 1907, A/N12/5, Manchester Guardian Archives (MGA), The John Rylands University Library, University of Manchester.

5 *More C*, p. 228. The quotes in this chapter, unless otherwise indicated, are from NevJ. e 614/2 – 614/4, 1907–8.

6 C. Kaul, *Reporting the Raj: The British Press and India c.1880–1922*, Manchester, 2003, pp. 259, 266.

7 *More C*, p. 228.

8 3 October 1907, D573/2, Morley Papers.

9 By the time he wrote his autobiography, Henry had read Morley's printed correspondence and appreciated his courage in standing up to his Indian Council and Anglo-Indian authorities.

10 With her 1907 novel *Nicolette*.

11 K. O. Morgan, *Keir Hardie: Radical and Socialist*, 1988 edn, pp. 190–6; C. Benn, *Keir Hardie*, 1997, p. 231.

12 *MG*, 22 November 1907.

13 N. Owen, 'British Progressives and Civil Society in India, 1905–1914' in J. Harris (ed.), *Civil Society in Britain: History, Ideas, Identities, Institutions*, Oxford, 2003, pp. 149–75.

14 He wrote for this journal edited by the Moderate G. A. Nateson.

15 *NSI*, p. 181.

16 A. Tripathi, *The Extremist Challenge: India between 1890 and 1910*, New Delhi, 1967, p. 128.

17 They devoted their lives to India 'in a religious spirit', promoting 'by all constitutional means, the national interests of the Indian people', *NSI*, p. 38. Henry's printed accounts conflate several meetings with Gokhale.
18 *Nation*, 27 February 1915.
19 B. R. Nanda, *Gokhale, Gandhi and the Nehrus: Studies in Indian Nationalism*, 1974, p. 13.
20 *More C*, p. 237; *Indian Review*, XVI/3, March, 1915: Henry's eulogy was the longest of eighteen.
21 *Glasgow Herald*, 2 December 1908. For Crete see Chapter 1.
22 *MG*, 22 November 1907. The term 'Anglo-Indian' did not then have its modern meaning. It instead signified British officials and any long-term British resident in India.
23 Gokhale to Krishnaswami Iyer, 16 November 1907, microfilm 11701, Gokhale Papers, National Archives of India, IOR.
24 Henry wore a helmet as protection from the heat and was known for his ruddy complexion.
25 Morley to Minto, 3 January 1908, D573/3, Morley Papers.
26 Quoted in M. N. Das, *India under Morley and Minto: Politics behind Revolution, Repression and Reforms*, 1964, pp. 72, 84–5.
27 *Madras Standard*, 23 November 1907.
28 CIR, Proceedings B, 19 October 1907, also 30 November 1907, enclosed in D573/13, Morley Papers.
29 *NSI*, pp. 203–4.
30 *More C*, p. 282.
31 *Hindu*, 20 November 1907.
32 Kaul, *Reporting the Raj*, Chapter 2.
33 6 February 1908, Minto Papers, Add. MSS. 1272, IOR.
34 NevJ. e 615/3, 24 June 1909.
35 *More C*, pp. 258–62.
36 *MG*, 30 December 1907.
37 CIR, Proceedings A, 12 January 1908.
38 Ibid.
39 Copy of telegram from Reuters Calcutta to Reuters London, 20 December 1907, Dunlop-Smith Papers, MSS. Eur. F166/13, IOR.
40 Ibid., Buck to Dunlop-Smith; Kaul, *Reporting the Raj*, pp. 40–9.
41 *NSI*, p. 217.
42 Ibid., p. 218.
43 CIR, Proceedings B, 19 October 1907.
44 Ibid.
45 *MG*, 27 December 1907.
46 *NSI*, p. 248.
47 *MG*, 27 December 1907.
48 *NSI*, p. 257.
49 Ibid., pp. 257–8.
50 Argov suggests that Mehta's decision to bring into the pavilion forty hired men armed with sticks provides one of several clues to Moderates' pre-determination to expel Extremists. D. Argov, *Moderates and Extremists in the Indian Nationalist Movement*, Bombay, 1967, p. 261.
51 *NSI*, p.259.

52 When they met at Allahabad in April 1908 they drew up a constitution. The twenty-fourth Congress was the first exclusively for Moderates.

53 *MG*, 30 December 1907.

54 See Argov, *Moderates and Extremists*, p. 261.

55 *Nation*, 1, 22 February 1908.

56 Tripathi, *The Extremist Challenge*, p. 184.

57 S. A. Wolpert, *Morley and India 1906–1910*, Berkeley, CA, 1967, p. 98. C. F. G. Masterman, *In Peril of Change*, 1904, pp. 15–17 had discussed Henry's literary work and the new spirit dawning in England.

58 17 August 1910, microfilm 11704, Gokhale Papers. Henry also sent Gokhale letters of introduction to William Archer and the Webbs.

59 J. D. Rees, *The Real India*, 1908, p. 341.

60 *Glasgow Herald*, 14, 26, 30 December 1907.

61 *India*, 16 October 1908.

62 See D. Cannadine, *Ornamentalism: How the British Saw Their Empire*, 2001.

63 *NSI*, pp. 320–37.

64 Ibid., p. 103; *Indian Review*, IX/2, February 1908, p. 82.

65 *Madras Standard*, 23 November 1907.

66 Owen, 'British Progressives and Civil Society in India, 1905–1922', draft version, p. 12.

67 Compare the Simla scheme of reforms proposed by Morley (*NSI*, pp. 22–4), Gokhale's response to them and Henry's ideas for reform (*NSI*, pp. 44–6).

68 *NSI*, p. 335.

69 *More C*, p. 265.

70 *Indian Review*, IX/2, February 1908, pp. 81–4.

71 *Glasgow Herald*, 11 December 1907.

72 *Indian Review*, IX/2, February 1908, p. 87.

73 Wolpert, *Morley and India*, Chapter 6. To achieve reforms Morley had to appease the Tory Viceroy, the House of Lords and the conservative Indian Council. He seems to have deliberately let Minto take the credit for the reforms.

74 Nevinson to Gokhale, 12 February 1909, microfilm 11704, Gokhale Papers.

75 *Nation*, 17 October 1908.

76 Ibid., 24 October 1908.

77 J. O. Baylen and N. J. Gossman, *Biographical Dictionary of Modern British Radicals*, 3, *1870–1914*, Hemel Hempstead, 1988, p. 14.

78 5 November 1908, D573/3, Morley Papers.

79 NevJ. e 628/2, 28 February 1941.

80 Ibid., e 626/3, 31 January 1936.

81 C. F. Andrews, *Rabindranath Tagore: Letters to a Friend*, 1928, p. 152.

Chapter Seven

1 The quotes in this chapter, unless otherwise indicated, are from NevJ. e 612/1 – 618/4, 1903–15.

2 *More C*, p. 2.

3 Nevinson to Scott, 16 September 1903, 124/153, MGA.

4 Noel Buxton financed this himself. Resigning from the family brewery firm

in 1904, he became Liberal MP for Whitby. He, his brothers Charles Roden, Leland and Harold and sister Victoria were also Henry's friends.

5 V. Goldsworthy, *Inventing Ruritania: The Imperialism of the Imagination*, New Haven, 1998, p. 118.

6 L. S. Stavrianos, 'The Balkan Committee', *Queen's Quarterly*, xlviii/3, 1941, pp. 258–67.

7 The Balkan Committee. List of Members, Noel Buxton Papers, 56/2, McGill University Library, Montreal, Canada. Henry became a vice-president.

8 *DC*, 5 January 1904.

9 *More C*, p. 11.

10 *The Times*, 23 November 1903.

11 See Chapter 5.

12 *Speaker*, 30 January 1904.

13 *The Times*, 23 November 1904.

14 *More C*, p. 16.

15 Scotia referred to his 'northern voice'. A surviving broadcast of the elderly Henry does not suggest his Leicestershire roots though his voice is unlike that of his BBC interviewer. 'Scrapbook for 1900', 25 February 1938, 9CL0001499, British Library Sound Archive.

16 M. Glenny, *The Balkans 1804–1999: Nationalism, War and the Great Powers*, 2000, p. 216.

17 *Nation*, 21 October 1911.

18 *More C*, p. 362.

19 D. Birkett, *Spinsters Abroad: Victorian Lady Explorers*, Oxford, 1989, p. 161.

20 M. E. Durham, *Albania and the Albanians: Selected Articles and Letters, 1903–1944*, ed. B. Destani, 2001, p. 103.

21 H. W. Nevinson, 'The Land of the Eagle', 10 November 1927, BBC Written Sound Archives, Caversham.

22 Henry had been about to write about relations between Albanians and Turks for the *Guardian* and had started a *Nation* article. The Foreign Office assured the Turks that Henry's mission was not political.

23 Henry chose to tell this differently post-war, writing that, in response to the officer's cry that 'Only England can save us', Edith declared 'It is the beginning.' *More C*, p. 367.

24 *DN, Nation*, 21 October 1911.

25 ESNev. MS. Eng. Misc. Diary iv, e 636, 16 November 1944.

26 R. C. Hall, *The Balkan Wars 1912–1913: Prelude to the First World War*, 2000, p. 132.

27 Arthur Moore used the pseudonym of Antrim Oriel. A. Oriel, *The Miracle*, 1908, pp. 11, 187, 204.

28 *Nation*, 5 April 1917.

29 Ibid.

30 24 October 1912, A/N12/19, MGA.

31 *DC*, 28 November, 10 December 1912.

32 Ibid., 4 January 1913.

33 *Economist*, 4 January 1913.

34 *More C*, p. 387.

35 For £10 per article, paying his own expenses. The articles appeared in July and August.

36 *IDB*, p. 86.

37 *DC*, 23, 26, 29, 31 July, 1 August 1913.

38 Ibid., 30 July 1913.

39 Quoted in J. Hodgson, 'Edith Durham, Traveller and Publicist' in J. B. Allcock and A. Young (eds), *Black Lambs and Grey Falcons: Women Travellers in the Balkans*, Bradford, 1991, p. 31. See too her later accounts of this in which the telegram drafted by Henry 'saved Korche'. Durham, *Albania and the Albanians*, pp. xiv, 200.

40 H. W. Nevinson, *Original Sinners*, 1920, pp. 173–204.

41 H. W. Nevinson, 'Memories of War Correspondence', 28 January 1930, BBC Written Sound Archives.

42 M. J. Farrar, *News from the Front: War Correspondents on the Western Front 1914–18*, Stroud, 1998, p. 7.

43 C. Lovelace, 'British Press Censorship during the First World War' in G. Boyce, J. Curran and P. Wingate (eds), *Newspaper History from the Seventeenth Century to the Present Day*, 1978, p. 307.

44 *Nation*, 12 September 1914.

45 *Last C*, p. 19.

46 Ibid. It was published in the *New Republic*. The editor told Henry it 'sent a thrill through all its readers'.

47 See Richard's painting *La Patrie* (1916).

48 *Last C*, p. 22. Fighting around Ypres would 'flicker on' until 22 November. The BEF had sent 160,000 troops to France. The October and November conflict resulted in more than 24,000 British and 50,000 German deaths. J. Keegan, *The First World War*, 1998, pp. 142–6.

49 *Nation*, 28 November 1914.

50 Ibid., 4 November 1914.

51 E.g. M. Burr, *Slouch Hat*, 1935, p. 121.

52 *DN*, 12, 16 March 1915.

53 H. Spender, *The Fire of Life: A Book of Memories*, 1926, p. 201.

54 Quoted in Farrar, *News from the Front*, p. 54.

55 Perry Robinson, who joined the group in 1916, was also in his fifties but younger than Henry.

56 The Germans had used tear gas on the Eastern Front but it had frozen instead of vaporizing. Now chlorine released from pressurized cylinders in windy conditions literally had deadly effects. *DN*, 19 May 1915.

57 HWNP, MS. Eng. Misc. c 497a.

58 *Nation*, 24 October 1914.

59 *NL*, 30 October 1925.

60 *PW*, pp. 49–50. After a rising in Barcelona in July 1909, workers took over the city for nearly a week. Henry called the war in the Spanish North African enclave on the Mediterranean coast of Morocco 'the most futile and disagreeable campaign I have shared'. He saw it as a petty conflict designed to protect Spanish and French business interests using Spanish conscripts against Riff tribesmen. *More C*, p. 300; *DN*, 7–12 August 1909.

61 *Atlantic Monthly*, November 1916; *Nation*, 12 February 1916.

62 *Nation*, 5 August 1916.

63 *BW*, p. 231. Written May 1918.

64 *Nation*, 5 April 1917.

65 Ibid.
66 By 1940 Richard had alienated many art critics. When he was not included in a projected National Gallery show of British artists since Whistler, Henry persuaded Edward Marsh to lend it one of his Nevinson paintings.
67 C. R. W. Nevinson, *Paint and Prejudice*, 1937, p. 43.
68 G. Cannan, *Mendel: A Story of Youth*, 1916, pp. 119, 185–7. Henry called it a 'silly but venomous libel'. For more information about Richard, see A. V. John, 'A Family at War: The Nevinson Family' in M. J. K. Walsh (ed.), *C. R. W. Nevinson: The Lives of a Modern Bohemian*, Newark, DE, forthcoming.
69 *The Vote*, 31 December 1910.
70 *V&M*, pp. 78–9.
71 Ibid., p. 80.
72 *V&M*, p. 86.
73 NevJ. e 621/2, 1 January 1920.
74 Richard's service card stated 'business reasons', not sick leave. Walsh, *C. R. W. Nevinson*, p. 98.
75 R. Cork, 'A Sudden Maturity'. Lecture to the C. R. W. Nevinson: Life, Art and Legacy Conference, University of Greenwich, 6 July 2002.
76 Information provided by Knowlman descendants.
77 J. Black, 'A Curious, Cold Intensity: C. R. W. Nevinson as a War Artist 1914–1918' in R. Ingleby *et al.*, *C. R. W. Nevinson: The Twentieth Century*, 1999, p. 31.
78 Quoted in R. Ingleby, 'Utterly Tired of Chaos' in Ingleby *et al.*, *C. R. W. Nevinson*, p. 16.
79 P. Whitebrook, *William Archer: A Biography*, 1993, p. 318.
80 Walsh, *C. R. W. Nevinson*, p. 137.

Chapter Eight

1 Salary plus expenses were £40 weekly. The quotations in this chapter, unless otherwise indicated, are from NevJ. e 619/1–620/4, 1915–19.
2 S. Moseley, *The Private Diaries of Sydney Moseley*, 1960, pp. 145–6, 150.
3 17 May 1915, Edward Clodd Collection, The Brotherton Collection, Leeds University Library.
4 Henry had told Brooke that he liked his poems very much but that a few phrases of 'A Channel Passage' were 'too strong' for current public taste. He suggested that there would have been no problem had he had sole editorship. *Nation*, 1 May, 26 June 1915; N. Jones, *Rupert Brooke: Life, Death and Myth*, 1999, p. 124. Henry later dedicated *FT* to the memory of 'Ka' Arnold Forster (Brooke's former lover) and Philip Webb.
5 Some of the Ottoman troops would not have been Turks but Henry refers to them thus, so his term is used.
6 29th Division (86th, 87th and 88th Brigades), the Royal Naval Division, 1st Australian Division, Australian and New Zealand Army Corps and the French Corps.
7 J. Lee, *A Soldier's Life: General Sir Ian Hamilton 1853–1947*, 2001 edn, p. 156.
8 Margaret's nephew Mervyn served with the Anzacs and was wounded at Gallipoli.

9 *Last C*, p. 35.

10 K. Fewster (ed.), *Gallipoli Correspondent: The Front-Line Diary of C. E. W. Bean*, Sydney, NSW, 1983, p. 155.

11 C. Mackenzie, *Gallipoli Memories*, 1929, pp. 205, 237–8, 389.

12 H. W. Nevinson, *The Dardanelles Campaign* [*TDC*], 1918, p. 207.

13 Ibid., p. 209.

14 *MG*, 30 July 1915.

15 *TDC*, p. xi.

16 *IDB*, pp. 1–12.

17 He became Honorary Lieutenant of the Tower of London.

18 Quoted in Lee, *A Soldier's Life*, p. 22. He was Deputy Quartermaster General at Simla in 1896 and Quartermaster General of the British army in 1903.

19 When *The River Clyde* was torpedoed Cather gave his lifebelt to a drowning man. Henry discovered that he had with him Evelyn's latest book.

20 *Last C*, p. 31.

21 *Votes for Women*, 29 October 1915.

22 *MG*, 9 August 1915. The New Zealander Colonel Malone had commented that 'the art of warfare is the cultivation of the domestic virtues'.

23 Ibid., 25, 26, 28 August 1915.

24 *TDC*, p. 407.

25 *MG*, 2 December 1933.

26 *Nation*, 29 April 1916.

27 *Last C*, p. 54.

28 *The War Illustrated*, 15 July 1916.

29 E. M. Forster Papers, vol. 8/24, p. 101, King's College Library, Cambridge.

30 He wrote Australia's official war history. Fewster, *Gallipoli Correspondent*, pp. 159, 165.

31 Ibid., pp. 160, 165.

32 Elizabeth Robins Diary, 4 November 1915, Robins Papers, Fales Library, New York University Library.

33 K. Denton, *Gallipoli: One Long Grave*, Sydney, Australia, 1986.

34 P. Knightley, *The First Casualty: From the Crimea to Vietnam. The War Correspondent as Hero, Propagandist and Myth Maker*, 1975 edn, pp. 108, 536.

35 3, 5 May 1917, Ian Hamilton Papers, 8/1/50, Liddell Hart Centre for Military Archives, King's College, London.

36 Ibid., 4 May 1917. In 1928 Hamilton told Henry that Ashmead-Bartlett was removed because he broke his word a second time with remarks 'calculated to spread despondency and alarm' and reported to the Chief of Staff. Ibid., 13 April 1928, 13/81.

37 N. Hiley, 'Enough Glory For All: Ellis Ashmead-Bartlett and Sir Ian Hamilton at the Dardanelles', *Journal of Strategic Studies*, 16/2, June 1993, p. 264.

38 He now had overall command of British forces in the Mediterranean east of Malta (excepting Egypt). The Dardanelles army was under General Birdwood.

39 *Last C*, p. 63; Committee of Imperial Defence, Copy of K. A. Murdoch's letter to the Prime Minister of the Australian Commonwealth, 23 September 1915, CAB 19/30, TNA: PRO.

40 *TDC*, p. 406.

41 *MG*, 31 December 1915.

42 1, 2 February 1917, Hamilton Papers, 8/1/50. Masefield told Henry that he had recommended him as the author but the government wanted the well-known poet in order to boost US sales.

43 Confidential report to the Secretary of the War Office by A. J. Murray, General Commander-in-Chief, Egyptian Expeditionary Force, CAB 19/30, 87, TNA: PRO. Sir Archibald Murray had been one of Henry's censors at Ladysmith. The two men met again in Egypt in 1916.

44 Henry knew several of the Commission's members and was most impressed by the questions from Walter Roch, Pembrokeshire MP and suffrage supporter. Stephen Gwynn MP later told Henry that his evidence was thought to be amongst the best.

45 J. Macleod, 'General Sir Ian Hamilton and the Dardanelles Commission', *War in History*, 8/4, 2001, pp. 418–41. On 5 May 1917 a letter from Hamilton to Henry asks if he could 'rough draft my idea of something you might say to me' (about Ashmead-Bartlett) ready for the Commission, 8/1/50, Hamilton Papers.

46 See too *MG*, 18 November 1919. In 1944 Hamilton wrote that part of the problem was making the War Office understand the race against time and 'that Gallipoli was not in France'. General Sir I. Hamilton, *Listening for the Drum*, 1944, p. 164.

47 Generals Birdwood and Godley and Admiral Sir Roger Keyes also assisted.

48 General Sir I. Hamilton GCB, *Gallipoli Diary*, vol. 1, 1920, p. viii.

49 15 February 1918, 8/1/50, Hamilton Papers; *TDC*, p. 273.

50 *MG*, 14 November 1918.

51 D. Jerrold, *The Lie about the War: A Note on Some Contemporary War Books*, 1930, p. 13; NevJ.e621/4, 18 April 1921; A. Moorehead, *Gallipoli*, Ware, 1997 edn, p. 305 calls it a 'graceful and accomplished account'.

52 P. Doyle, 'World War One: Disaster at Gallipoli', Channel Five, 14 May 2003, and personal communication.

53 D. French, 'The Origins of the Dardanelles Campaign Reconsidered', *History*, 68/223, June 1983, p. 224; K. Fewster *et al.*, *Gallipoli: The Turkish Story*, Crows Nest, NSW, 2003 edn; T. Travers, *Gallipoli 1915*, 2001.

54 *TDC*, pp. 407–8.

55 *Nation*, 29 April 1916; *NL*, 2 November 1923, 20 March 1925.

56 *Nation*, 23 September 1916.

57 27 April 1932, 13/81, Hamilton Papers.

58 *Last C*, p. 69.

59 *MG*, 22–24 November, 1 December 1915, 1, 11 January, 2 February 1916.

60 M. Burr, *Slouch Hat*, 1935, p. 121.

61 The sister of the suffrage leader Charlotte Despard ran the Scottish Women's Hospital at Salonika.

62 *Last C*, p. 86.

63 The paper requested his service in June but, embroiled in proofs, he had delayed. Gibbs and Henry also reported for the *Daily Telegraph*.

64 C. E. Montague, *Disenchantment*, 1922, p. 100. Henry thought this book the finest critique of the war. Montague had been a leader writer on the *MG*.

65 BBC, *Anywhere for a News Story*, 1934, p. 13.

66 In charge was Major Neville Lytton, whose pro-suffrage sister and brother Henry knew well.

67 *Last C*, p. 138.

68 Montague, *Disenchantment*, p. 172; *MG*, 6 December 1933.

69 *Last C*, pp. 142–3.

70 Ibid., pp. 144–5; *DC*, 26 August 1918.

71 *DN*, 9 November 1918.

72 Ibid., 12 November 1918; *MG*, 11 November 1918. Henry's short wire was not, however, appreciated by the British press. He complained that they expected 'columns of gush' as well as a terse, unique account of a historic moment. *Last C*, p. 148. But by mid-November he was describing it as 'one of the most dramatic and historic scenes I have ever witnessed'. *DN*, 14 November 1918.

Chapter Nine

1 *The Irish Times*, 12 November 1941.

2 *Nation*, 15 January 1921.

3 H. W. Nevinson, 'Sir Roger Casement and Sinn Féin', *Atlantic Monthly*, cxviii/2, 1916, p. 237.

4 *ER*, pp. 50, 52.

5 Founded by the Trinity historian and Home Ruler C. H. Oldham, it discussed politics and literature weekly.

6 Founded two years earlier, it advocated land reform and Home Rule.

7 H. W. Nevinson, 'The Chance in Ireland', *Contemporary Review*, lxxxiii, March 1903, pp. 337–43. He was writing about the Land Purchase Bill (Wyndham's Act). It organized state purchase from landlords, allowing tenants to buy their land through state loans.

8 H. M. Tomlinson, *The Day Before: A Romantic Chronicle*, 1940, pp. 253–9.

9 NevJ. e 610/1, 26 February 1893. The quotes in this chapter, unless otherwise indicated, are from NevJ. e 619/3–622/4, 1916–22.

10 *Nation*, 7 December 1912. In the *Baltimore Sun*, 9 January 1922, he wrote how he longed to feel pride in his country but 'the shadow of Ireland spread her dark and chilling hand over my heart and froze me into silence'.

11 *Nation*, 20 April 1907.

12 *RA*, pp. 174–201.

13 G. P. Peatling, 'British Ideological Movements and Irish Politics 1865–1925', D.Phil., University of Oxford, 1997; Idem, *British Opinion and Irish Self-government, 1865–1925: From Unionism to Liberal Commonwealth*, Dublin, 2001, Chapters 3–6.

14 S. Weaver, *The Hammonds: A Marriage in History*, Stanford, CA, 1997, pp. 167, 170.

15 It stated that Home Rule would be disastrous to the whole of Ireland, subverting civil and religious freedom, destroying citizenship and imperilling the unity of empire.

16 Nevinson to C. P. Scott, 18 August 1912, A/N12/12, MGA.

17 Nevinson, 'Sir Roger Casement', p. 239; *New Weekly*, 18 April 1914.

18 *DN*, 12 February 1912; *MG*, 25–30 March 1914.

19 *MG*, 30 September 1912.

20 *Nation*, 5 October 1912.

21 M. Ward, *Unmanageable Revolutionaries: Women and Irish Nationalism*, 1983, pp. 68–70.

22 M. Hughes, *Ireland Divided: The Roots of the Modern Irish Problem*, Cardiff, 1994, p. 40.

23 Henry was attacked in the *Nation* (4 April 1914) for romanticizing the garrison in the Curragh. He responded (8, 25 April 1914), distinguishing between an army and an army of occupation. Garrisons in Ireland resulted from British misgovernment so British politicians, not the army, were culpable.

24 Nevinson, 'Sir Roger Casement', p. 243.

25 Ibid., p. 241.

26 *Last C*, p. 88.

27 *DN*, 12 February 1912.

28 D. Ryan, *James Connolly*, 1924, p. vii.

29 Nevinson to E. Carpenter, 11 July 1916, MSS. 386/273, Carpenter Collection, Sheffield Archives.

30 *Nation*, 19 August 1919.

31 Nevinson, 'Sir Roger Casement', p. 242.

32 *MG*, 8 May 1916.

33 M. Ward, *Hanna Sheehy Skeffington*, Cork, 1997, p. 165.

34 NevJ. e 613/1, 21 September 1905.

35 In A. Mitchell, *Sir Roger Casement's Heart of Darkness: The 1911 Documents*, Dublin, 2003, p. 427.

36 Ibid., pp. 426–7.

37 *Nation*, 1 July 1911.

38 HWNP, MS. Eng. Misc. c 497.

39 Nevinson to E. Clodd, 12 July 1916, Edward Clodd Collection, The Brotherton Collection, Leeds University Library.

40 NevJ. e 611/4, 10 February 1903.

41 H. W. Nevinson, 'The Casement Trial', *War and Peace*, in E. D. Morel Papers, F8/25, The British Library of Political and Economic Science.

42 *Guardian*, 28 February 1998, 8 May 2000. A panel of independent experts examined them for BBC/RTE documentaries in 2002, though divergent views are likely to persist.

43 Nevinson, 'The Casement Trial'.

44 There are slight differences between the wording in the diary and in *Last C*, pp. 101–2.

45 Poet and diplomat, formerly imprisoned for the Irish cause.

46 Gertrude Parry later told Evelyn that Henry strode up to the dock and took Casement's hand. Henry's diaries do not mention it. Had it happened, it is unlikely that he would have omitted it. 12 November 1941, ESNev. MSS. Eng. Lett. d 280.

47 Henry later included this speech (and extracts from the writings of Swift, Shaw, Carlyle and W. H. Davies) in his anthology *England's Voice of Freedom: An Anthology of Liberty* (compiled by and with Introduction by H. W. Nevinson), 1929; New York, 1929), reproducing the words of over 100 people from the sixth to twentieth centuries.

48 *Guardian*, 15 June 1998.

49 *Last C*, pp. 101–4.

50 6 July 1916 in D. H. Laurence (ed.), *The Bernard Shaw Collected Letters 1911–1925*, 3, 1985, p. 405.

51 Other key supporters included Llewelyn Davies, Clement Shorter and Sir Arthur Conan Doyle. Henry also tried to organize a 'brief petition for Congo people to sign' but the Anti-Slavery Society decided against it. Nevinson to G. Bannister, 10, 12 July 1916, Roger Casement Papers, MSS. 13075, National Library of Ireland.

52 *MG*, 25 July 1916.

53 Wilfred Scawen Blunt Papers, MS.141–1975, 142–1975, Fitzwilliam Museum, Cambridge.

54 Ibid., 431–1975, Blunt's diary, 11 July 1916.

55 *LL*, pp. 81–9.

56 Yet another was Agnes Harben, married to suffragist Henry Harben. Henry described her as 'so beautiful, so exquisite, so clever'. His diary says she mentioned 'that little thrill of happiness' he gave her. She apparently added that they 'must be good next time we meet'.

57 *Nation*, 18, 25 May 1918.

58 *Last C*, pp. 131–2.

59 *DH*, 1 April 1919.

60 *Nation*, 19 August 1919.

61 *Last C*, p. 170.

62 See Chapter 10.

63 D. G. Boyce, *Englishmen and Irish Troubles: British Public Opinion and the Making of Irish Policy 1918–22*, 1922, pp. 193–5.

64 *Last C*, p. 175. The release of the MacSwiney Home Office file in 2002 revealed that George V had unsuccessfully pleaded for his life to be saved.

65 *DH*, 1 November 1920.

66 M. Pottle (ed.), *Champion Redoubtable: The Diaries and Letters of Violet Bonham Carter 1914–1945*, 1999 edn, p. 132.

67 *DH*, 18 November, 2, 14 December 1920.

68 *Nation*, 18 December 1920.

69 *Last C*, p. 189.

70 *DH*, 22 December 1920.

71 Evelyn spent a fortnight in Ireland in January to see the effect of reprisals.

72 MacDonald (Labour) stood for Woolwich East, focusing on unemployment and Ireland, losing by 682 votes.

73 *Last C*, p. 190.

74 *Nation*, 3 September 1921.

75 Terms included Dominion constitutional status in the British Empire.

76 Nevinson to Campbell, 30 July 1922, MS. 10171/980, Trinity College, Dublin.

77 Ibid.

78 *Nation*, 25 March 1922.

79 But in 1923 he heard that she was no longer 'an extremist Republican'. NevJ. e 623/1, 20 September 1923.

80 Nevinson to C. E. Montague, 22 March 1922, CEM/2/2/2/4, Montague Collection, The John Rylands University Library, University of Manchester.

81 *Last C*, p. 265. He gives the wrong date (a week late) for the attack.

82 *Nation*, 8 July 1922.

83 He attended the opening of the Dáil in September 1923.

84 Nevinson to P. Webb, 9 October 1927, ESNev. MSS. Eng. Lett. c 278.

85 E.g., for Boyce, Henry's reports are 'marred by a polemic tone and an apparent determination to find against the Crown forces on every front'. Boyce, *Englishmen and Irish Troubles*, p. 71.

86 Peatling, *British Opinion and Irish Self-government*, p. 71.

87 He was now writing his memoirs, which included much Irish material.

88 *Cork Examiner*, 29 December 1932.

Chapter Ten

1 25 December 1918, Nevinson MS.13,075(2), Roger Casement Papers, National Library of Ireland. Compare the television correspondent Jeremy Bowen's comment on war reporting: 'After fifteen years and eleven wars I don't seek it out any more. But I can't say I'll never do it again', 'Jeremy Bowen on the Front Line', BBC1, 16 January 2005. The quotes in this chapter, unless otherwise indicated, are from NevJ. e 620/4–628/4, 1918–41.

2 Compare similar, more recent sentiments: C. Moorehead, *Martha Gellhorn: A Life*, 2004 edn, p. 471; J. Simpson, *Strange Places, Questionable People*, 1999 edn, p. 5.

3 *Baltimore Sun* subjects included the General Strike of May 1926 when Henry and Evelyn walked round London talking to strikers and blacklegs.

4 NevJ. e 620/3, 17 December 1917.

5 He had exhibitions in New York in 1919 and 1920.

6 *DN*, 21 November 1918, shows him and his colleagues as 'almost' the first. A decade later *Last C*, p. 148 makes him the first!

7 H. W. Nevinson, 'Earl Haig' in W. R. Inge, *The Post Victorians*, 1933, p. 199.

8 *Freeman*, 7 July 1920.

9 *Nation* 15 February 1919.

10 W. Rothenstein, *Men and Memories 1900–1922*, 2, 1932, p. 358.

11 E. Sharp, *Unfinished Adventure: Selected Reminiscences from an Englishwoman's Life*, 1933, p. 172.

12 *Last C*, p. 159.

13 Evelyn spent four months in Germany in 1920 doing relief work with the Society of Friends. She never joined the Quakers but, attracted by their pacifism and social vision, worked closely with them. Evelyn Sharp's life is the subject of my forthcoming biography published by Day Books. ESNev. MSS. Eng. Misc. f 403.

14 *Last C*, p. 282.

15 Morgan Philips Price, *Dispatches from the Weimar Republic: Versailles and German Fascism*, ed. T. Rose, 1999, p. 169.

16 *Nation and Athenaeum*, 10 February 1923.

17 See Frederic Whyte's annotation of a letter he received from Henry, 17 February 1923, FW107 (135) Special Collections, the Robinson Library, University of Newcastle.

18 *NL*, 2 March 1923. After Massingham's resignation from the *Nation* early in 1923, Henry wrote regularly for Brailsford's *New Leader*. He also contributed to the *Venturer*, edited by the pacifist poet Gilbert Thomas.

19 18 October 1923, A/N12/27 to 2 December 1923, A/N12/31, MGA.

20 *Last C*, p. 291.

21 *MG*, 6 November 1923.

22 Ibid., 8, 10 November 1923.

23 5 November 1923, B/N82A/4, MGA.

24 Sharp, *Unfinished Adventure*, pp. 283–4.

25 *Last C*, p. 295.

26 Ibid.

27 Programme in Elmhirst Papers, Dartington Hall Trust, Devon. Leonard Elmhirst (then a mature student at Cornell) secured Henry's invitation there.

28 *Last C*, p. 225.

29 Nevinson to L. Elmhirst, 20 June 1920, Elmhirst Papers.

30 *Last C*, p. 205.

31 HWNP, MS. Eng. Misc. c 497.

32 Margaret visited America separately to see its probation system.

33 Lieutenant-Colonel C. À. Court Repington, *After the War: A Diary*, 1922, pp. 433–4.

34 In 1922 Henry lectured to university students in Geneva about the conference. His controversial report for the *MG* on the Geneva Naval Conference of 1927 raised questions about American agents in Geneva working for steel trusts with vested interests in a large US navy.

35 *Last C*, p. 231.

36 Repington, *After the War*, pp. 433–4, 465.

37 *MG*, 2 January 1922.

38 A. Nevins, *American Social History*, Oxford, 1946, pp. 551–5. Henry features alongside Cobbett, Dickens, Martineau and Trollope.

39 See Henry's sixpenny book *The English* and his *Rough Islanders*, 1930 for explorations of Englishness.

40 *NL*, 23 October 1924, misleadingly entitled 'With the PM through England'.

41 18 September 1929, B/N82/11a, MGA.

42 *MG*, 14 October 1929.

43 *More C*, p. 210.

44 *Last C*, p. 236; Introduction to D. R. Kahn, *Spring Up, O Well*, 1936, pp. 7–12.

45 HWNP, MS. Eng. Misc. c 497.

46 *IDB*, p. 71.

47 *MG*, 19 October 1926.

48 Ibid., 15 November 1926.

49 *Last C*, p. 336.

50 *NL*, 4 March 1927.

51 HWNP, MS. Eng. Misc. c 497.

52 *MG*, 1 January 1927; *FT*, pp. 1–23.

53 *Last C*, p. 90.

54 *EPT*, p. 8.

55 MS. Eng. Lett. c 269, Bodleian Library, Oxford.
56 H. W. Nevinson, Introduction to H. J. Ripper, *Vital Speech: A Study in Perfect Utterance*, 1938, pp. ix–xi.
57 H. W. Nevinson, *Fire of Life* [*FL*], 1935, pp. 5–6. The journalist Ellis Roberts abridged the volumes into one.
58 In February 1942 the BBC broadcast a tribute to Henry, calling him 'one of the greatest of war correspondents'. Richard introduced it.
59 He proposed a memorial to Sharp: Cecil Sharp House in Regent's Park opened in 1930.
60 *Labour Magazine*, 24 October 1924.
61 21 April 1928, 911/3/X, John L. Nevinson Diaries, The Society of Antiquaries of London.
62 4 June 1932, Series 2B/6/136, Robins Papers, The Fales Library, New York University.
63 There was no post-mortem. The death certificate states her age as 75. She was actually 74.
64 In fact he left £12,902 when he died.
65 MS. Eng. Lett. f 825, Bodleian Library, Oxford. Grinling was a leading figure in the Woolwich labour movement. Henry visited him for many years. They had met at Toynbee Hall.
66 H. W. Nevinson, 'Edward Carpenter 1844–1929' in Barrett Brown (ed.), *Great Democrats*, 1934, p. 106.
67 *NL*, 8 May 1925; *Spectator*, 2 March 1934. In 1921 Henry had visited Howard University and briefly glimpsed segregation in Virginia.
68 *MG*, 10–13, 15 June 1925 (reprinted as a pamphlet), 3 July 1931.
69 http://sunsite.berkeley.edu/Goldman/Writings/Speeches/foyles.html
70 Nevinson to P. Webb, 19 August 1936, ESNev. MSS. Eng. Lett. c 279; *The Times*, 19 August 1936.
71 *MG*, 15 November 1938.
72 I. Brown, 'The Poets' in I. Norrie (ed.), *The Heathside Book of Hampstead and Highgate*, 1962, p. 28. In 1936 he wrote a Preface to *Hitler The Man*, a Friends of Europe pamphlet urging co-operation for the prevention of war and providing information about Nazi Germany.
73 In June 1940 Henry chaired their conference on wartime compulsory censorship and led a deputation to the Minister of Information. He wrote a Foreword to *British Liberty in Danger* (1940) by the NCCL's co-founder, Ronald Kidd.
74 D. K. Roberts to E. Sharp, 14 November 1941, ESNev. MSS. Eng. Lett. d 280.
75 HWNP, MS. Eng. Misc. c 496.
76 H. and M. Cecil, *Clever Hearts: Desmond and Molly MacCarthy*, 1991 edn, p. 290.
77 Quoted in S. Jameson, *Autobiography of Storm Jameson: Journey from the North*, 1, 1984 edn, p. 369.
78 When Lord Runciman was billed as guest of honour for a Society of Authors dinner, Henry and Evelyn (separately) returned their tickets. Henry argued that it would be 'a crime against literature' to show any approval of the German government. The Runciman Mission to Czechoslovakia in August 1938 had looked at the Czech–German question. The

following day the Society wrote to say that Runciman would not, after all, be attending. Evelyn Sharp correspondence with D. K. Roberts, Society of Authors, October 1938, Add.56804. A224, British Library.

79 Her sister, Maud Karpeles, was yet another of Henry's 'admirers'.

80 *V&M*, p. 179. A letter from Evelyn to Henry's relative Ethel G. Woodd, 8 August 1941, privately owned, stressed how he longed to return to Hampstead.

81 E. Sharp to Mr Villard, 22 February 1942, EsNev. MSS. Eng. Lett. d 279. Bill Adams's talk to the Campden Society (1984) recalled Henry as the most appealing of the settlers.

82 Although reprinted several times in the 1970s, this did scant justice to Henry as writer. There were some factual inaccuracies and it ignored recent insights. Yet it was started during the Blitz when Henry was 84. See my forthcoming study of Henry's literary work.

83 Personal communication.

84 Penguin 02.0095, DN1107, Special Collections, University of Bristol. Originally entitled *Scenes and Men*.

85 Three versions of this are known to exist. 'A Study for a Portrait of Henry W. Nevinson' in pencil and coloured chalks was sold at Sotheby's in December 1981. In 1978 Birmingham Museum and Art Gallery acquired from PEN (for £350) a completed version. Evelyn bequeathed a tempera portrait to Christ Church. Hung in the Senior Common Room until 1978, it was later put in the College's Picture Gallery.

86 HWNP, MS. Eng. Misc. c 496.

87 Evelyn's words in Henry's last diary.

Afterword

1 HWNP, MS. Eng. Misc. d663.

2 *New Leader*, 2 October 1925.

3 NevJ. e 611/3, 22 March 1902.

4 S. Jameson, *Autobiography of Storm Jameson: Journey from the North*, 1, 1984, p. 377.

Index

CPSIA information can be obtained
at www.ICGtesting.com
Printed in the USA
LVHW041742180423
744640LV00003B/37

9 781350 382060